Beyond The Labyrinth

BEYOND
THE LABYRINTH

A Study of Edwin Muir's Poetry

CHRISTOPHER WISEMAN

1978

SONO NIS PRESS

1745 BLANSHARD STREET, VICTORIA, BRITISH COLUMBIA, CANADA V8W 2J8

Canadian Cataloguing in Publication Data

Wiseman, Christopher, 1936-
  Beyond the labyrinth

  Bibliography: p.
  Includes index.
  ISBN 0-919462-66-9

  1. Muir, Edwin, 1887-1959. I. Title.
  PR6025.U6Z93   821'.9'12   C78-002158-4

Published by
SONO NIS PRESS
Victoria, British Columbia

Designed and printed in Canada by
MORRISS PRINTING COMPANY LTD.
Victoria, British Columbia

For my mother
and in memory of
my father
STEPHEN WISEMAN

An absurd thing I realized after reading Bowra's book was that I had been writing symbolist poetry very frequently for years without knowing it.

— EDWIN MUIR

ACKNOWLEDGEMENTS

My thanks go to Faber and Faber, Ltd. for permission to quote from Edwin Muir's *Collected Poems* and from *Four Quartets* by T. S. Eliot; to The Hogarth Press for permission to quote from Edwin Muir's *An Autobiography*; to Gavin Muir for permission to quote from other works by Edwin and Willa Muir. I should also like to thank the editors of *Scottish Literary Journal, Studies in Scottish Literature,* and *The University of Windsor Review,* in whose journals articles based upon material in this book first appeared.

As do all critics of Muir's work, I owe a particular debt to Professor Peter Butter. My own work has also been helped in various ways by Kathleen Raine, Professor George Wing, Donald Gordon, the late Keith Wright, Professor I. F. Clarke, Professor Robert H. Carnie and Professor Robert Tener. To these, and others, I express my gratitude, as I do to Mrs. Betty O'Keeffe and Miss M. Archibald for their help in preparing the manuscript.

I wish to thank the Canada Council for a Leave Fellowship which made it possible for me to complete my work. This book has been published with the help of a grant from the Humanities Research Council of Canada, using funds provided by the Canada Council. I am extremely grateful.

Finally, and above all, I wish to thank my wife for much more than I could express here.

CHRISTOPHER WISEMAN
Calgary, 1978

CONTENTS

CHAPTER ONE

The Fall Into Time

Those critics who have written on Edwin Muir have concentrated on his life, his system of beliefs and the embodiment of those beliefs in his work. There has been surprisingly little systematic analysis of the poems, especially from a technical point of view; in fact most of Muir's critics have appeared reluctant to expose individual poems to more than generalized treatment. Typically, Muir has been regarded, even by those who admire his poetry, as a writer whose language and techniques are somehow impervious to the analytic methods of modern criticism. Helen Gardner's approach is representative:

It has been an era of metrical experiment, linguistic experiment, and great concern with the technique of writing in verse. Muir's poetry retained to the end a certain artistic naivety.[1]

And this view of Muir as a poet who lacks technical dynamism and who therefore is out of step with his time has become almost a critical cliché. Charles Tomlinson believes that Muir's poetry lacks "that linguistic vigour without which true poetry cannot exist"; that his work fails "to bring to bear those rhythmic overtones and linguistic resonances whereby the poetic intuition is primarily kindled."[2] And this sense that something is lacking in the texture of Muir's work is shared by Kenneth Allott, who is concerned that "the poems so rarely 'explode' into meaning — for me Muir remains an extremely honest and often rewarding but not very exciting poet."[3] Graham Hough has claimed that "there is no novelty of technique and no startling imagery in his work";[4] J. A. M. Rillie that "He is given to the comfortable cliché, is conventional in purely descriptive poems . . . and rhythmically he is all thumbs";[5] Edwin Morgan that "he never did develop an entirely surefooted technique: even his last poems are liable to be flawed by some awkward rhythm, some clumsy inversion, some flatness of vocabulary. . . ."[6] Even the grave voice of Eliot, who came to admire Muir's poetry late in his life, joined in the chorus with the gently dismissive words: "I do not believe that technique was ever a primary concern with Edwin."[7]

Together with this sense that Muir was less than interested in technique has been a widespread feeling that the poet did not, in a technical sense, belong to his time, and again the implication is that this allows us to take him slightly less seriously, to treat his work as somehow not completely relevant to the mid-twentieth century. Morgan has written that Muir was "out of step with his time" because he relies on traditional verse-forms and avoids startling and broken imagery. Helen Gardner believes that Muir's poetic style "has no relation to the styles of the most powerful poetic masters of this century, Pound, Eliot and Yeats."[8] A. Alvarez, even more provocatively, takes this further:

Muir was not a "modern" poet; the experiments of the great American innovators touched him not at all; he used symbols but was never a Symbolist. . . . Spiritually and technically in fact, he belongs to the generation of poets which was killed off in the First World War. . . . "[9]

It is obvious that Muir is being judged from a particular critical standpoint. Clearly his poetry, to critics accustomed to modernism, seems strange and even quaint, and their typical reaction has been to treat him as some sort of exception to the rule; a writer of fable, allegory or parable, whose individual poems may be hurried over in order to discuss the ideas behind them. To most of Muir's critics, his poetry has not proved amenable to close textual examination, lacking, as they obviously think, the broken imagery, the dynamic use of language, the experimental structure and the urban settings of so many modern poets. Implied in many of these critical reservations is a worried belief that Muir does not deal adequately with contemporary reality and attitudes; that his traditional verse-forms demonstrate that he never comes to grips technically with the modern movement; and that these two limitations necessarily restrict his relevance and, ultimately, his importance as a poet. Frederick Grubb, in a study of Kathleen Raine's poetry, somewhat patronizingly states: "She considers what T. S. Eliot adopts as symbolism and Edwin Muir relegates into fable."[10] This suggests, though obscurely, that Muir is somehow unable to consider certain material directly and that he writes "fable" as a kind of evasion. And, extremely, Muir's poetry has elicited responses from fellow poets like that of

Philip Larkin, who admits to finding Muir "unreadable,"[11] and C. M. Grieve, who claims that, after Muir gave up socialism and turned to religious themes, his poetry "became tepid and static and full of nonsense."[12]

It is one of the central purposes of this book to challenge these critical views and show their inadequacy. By an examination of much of Edwin Muir's later poetry, I hope to show that his techniques are not only highly sophisticated but essential to the successful incarnation of his ideas. In particular I hope to demonstrate that he is a poet who often uses complex symbolist techniques and that his use of syntax and prosody, far from being weak, is creative and vital. As far as I know, Muir has never been seriously considered as a symbolist poet. Kathleen Raine has used the term:

He discovered late what was known early to Dante and Milton, and discovered in the course of their poetic thought by Coleridge, Shelley, Blake and Yeats, the great symbolic language of tradition.... Muir came to the great source of vision without this learning, with little knowledge of the traditional forms. He was a symbolist poet by natural gift.... [13]

And J. M. Cohen, more vaguely, describes Muir as "both a symbolist and a writer of parables in the Biblical spirit."[14] But no critic has examined Muir's poetry in terms of symbolist techniques, and I believe that it is only through an examination of this sort that his technical qualities become understandable and significant. It is, further, a way into a fuller understanding of meaning and a deeper response to feeling and idea in the poetry.

Alvarez's claim that Muir "used symbols but was never a Symbolist" seems demonstrably inaccurate and regrettably typical of the lack of attention paid by some critics to the poet's techniques. In fact the development of Muir's poetry may be usefully seen as the largely intuitive development of symbolist technique; a development intimately connected with both theme and quality. His poetry may not *sound* like that of Eliot, Pound, Stevens or Yeats, but symbolist techniques are just as essential to the structure and meaning of many of his poems as they are to the work of the other great post-symbolists. The differences derive not as much from the deployment or non-deployment of symbolist technique as such, as from tone, dramatic intensity, the use of openly contemporary, and especially urban, subject-matter, and inherent beliefs about society and its values, about time and mortality.

Muir's symbols were discovered early in his life, but it is only in *The Labyrinth* (1949) and the subsequent poetry that he acquired the specialized techniques by which he could free his symbols and draw out their full range of meaning. Metre, syntax, tense, sound, tone; the relationship of the poet to his material; specific exploratory properties of language and image — these are fundamentally connected with the presentation of symbol in poetry and hence with idea and belief. Such great concepts as time and eternity are not incorporated rationally and logically in Muir's poetry, but explored and released into meaning through symbol. As I shall try to show, poetic symbols must be worked towards and presented as an essentially exploratory act, and a sophisticated employment of language, prosody and sound is required if the symbols are to become sufficiently free to manifest their highest value and significance.

My purpose, then, is twofold. Firstly, by concentrating on Muir's techniques for using symbol, I shall attempt to place him squarely in the tradition of post-symbolist poetry. Secondly, I shall examine much of his later poetry in some detail, in the hope that this will help to shift the emphasis from heavily biographical criticism to the individual poems, many of which have previously been ignored. The biographical element, however, cannot be completely neglected. There is a strong and obvious connection between the life and the poetry; between the poet's personal journey towards integration of personality and the poetic journey towards an inclusive symbology and a technique with which to release and explore that symbology. The major opposing symbols in Muir's poetry, for example, derive largely from extremes of experience in his childhood and youth, modified by his two breakdowns, his psycho-analysis and his response to events in Europe. In a very real sense, Muir's poetry is the record of an often tragically blocked personality which only towards the end of life manages to achieve a healthy and creative balance between strongly conflicting extremes of experience, and before I examine his work, it is essential to understand something of the beliefs, ideas and intuitions which produced not only individual symbols but the rich and coherent pattern which informs all Muir's writing and thought.

Muir's symbols derive partly from dreams and visions, partly from his knowledge of religion and myth, and partly from the events of his own life, which he saw as both unique and yet simultaneously representative of a universal human pattern, containing symbolic experiences of good and evil and apprehensions of heaven and hell

14

which he believed have been felt by all men at all times. He called the critical events of life, the day to day experience of each individual, the Story. That other reality, outside the pull of time and local events, which underpins and sustains this exterior life, and which puts every man in touch with every other, he called the Fable. In every man's Story there are intimations of, glimpses into, the timeless Fable; the most common access to it being through dreams. Thus Muir's central belief implies a division of reality into conscious and unconscious, into worldly and numinous, into time and eternity. This duality saturates all Muir's writings. Early in his autobiography he makes clear his ideas about the Story and the Fable:

It is clear that no autobiography can begin with a man's birth, that we extend far beyond any boundary line which we can set for ourselves in the past or the future, and that the life of every man is an endlessly repeated performance of the life of man. It is clear for the same reason that no autobiography can confine itself to conscious life, and that sleep, in which we pass a third of our existence, is a mode of experience, and our dreams a part of reality. In themselves our conscious lives may not be particularly interesting. But what we are not and can never be, our fable, seems to me inconceivably interesting. I should like to write that fable but I cannot even live it; and all I could do if I related the outward course of my life would be to show how I have deviated from it; though even that is impossible, since I do not know the fable or anybody who knows it. One or two stages in it I can recognize: the age of innocence and the Fall and all the dramatic consequences which issue from the Fall. But these lie behind experience, not on its surface; they are not historical events; they are stages in the fable.[15]

Edwin Muir's poetry bears witness to a long search for the symbols and techniques which would allow him access to the permanent rhythms and timeless values of the Fable by transcending the time-ridden world of the Story. He believed that the symbols of his poetry came from this permanent reality and only by following them back towards their source could he gain a knowledge of that other reality:

The longer he lived the more sure he became that cosmic radiation from far outside conveyed this aspiration (love) to mankind, from an unknown source to which one's unconscious gave access and which he called "The Fable" of one's life. Much less decisive was "The Story", the sum of conscious happenings from day to day on earth. His poetry, he was sure, came ultimately from The Fable.[16]

Willa Muir's words here are reinforced by the last paragraph of her book:

In reaching this personal harmony we made at least a start, we took a step or two along the road towards that greater world harmony which haunted us like a dream from the Fable. Edwin believed that it *was* a dream from the Fable which would ultimately come to pass, and he felt himself to be a spokesman for it in his poetry.[17]

The difficulties of precise description are, of course, immense when one attempts to define such a concept. It is as vague or precise as the psychologist's "unconscious," the religious man's God, or Plato's visions of harmony. It is, I think, of little value to explore it further here. In my analysis of the poetry, where the discipline, focus and pattern of art are brought to bear, over and over again, upon this intimation of order and transcendence, we will perhaps understand more clearly what Muir felt about the Fable. But an examination of Edwin Muir's personal Story and his own response to it will be of help in understanding both the sources of his symbols and the forming of his ideas under the pressure of experience.

Only a brief outline of Muir's life need be given here, as it has been thoroughly documented elsewhere. He was born in 1887 on a farm in the Orkneys, the youngest of six children. When he was two, the family moved to a rented farm on the small island of Wyre, accompanied by the father's sister and the children's cousin. After six years, they moved to a neighbouring farm, and Edwin started school. Failing to make a profit on that farm, the Muir family moved to a farm near Kirkwall, on the Orkney mainland, but instead of settling, the family started to break up, and Edwin's brothers and sisters left one by one for Kirkwall or Glasgow. His father, once again unable to make the farm pay, had to give it up, and the family moved into Kirkwall. After a year, when Edwin was fourteen, the family moved to Glasgow, where the Muirs felt uprooted and lost, and the misery was made worse by a tragic series of illnesses and deaths, as in the space of four years, both Edwin Muir's parents and two of his brothers died. Muir worked in various offices in Glasgow, although he, too, suffered from ill-health. He became interested in socialism and joined literary and political discussion groups. In 1912, he took a job in a bone-factory in Greenock, and also around this time he started to read Nietzsche with great excitement, finding some strength in the idea of the Superman. He returned to Glasgow in 1914, was rejected as physically unfit for the army, and remained there until 1919. In that year, he married Willa Anderson and went to London. After some time, he became Orage's assistant in the

New Age office, but his tragic experiences in Glasgow had left him unbalanced and repressed and eventually he submitted to a course of psycho-therapy. This released a flood of images from his unconscious and the therapy had to be stopped before it became overwhelming. In 1921, Edwin and Willa Muir moved to Prague, where he lived by writing for an American magazine, *The Freeman*. His health greatly improved, Muir and his wife moved to Dresden and Hellerau in Germany, where Edwin started to write poetry. Living by translating from German and by contributing to various magazines, they moved around Europe. In 1923 they travelled to Italy, then returned north to Austria, where they lived until the summer of 1924. After two years back in Britain, they moved to the South of France, returning in 1927 to Surrey, where their son Gavin was born. Then for seven years they lived in Hampstead, only moving when their son was run over and needed to recover away from the city. By now, Muir was a reasonably successful writer, having published three collections of poetry as well as criticism and translations, and clearly his personality was much better balanced than it had been in Glasgow and London. From 1939 to 1945, the Muirs lived in St. Andrews and Edinburgh. Both were seriously ill at various times but he managed to find congenial employment with the British Council in Edinburgh after a dull job in a Food Office. When the war ended, he continued his association with the British Council and was appointed Director of the British Institute in Prague where he remained until after the 1948 "Putsch." This event, so soon after the horrors of the war, shattered the Muirs, and led not only to Edwin's most pessimistic poetry, but to a second breakdown, after he had returned to England, which lasted several months. At the beginning of 1949, he was appointed Director of the British Institute in Rome. Here he was extremely happy but the Institute was closed down after a year as a result of a reduction in British Council funds. Muir accepted the position of Warden at the experimental Newbattle Abbey College in Scotland where he remained, in spite of some unpleasant opposition from certain quarters, until 1955. In that year he was invited to be the Charles Eliot Norton Professor at Harvard, which provided both money and a reasonably enjoyable year in the United States. Returning to England in 1956, the Muirs moved into a small house in the village of Swaffham Prior near Cambridge. Now nearing seventy, Muir was writing some of his finest poetry. He was given, in 1958, an Honorary Doctorate of Letters degree at Cambridge, and greatly enjoyed the friendship and company of Kathleen Raine, John Holloway and other members of the university community. On the third of January 1959, Edwin Muir died.

Dominating his entire life were Muir's early years in Orkney; an experience which clearly sustains his powerful visions of Eden. The Orkney Edwin Muir grew up in was, as it is today, a place of extreme natural beauty, where small islands sit in a remote northern sea under light of amazing clarity and startling colour. Throughout the islands are visible reminders of the Viking civilization in Orkney, from the magnificent St. Magnus Cathedral in Kirkwall to the incredibly preserved burial mound at Maeshowe. Earlier civilizations, too, have left their obvious marks on Orkney in such places as the standing stones at Brogar and Stenness, the earth-house at Renibister, and the village of Skara Brae, dug into the sand by the west coast. Removed from the British mainland, Orkney is still, today, proud of its distinctive history and culture and somewhat suspicious of the frenzied modern world south of the Pentland Firth. In the late nineteenth century, when Edwin Muir was a child, Orkney was virtually untouched by progress and industry. It was a place of wonder and simplicity to Muir; a place of integration between past and present, between man and environment, between earth and sea and sky, human and animal, mundane and magic. As Muir puts it: "The Orkney I was born into was a place where there was no great distinction between the ordinary and the fabulous; the lives of living men turned into legend."[18] On the island of Wyre, where the Muirs farmed, was

a little green knoll called the Castle. In the eleventh century this had been the stronghold of a Viking freebooter called Kolbein Hruga, or Cubly Roo. . . . There were only two things that rose from those low, rounded islands: a high, top-heavy castle in Shapinsay, standing by itself with the insane look of tall, narrow houses in flat, wide landscapes, and in Egilsay a black chapel with a round, pointed tower, where St. Magnus had been murdered in the twelfth century. It was the most beautiful thing within sight, and it rose every day against the sky until it seemed to become a sign in the fable of our lives.[19]

This landscape was to dominate Muir's symbolic thinking for the rest of his life. It was, to his child's imagination, a place outside time; a landscape in which the human pattern of life and death was totally simple, even archetypal. Describing his parents, Muir writes:

I never thought that they were like other men and women; to me they were fixed allegorical figures in a timeless landscape. Their allegorical changelessness made them more, not less, solid, as if they were condensed into something more real than humanity; as if this image 'mother' meant more than 'woman' and the image 'father' more than 'man'.[20]

This timeless, archetypal quality is emphasized again and again by Muir. His childhood was a time when the Story and the Fable were joined without strain and the individual was in contact with and sustained by deeper and richer patterns:

That world was a perfectly solid world, for the days did not undermine it but merely rounded it, or rather repeated it, as if there were only one day endlessly rising and setting. Our first childhood is the only time in our lives when we exist within immortality, and perhaps all our ideas of immortality are influenced by it.[21]

The twin qualities of harmony and timelessness which inform Muir's later symbolic vision of Eden and the unfallen state are clearly adumbrated in these pages:

And a child has also a picture of human existence peculiar to himself, which he probably never remembers after he has lost it: the original vision of the world. I think of this picture or vision as that of a state in which the earth, the houses on the earth, and the life of every human being are related to the sky overarching them: as if the sky fitted the earth and the earth the sky. Certain dreams convince me that a child has this vision, in which there is a complete harmony of all things with each other than he will never know again.[22]

Thinking back to this time, Muir writes:

If I were recreating my life in an autobiographical novel I could bring out these correspondences freely and show how our first intuition of the world expands into vaster and vaster images, creating a myth which we act almost without knowing it, while our outward life goes on in its ordinary routine of eating, drinking, sleeping, working. . . . [23]

It is clear that his poetry does exactly what Muir envisaged for his hypothetical autobiographical novel, taking images from his childhood and early manhood and developing them into a structured body of symbol which takes on the coherence and interpretative amenability of myth. Just as Edwin Muir's life was a constant search to find the sort of balance, harmony and integration of Story and Fable which he knew in his childhood, so his poetry is a constant search for the symbols and techniques which allow a transcendence of the surface reality of time and place, and a penetration to a wider, more fertile, world of experience:

Human beings are understandable only as immortal spirits; they become natural then, as natural as young horses; they are absolutely unnatural if we try to think of them as a mere part of the natural world. They are immortal spirits distorted and corrupted in countless ways by the world into which they are born. . . . I do not have the power to prove that man is immortal and that the soul exists; but I know that there must be such a proof, and that compared with it every other demonstration is idle.[24]

This manifesto, written in 1939 before his greatest poetry appeared, is central to an understanding of Edwin Muir's thinking. All his poetry can be seen as an attempt to demonstrate, symbolically, that "man is immortal and that the soul exists." This belief is the core of Muir's thought and vision, unifying all his work. Without it, he felt that human life would be inconceivable and monstrous, as indeed his own life seemed to be in London and in Prague when he lost the vision of Eden and almost broke under the strain.

Orkney, then, gave Muir the timeless landscape and the sense of deep harmony which characterize his poetry. Even in his childhood reading, when he first came to poetry, the islands became, to him, the perfectly natural setting for myth and legend:

. . . it seemed to me that I was watching the appearance of a new race in my familiar countryside: a race of goddesses, beautiful women, and great warriors, all under the low Northern sky, for even the Greek stories unfolded for me in a landscape very like Orkney.[25]

It can be argued that every childhood seems like Eden and is inevitably recalled this way, but, for Muir, the remote and intense beauty of Orkney, the totally agrarian way of life, the preserved remnants of centuries of civilization around him, all opened his eyes to wider than usual possibilities of human life. From Orkney he took a fierce apprehension of harmony between man, beast and nature, and of the interpenetration of the real and the fabulous, the temporal and the eternal. Orkney is clearly the main source of his vision of Eden and unfallen man, Muir's great symbol of order and grace where all things are in their place without tension or complexity. And yet even these years were not wholly ones of joy and harmony. When Muir was six or seven, he had a frightening experience of unhappiness — "a sort of convulsion which I can't entirely put down to growth"[26] — and when he came out of it the innocent world of childhood was never quite the same. It was an intimation of guilt and suffering, but this strange event in his childhood was, I believe, of much less significance for his life and work than the "Fall" into time and suffering when he left Orkney and went to Glasgow, anticipating though it did his vulnerability to the pressures of negative experience.

After Orkney, the move to Glasgow was brutal and shattering. It is difficult to imagine an environment more calculated to smash the vision of harmony than Glasgow, with its massive sprawl of slums, its violence, its industry and blackness, its moral and physical squalor. By a journey of a few hundred miles, the Muir family moved into a completely new world, which virtually destroyed them and provided Edwin Muir with memories so terrible that he could not contemplate them for many years. It is partly from Glasgow that the symbols of the Fall and the labyrinth derive — the anti-symbols which ceaselessly war with the Eden-vision in Muir's poetry. The move to Glasgow was a move through time and space, divorcing Muir from the experience of harmony and throwing him into a world in which he could find no symbols of hope, no thread to connect him back to his true origins. It was his first contact with time, and an unhappy one:

I was born before the Industrial Revolution, and am now about two hundred years old. But I have skipped about a hundred and fifty of them. I was really born in 1737, and till I was fourteen no time-accidents happened to me. Then in 1751 I set out from Orkney for Glasgow. When I arrived I found that it was not 1751, but 1901, and that a hundred and fifty years had been burned up in my two days' journey. But I myself was still in 1751, and remained there for a long time. All my life since I have been trying to overhaul that invisible leeway. No wonder I am obsessed with time.[27]

Edwin Muir had fallen from eternity into time, from Eden to "a tenth-rate hell."[28] The great opposing symbols had already appeared, although he did not as yet realize it, and were starting to pull him apart. The one foot he tried to keep in Eden, in 1751, was gradually loosened as the squalor and tragedy of his life in Glasgow swallowed him.

Already savagely uprooted, Edwin Muir was further shattered by the deaths of his brothers and his parents in a space of four years. It was as if this gentle farming family was physically unable to live in the industrial world; that whatever nourished them in Orkney was lacking in Glasgow. The effect of these deaths on Edwin Muir was great. The pages describing this time in *An Autobiography* make frightening reading, for even then, more than thirty years later, Muir could scarcely bring himself to discuss what happened:

I have hurried over these years because they are still painful and still blurred in my mind: I was too young for so much death. All that time seemed to give no return, nothing but loss; it was like a heap of dismal rubbish in the middle of which, without rhyme or reason, were scattered four deaths. I climbed out of these years like a man struggling out of a quagmire, but that rubbish still encumbered me for a long time with *post-mortem* persistence.[29]

For the rest of his life, Muir attempted to find ways of contemplating this experience, of dragging it into the light in order to make sense of it. Even in his late poems the echoes of his first years in Glasgow sound just below the surface, and his great negative symbols — the Fall, the labyrinth, the intercepter — with their emphasis on blockage, sterility, lack of meaning, unnatural events — draw heavily on this time. The alienation from Eden, eternity, harmony, together with the shock of the experience of death, pain, and meaningless suffering, left Muir stunned. He grew "silent, absent, dingy,"[30] unable to reach back for the wholeness of his childhood or to find consolation in any transfiguring image:

Something in myself was buried, and I was only half there as I worked in the office and wandered about the roads. I felt that I had gone far away from myself.[31]

This loss of the real self, the blocking off of the images of health and harmony, lies at the heart of Edwin Muir's neurosis, which only began to be cleared during his analysis in London. It is no wonder that the Fall, the sudden sickening removal from the land of wholeness and timelessness, should have come to dominate his thought and his symbology. The Fall, in terms of his Glasgow years, is primarily the loss of the experience of transcendence, the movement from eternity into time, from Eden into the labyrinth, from Fable into Story. Reinforced by the new experience of poverty, violence and appalling social conditions, Muir tried to compensate for this loss by embracing both socialism and Nietzscheanism — structures of ideas which might replace the ordered certainties of his early life. It is not difficult to understand Muir's hunger for intellectual structure. Having once had strong intimations of a different and better reality underlying the surface of life, "a sort of parallel world,"[32] Muir was desperately trying to will into existence a personal vision which again might reveal that other world. But the Nietzschean and socialist modes of perception could never fully satisfy him, being, on the one hand, short of the sympathy and the harmonious, deeply human qualities he knew in Orkney, and, on the other, unable to provide the imaginative, symbolic transfiguration of this world which, as he knew, could cut through time and place and comprehend the human situation in terms of something permanent and of lasting value. In Muir's own words:

Actually, although I did not know it, my Nietzscheanism was what psychologists call a "compensation". I could not free my life as it was, and so I took refuge in the fantasy of the Superman.[33]

And yet, in spite of these confused intellectual exercises, his thought, at the time he was writing his aphorisms in *The New Age*,[34] was already playing, at some deep level, with the ideas he was later to develop and turn into a symbology. "I wondered," writes Willa Muir, "... why he should bother himself so much about Original Sin."[35] In the aphorisms, too, is the idea of the unconscious, where innocence is retained, though the ideas of the Fall, the unconscious and Nietzsche often become curiously mixed together:

Innocence and good conscience still exist in the unconscious, in the rapture and joy of Love. The instincts believe in Life entirely without questioning; doubt and guilt are simply not present in their world.[36]

The yearning for vision and integration in some of the aphorisms is unmistakable, but soon the Nietzschean, artificial personality is back at work. On the Crucifixion, for instance, Muir writes: "This belief in the miraculous virtues of death and of spilt blood was pardonable in savages who believed in magic, but in us today it is a degrading superstition."[37] The confusion of the perceptions, the deliberate masks, the violent discrepancies between gentle and tough attitudes, the deliberate suppression of traditional simplicity, show clearly the desperation in Muir's search for a satisfactory vision at this time. He is lost in an intellectual labyrinth, imposing his will upon his fragile, lost instincts. It is no wonder that Willa Muir, having read *We Moderns* before she met its author, sensed "a yearning for love, innocence, poetry and mystery."[38] Muir's neurosis did not let up after his marriage and move to London. His wife recalls how his fears affected him:

23

The way he walked showed how rigidly he had been repressing some of himself. His whole left side was somehow cramped, the left shoulder unevenly higher than the right and the left arm, never allowed to swing free when he walked, held stiffly close to his body. The pressure on him had now been loosened, partly by our marriage, partly because the familiar Glasgow framework was missing, partly because Nietzsche's inward armature was breaking up, and the repressed forces in his unconscious were beginning to assert themselves as fears.[39]

London's size and strangeness brought out further evidence of his neurotic state:

He had an awful nervous reaction, thinking that some of these houses might fall down on him. He used to scuttle along the streets and come back home and say that he felt that they were going to fall on him and I began to realize that I'd got a very delicately balanced nervous system to cope with and that all the effects of his terrible adolescence and later in Glasgow had got to be worked out somehow.[40]

Already interested in psychoanalysis, Muir agreed to Orage's suggestion that he should be analysed by Maurice Nicoll, and only with the analysis did some sort of release start for that part of him, the unconscious, which he had penned up for so many years. At this stage of his life, Edwin Muir had experienced the two mutually hostile kinds of experience which were to form the core of his symbology. In one sense, all his later experience, including his breakdown in 1948 after returning from Prague, was merely a deepening, or broadening, of the years in Orkney and Glasgow. He had known the timeless, fabulous world of Eden, with all its pattern and integration. He had been wrenched out of it into the fallen world of Glasgow, being forced to carry immense burdens of death, pain, suffering, ugliness, violence, loss of certainty, ill health, moral and spiritual confusion. His unconscious, the link with the Fable and the wider reality he had known, had been firmly repressed by his conscious mind; his links with the Fable had been lost under the terrible pressure of the Story. He was out of balance, in touch with nothing of value to him, plagued with neurotic fears and repressions. It was a classic neurosis, and it was imperative for Muir, if he were to become an integrated personality, to rediscover the contents of the unconscious and to raise them to consciousness. He had somehow to put himself in touch with the symbols of health which he had lost in Glasgow, and create a balance between the outer and the inner, the Fall and Eden.

The analysis produced dramatic results, well documented by Muir, releasing a flood of material from the unconscious in the form of dreams and waking visions. Muir's ideas changed under the pressure of this material, and the self-willed barriers, the Nietzschean intellectual structure, crumbled, as images of the fabulous poured back. In an initially painful and necessarily inchoate state, the symbols of permanence and health were imposing themselves once again. It is not too fanciful to see Muir's poetry as an extended record of this head-on confrontation of dark and light, chaos and harmony, conscious blockage and unconscious release. It was, for Muir under analysis, a violent shock, as what was in conflict was nothing less than two diametrically opposed modes of perception, or in other words, a strong false self in conflict with an uncertain, weak and shy real self. It was a struggle which Muir perhaps only solved in some of his late poems, after rehearsing the symbolic opposition many times. What is certain, however, is that it was through symbol, through the stuff of dream and vision and the unconscious, that Muir discovered his real self. This equation of symbol with reality and health, as a release from the tormented world of time and surface reality, was instinctively sensed by Muir in his childhood and only reconfirmed by his analysis. A large number of his poems derive from dream and vision material, often making it difficult to apprehend the poetry as separate from the life. The conflicts between two realities, the use of symbol to transcend the neurotic and rediscover lost harmony, the slow journey towards an inclusive symbology and a spiritual balance, a belief in the supreme value of the timeless and numinous — these belong simultaneously to Muir, the man, trying to reconcile his extremes of experience, and to the poet, struggling to integrate warring symbols and to find an adequate technique for such an integration.

With the dropping away of his Nietzschean obsessions, Muir became open to different ideas, and deeply influenced by his dreams and visions. One of the most important results of his analysis was a new conception of immortality and man's relationship with time:

I realized that immortality is not an idea or a belief, but a state of being in which man keeps alive in himself his perception of that boundless union and freedom, which he can faintly apprehend in time, though its consummation lies beyond time.[41]

The stuff from his unconscious, the beautiful and strange dreams and visions released by his analysis, confirmed to him the existence and the creative powers of this immortal world, and it made him start searching for an all-inclusive symbology which would contain these visions and give them significant form. In his wife's words:

Now, although he was beginning to distrust Nietzsche's Super-Man, he still looked for some great story, some cosmic pattern that would assign a place to every experience in life, relating it to an inclusive whole and justifying it. He was looking for that in his visions, and he kept on looking for it as long as he lived, until he thought he had found it.[42]

The emergence from the labyrinth of neurosis was a painful one. It is no wonder that "he was never quite free of preoccupation with the story of the Fall" and the new self that was slowly forming seemed to be often looking fearfully over its shoulder at what it was leaving behind.

When Muir left Britain for Prague in 1921, he was again making a significant journey towards a new life, but this time, with the extremes of Eden and the Fall behind him, his journey was more clearly one of renewal. The change of place and country was to give him a chance to build on the new possibilities of balance he had been given in London, and one of the ways — indeed the really vital way — he began to achieve this was by writing poetry. In the new landscape of Europe, away from the battlefield on which his self had been torn apart, he began, in his mid-thirties, to create an art in which the conflict would be patterned, developed and re-fought through symbol and imagination.

I have said that the search for a symbology implied the search for a technique. In Edwin Muir's early poetry it is clear that his ability to deal with, or release, the images and symbols presented to him is very restricted. The clumsiness of rhythm and metre, and the often diastrous mingling of Victorian poeticisms with conversational language severely modify the success of his first collections. In these works, the inadequacies of the technique constantly undermine the successful presentation of symbol. In Muir's own words:

I had no training; I was too old to submit myself to contemporary influences, and I had acquired in Scotland a deference towards ideas which made my entrance into poetry difficult. Though my inspiration had begun to work I had no technique by which I could give expression to it. There were the rhythms of English poetry on the one hand, the images in my mind on the other. All I could do at the start was to force the one, creaking and complaining, into the mould of the other.[43]

CHAPTER TWO

The Poetic Symbol

Edwin Muir's early and middle-period poetry is characterized by the struggle to locate and release the symbols appropriate to his developing vision. As well as his need to learn the basic craft of poetry, his vision of the Story and the Fable demanded a poetic means with which to explore the symbolic higher reality of the Fable, which had become closely linked to a vision of Eden and to the timeless world of dream and the unconscious. He had to find a symbolic landscape in which the extreme experiences of Orkney and Glasgow could confront each other and which could contain the great welling up of unconscious images which followed his analysis in London. Only by developing an adequate pattern of symbols could Muir successfully incorporate both Fable and Story, Orkney and Glasgow, eternity and time, unconscious and conscious. I intend to show how Muir introduced his symbols and how he slowly developed the appropriate techniques which would allow the symbols a proper function. But first I must say a little about symbolism in poetry. We may usefully take as a starting point Suzanne Langer's description of the genesis of symbols in the mind's processes:

The material furnished by the senses is instantly wrought into symbols, which are our elementary ideas. Some of these can be combined and manipulated in the manner we call 'reasoning'. Others do not lend themselves to this use, but are naturally telescoped into dreams, or vapor off in conscious fantasy.[1]

It is this discursive, non-conceptual symbol which is of primary interest in the study of poetic symbolism. The symbols which are "telescoped into dreams" or "fantasy" have certain powerful characteristics when examined more specifically.

Basically, of course, a symbol stands for something. It is one side of an analogy, containing within itself the implications of the other side. But symbols often mean more than this, seeming to attract to themselves layers of suggestion and feeling and becoming active objects in their own right. "In a symbol," wrote Carlyle,

There is concealment and yet revelation: here therefore, by Silence and by Speech acting together, comes a double significance. And if both the Speech be itself high, and the Silence fit and noble, how expressive will their union be! Thus in many a painted Device, or simple Seal-emblem, the commonest Truth stands out to us proclaimed with quite new emphasis.

For it is here that Fantasy with her mystic wonderland plays with the small prose demain of Sense, and becomes incorporated therewith. In the Symbol proper, what we can call a Symbol, there is ever, more or less distinctly and directly, some embodiment and revelation of the Infinite; the Infinite is made to blend itself with the Finite, to stand visible, and as it were, attainable there.[2]

In less florid terms, a symbol, because it is free from the exactness of analogous thought, can never be fully expressed in rational terms. An allegory is a sign for something, a way of expressing a known content, but a symbol can be more than this, something that cannot be expressed by rational concepts. Thus, as Carlyle states, the symbol can embody the finite and the infinite. As defined in *The Princeton Encyclopedia of Poetry and Poetics,* "a literary symbol units an image (the analogy) and an idea or conception (the subject) which that image suggests or evokes."[3] An aesthetic symbol then — Blake's sick rose; Frost's dark woods; Keats' Moneta; Yeats' tower — can never be fully explained. We can open up the rational, referential part of it to our critical consciousness, but the irrational part is elusive, suggestive, amenable only tenuously (though powerfully) to the feelings, the imagination, the intuitive response. Thus a symbol addresses the whole psyche, its conscious and unconscious parts and all its functions as well, and has become an essential tool for the visionary poet. In Jung's words:

The indefinite yet definite mythological theme and the irridescent symbol express the processes of the soul more aptly, more completely, and therefore infinitely more clearly than the clearest definition: for the symbol gives not only a picture of the process but also . . . the possibility of simultaneously experiencing or re-experiencing the process, whose twilight character can only be understood through a sympathetic approach and never by the brutal attack of clear intellectual definition.[4]

The symbol is a focus of significances and relationships, containing the potentiality of recreating experience for the receptive mind and making available areas of experience which the "either/or" of logical thought cannot adequately contain.

Charles Chadwick makes an interesting distinction between two kinds of poetic symbolism. Firstly, at its simplest, symbolism suggests ideas and emotions by recreating them in the reader's mind through the use of unexplained symbols, but there is a broader kind of symbolism, which we might call "transcendental" symbolism, in which, in Chadwick's words, "concrete images are used as symbols, not of particular thoughts and feelings within the poet, but of a vast and general ideal world of which the real world is merely an imperfect representation."[5] In this kind of symbolism, the world of experience is not merely recreated but transformed through symbol, in order to come at a reality beyond time and place. It is this kind of "transcendental" symbolism which is relevant to a study of Edwin Muir's poetry, as all his basic ideas revolve around the belief in two orders of reality, one timeless, perfect, all-inclusive, and one imperfect, caught in time and suffering. In order to present this vision, to link the finite and the infinite, the Story and the Fable, Muir had to turn to symbol. His great symbols of Eden, the Fall, the labyrinth, the journey, become, as his poetry develops, the means through which he reconciles the opposites in his experience and reaches out beyond objective reality into the world of vision, the place of the unconscious.

Symbolist poetry is notoriously difficult to define. Tindall catches its essence in his description of the French symbolists:

To do their transcendental job, words had to be relieved of their normal meanings, removed from their familiar contexts, until, purified, they could provoke reveries, resonances, ineffable suggestions. Poems built by meticulous craft from words deprived of syntax could suggest things too fugitive for expression and meanings at once precise and multiple. Poems built in this way were absolute. Free from meaning in the usual sense, they were also free from time, chance, life, passion and matter. A symphonic relationship among the parts of a poem took the place of comprehensible relationships with external things. The poem, said Mallarmé, "is a mystery to which the reader must hunt the key". Abandoning the hope of a single interpretation, he must discover the main images, observe the effect upon them of the peripheral images, and guess the idea generated by their interaction.[6]

Clearly the key to an understanding of symbolism is a more strenuous focus upon technique than is usual when confronting non-symbolist poetry. Tindall goes on:

Sometimes the symbol was an image, like Mallarmé's swan, or a system of images; sometimes it was a suggestive rhythm or combination of sounds; and sometimes it was a whole poem, a symphony of sounds, images, rhythms approximating the condition of music.[7]

We are not, then, looking for one precise thing. Baudelaire, Verlaine and Mallarmé all wrote very different poetry, as did Yeats and Eliot. Yet we are able to make some tentative conclusions. Symbolist poetry is a poetry of indirection, in which objects tend to be suggested rather than named, or to be used for an evocation of mood:

Ideas may be important, but are characteristically presented obliquely through a variety of symbols and must be apprehended largely by intuition and feeling . . . to arouse response beyond the level of ordinary consciousness. For the symbolists the power of the Word goes far beyond ordinary denotative verbal limits through suggestive developments in syntax and inter-related images and through what may be termed the "phonetic symbolism" of musicality and connotative sound-relationships.[8]

Symbolist method is a means of releasing the full significance of the chosen symbol; allowing it enough freedom to express itself, with all its clustered meanings, to its full potential. The symbolist mode implies an interest in syntax, in music and in time. As the symbol is potentially transcendent, the poet must free it from the confines of sequential logic and a consistent time pattern, and one way of doing this is through syntax and tense. The basic ambition of the symbolists to make poetry approach the condition of music is basically a concern with time. Normally literature lives in two times at once; the time we take to read it and also the time it describes as its language presents an experience or a sequence of experiences. On the other hand, music has only one time; the time it takes for its performance. Musical time is always present. The symbolists, aspiring to the purity of the musical time, saw that, in Davie's words: "One way to make poetry into music is to collapse the two times of literature into the one time of music, by making the poem refer to no time except the time it takes in the reading."[9] In short, the poet telescopes time by dislocating logical sequential pattern. "The Love Song of J. Alfred Prufrock" is a classic modern example of this technique. In this poem, Eliot shifts his tense constantly, using past, present, and future as if there were no distinction, and the only time is the one time of its reading. In this way, the symbols are freed from time and can release significances both in time and out of time, both past and future, both present and possible. Similarly, the symbolist poet often refuses to be precise about place. Many symbolist poems create a landscape which is deliberately not precise, but symbolic and timeless. Again, to use Eliot's poem as an example, we do not ever know *precisely* what Prufrock is doing, where he is going, whom he is addressing. The city is around him, but so are "the chambers of the sea." The poem shifts around from memory to desire, from room to room, city to shore, conversation to thought, deliberately disorientating the reader in terms of space and time by the means of tense shift and spatial dislocation. To add to this time-space dislocation, the symbolist technique sometimes fractures syntax, leaving fragments and phrases unrelated and seemingly lost. This is another device for escaping logic and time. The fractured syntax, refusing the reader the easy consolation of a completed pattern, hints of what is unsaid and reaches for meanings and stillnesses beyond normal propositional logic. The desire to be free of the rational and conceptual dominates the symbolist aesthetic, the main purpose of which is to provide the conditions under which the symbol, or symbols, may be free to exist fully.

Another symbolist technique concerns the place of the "I" — the confessional poet — in the poem. As Mallarmé, whose own cold glittering landscapes are the justification, said:

The pure work implies the elocutionary disappearance of the poet, who yields place to the words, immobilised by the shock of their inequality; they take light from mutual reflection ... replacing the old lyrical afflatus or the enthusiastic personal direction of the phrase.[10]

In a symbolic landscape, where time and place become fragmented, even irrelevant, and where the poem reaches upwards towards a numinous reality, the personal, concrete presence of the poet often has no place. The consciousness running through a symbolist poem is a human consciousness, but not always one which can be readily located in time or space. The poet himself does not describe his poem; his poem, his language, describes itself and comments on the creative act: "That is not it at all,/ That is not what I meant, at all."

This aesthetic is dominated by the overriding concern of escaping from reason and from logic, from time and from place, and of inventing a language and a syntax which can transcend ordinary reality. For the symbolist poet the attaining of the "other" world

31

means, in most cases, an abandoning of public and political themes, though clearly not with Yeats (and, as we shall see, with Muir) who used symbolist techniques only some of the time. In Bowra's words: "The essence of Symbolism is its insistence on a world of ideal beauty, and its conviction that this is realised through art."[11] But this seems only partially satisfactory. The "world of ideal beauty" is perhaps misleading, inasmuch as the "other," ideal world may produce terror as well as beauty. It is a risk to sever yourself from time and place and to release yourself to the full meaning of the unconscious and its flood of images. The terror and pain implied in the poetry of, say, Blake, Baudelaire, Eliot and Muir reveals something of the vulnerability of the visionary poet. At its lowest, the desire to experience the timeless can lead to the pain of always knowing that, as humans, we are caught in time and place, for all our intimations and intuitions of the "other" world. To the mind living in two places and trying to reconcile them, the threat of schizophrenia, of inordinate, if idealistic, pressure, is very real. The most a man can have is one foot in Eden. As Engelberg puts it, the symbolist poet

seems forever alienated from an ideal world and also forever acutely conscious not only of this separation but also of the sordid reality from whose perspective he is obliged to seek the azure of the ideal world. In short, the poet is trapped between his impulse to recover the transcendent world and his awareness of the utter impossibility of ever doing so. ... This tension lies behind most Symbolist poetry, and these poets, however they may differ in style or substance, will repeatedly create symbolic landscapes, seascapes, cityscapes, and dreamscapes in which despair, a sense of loss and fear, a hunger for beauty and release, and a horrible awareness of sullen, leaden reality pervade their work. Such awareness will lead to dream, to nightmare, to seeing the beautiful in the ugly (and vice versa), to boredom, to fatigue — *and* to the magnificent visions that lie beyond the windowpane.[12]

The reality to which the symbolists aspire is ultimately the same thing which Edwin Muir lost in Glasgow — the vision of Eden, of harmony, of the past existing in the present, of eternal time, of the dream and the unconscious, of the transcending symbol. In the unconscious there is no time, no ordinary logic or reason.

We may say, then, that symbolist poetry uses sophisticated techniques of language and syntax in order to escape from the everyday reality of time and place. In the case of Dante, Blake, Yeats and

Muir, and others, this implies a *system* of symbols, not merely a symbol, or group, existing separately for each poem. Yeats' tower, gyres, birds, tree, dancer become an integral part of his poetry in the way that for Muir, the journey, the Fall, Eden, the labyrinth become a patterned symbology, a series of key symbols which are used over and over in slightly different circumstances. The poet releases these symbols into language in poem after poem, each time hoping they will generate more significance. And by sheer accumulation, they become richer and more meaningful. But, like Yeats, Muir is not a symbolist poet all the time. Only in certain key poems does he seem under sufficient pressure to use the full symbolist techniques of fractured syntax, tense-shift, disorientation of place, language commenting on itself, the elocutionary disappearance of the poet. But in nearly all his poems he displays a characteristically symbolist indirectness and suggestiveness. His landscapes are rarely other than symbolic and unlocated; the precise vagueness of dream haunts his verse; the pressure of the here-and-now, in a confessional sense, is remarkably absent; and the reader trained on a poetry of concept and logic soon finds himself bewildered when confronted with freely moving, unlocated symbols and the sort of mind to which the unbelievable violence of our century is imagined in an almost surrealistic and slow-motion dream of two unidentified creatures fighting.

Symbolist poetry, then, is a poetry using specialized techniques. The presence of a symbol in a poem does not presuppose that it is a symbolist poem. It is perhaps useful to make a distinction between merely symbolical, which implies any use of symbol, and the symbolist, which implies the use of the sophisticated attitudes and techniques I have briefly discussed here. Certainly we must distinguish between symbolism and allegory, where the allegorical experience is referentially (and usually intellectually) linked to specific properties in order to define and comment upon them. Blake insists upon the distinction:

Fable or Allegory are a totally distinct and inferior kind of Poetry. Vision or Imagination is a Representation of what Eternally exists, Really and Unchangeably.[13]

Symbolism and the poetry of vision hope to penetrate to "what Eternally exists," and this is what Muir aspired to. He is not an allegorist, nor is he always a symbolist in the strictest sense of the word. But in his mature poetry he almost invariably uses symbol, and, as I shall attempt to show, he is often forced, by pressure of experience, into using classic symbolist techniques which alone seem able to contain his vision at its most powerful and complete. And these symbolist poems, almost all of them written late in his life, are undoubtedly his greatest achievements.

CHAPTER THREE

The Early Poetry

Muir's first two volumes of poetry are not particularly interesting in terms of the growth of his symbology and technique. They are the books of a beginning poet for whom basic problems of language and metre seem to be dominant. Only nine of twenty-four poems in the first volume have survived in the *Collected Poems*[1] and none at all of *Chorus of the Newly Dead*.

Technically, *First Poems* is characterized by clumsiness of various kinds. The metres are often plodding and mechanical; the diction belongs largely to the nineteenth-century, with many inversions and archaisms like "o'er" and "ere"; many words are rhyme-forced; poetic energy is constantly dissipated by a preponderance of adjectives and purely decorative phrases; and clear echoes — especially of Wordsworth, Coleridge and the Scottish ballads — are often instrusively evident. It is a derivative, literary volume, using the techniques of Romantic and Victorian poetry too uncritically. And yet already visible is Muir's determination to go back to his roots, to retrace his steps from childhood, to reshape his life in imaginative terms. Several of these poems go back to his beginnings. "Childhood" remembers Orkney:

> Long time he lay upon the sunny hill,
>   To his father's house below securely bound.
> Far off the silent, changing sound was still,
>   With the black islands lying thick around . . .
>
> The evening sound was smooth like sunken glass,
>   And time seemed finished ere the ship passed by.

The poem evokes the glassy timelessness of his childhood, but it is merely *described*, not presented dramatically. The poem is unable to enact its meaning.

Similarly, in "Horses," the tentative gestures towards a timeless landscape and an emblematic reality are modified and weakened not

35

only by the archaisms, but by the intrusive presence of the "I," who grabs the reader and describes insistently without letting him see for himself:

> Ah, now it fades! it fades! and I must pine
> Again for that dread country crystalline,
> Where the blank field and the still-standing tree
> Were bright and fearful presences to me.

It is clear what Muir is trying to do, but his lack of a suitable technique prevents him from entering that world of vision and timeless meaning he aspires to. And throughout this volume there is a yearning for simplicity, for Eden, for the timeless magic of childhood which might compensate for the complexities of adult life. Muir is trying to digest, present and understand the mass of images which were released by his analysis — dreams of lost lands and seas, the poet standing "self-tranced between the earth and sky." This is a primitive adumbration of the symbol of Eden, though as yet the poet has no language which can embody it and it remains an anguished hint. One of the more interesting poems in *First Poems* is "Betrayal," where Muir, for the first time, uses the symbolic mode. The poem concerns a beautiful girl caught in a snare, imprisoned by a gaoler until she rots away. It is a traditional utterance of the time versus beauty theme; the inevitable mutability of the flesh:

> For still she smiles, and does not know
>   Her feet are in the snaring lime.
> He who entrapped her long ago,
>   And kills her, is unpitying Time.

This kind of poem is best left to act out its own significance, but Muir at this stage has not learned to leave his symbols to interact and present their own meaning. This poem, with all its flaws, is perhaps the clearest pointer to the way the poet will develop, using dream-like, indirect presentation in an unlocalized time and place where concept is modified effortlessly into symbol. There are premonitions here, too, of Muir's own strong lyric voice, especially in the third stanza which stands out firmly from the derivative stylization of the rest of the poem:

> And there she waits, while in her flesh,
>   Small joyless teeth fret without rest.
> But she stands smiling in the mesh,
>   While she is duped and dispossest.

It is interesting that, in his own copy of *First Poems*,[2] Edwin Muir wrote the words "Very bad" against this poem, presumably when he was going through the volume trying to find material for his *Collected Poems*. Many of the poems received such comments, ranging from "Awful!" ("On the Mediterranean") to "This, pretty bad" ("Remembrance"), showing Muir's strong dissatisfaction with these early poems when he looked at them much later in his life. *First Poems* deals with time and place, but in a wavering uncertain way. The idea of opposition between eternity and time lies unassimilated under the often clumsy surface of many of these poems.

The volume concludes with six ballads, two of which are written in Scots. "Ballad of the Soul" is perhaps the most interesting, though it has serious limitations:

On "Ballad of the Soul" (originally called "Ballad of Eternal Life"), based on the waking trance he had experienced in London, Muir commented much later: "The dream was wonderful, but the poem is all wrong." The trouble was that he was trying merely to reproduce the dream, not working creatively on it. . . . Too many of *First Poems* merely reproduce dreams. . . . [3]

Professor Butter is right about this poem. The conception is vast but Muir relies almost completely on the dream itself to provide the necessary dramatic interest, and his language is not adequate for the job:

> I struck it prone;   I walked alone
>   In alien horizons;
> The low-browed voiceless animals
>   Were my companions.
>
> Asleep, a huge forgotten brood
>   Lay round like tree-stumps old:
> The dragons.   From their eyelids fell
>   Soft-rayed, the rustling gold.

Here the syntax is clearly at war with the metrical system and the rhyming is dominating the sense. In short, the form is wrong for the content and the two are incompatible. Admittedly, many of the worst stanzas (including the two above) were later excised in *Collected Poems*, but the poem still fails. The prose description of the trance in *An Autobiography* is much more impressive.

The ballads in Scots, especially "Ballad of the Flood," are more interesting. The story of Noah is perhaps more appropriate to the

ballad form than a deeply personal vision, and, although "Ballad of
the Flood" is derivative, and literary, it does manage to capture the
characteristic movement of the ballad with some success:

> "Last night I dreamed a ghastly dream,
>   Before the dirl o'day.
> A twining worm cam out the wast,
>   Its back was like the slae. . . .
>
> "And we sall joy to-day, my luve,
>   Sall dance to harp and horn,
> And I'll devise anither play
>   When we walk out the morn.

In "Ballad of Hector in Hades," the speaker is Hector, returned
from his death to run again his race with Achilles around Troy. For
this reason the poem has a certain interest, not the least of which is
that it is Muir's first poetic treatment of Troy. The poem moves
from a ghostly "burnished stillness" to the frenzy of the race which
seems to involve the whole universe, and, throughout, this juxtaposition of movement and stillness gives the poem its tension. In the
last stanza the two states are combined in a superb hyperbolic
resolution:

> The race is ended.   Far away
>   I hang and do not care,
> While round bright Troy Achilles whirls
>   A corpse with streaming hair.

The poem's origin, however, lies not only in Homer, but in personal
experience. It recreates a significant moment of Muir's childhood
when he ran away from a boy named Freddie Sinclair and felt great
shame and guilt afterwards. In this poem, writes Muir, "I got rid of
that terror."[4] Again the impulse is to examine childhood, but this
time to be rid of one of the few unpleasant memories of those years
in Orkney.

The poem suffers a little from a thumping, over-insistent rhythm,
which works unsubtly upon the ear. And again the language occasionally breaks down in the face of a tight form; but it does point
clearly forward to later poems of nightmare where forces move
across legendary still landscapes in vast dances of life and death.

As a whole, this volume cannot be judged a poetic success, but in
the light of the later poems and Muir's personal situation following
his breakdown and analysis, it can be seen as the first sign of his

being able to express himself in terms of time, memory and place. He introduces, under the instinctive pressures of dream and vision, partial images of early childhood in an effort to relate them to the present, and, for all the technical uncertainties, he explores occasionally the possibilities of indirect presentation based on image instead of concept. It is a tentative beginning but a valuable first step on the long road towards personal integration and poetic maturity. As yet he has not contemplated the hell of Glasgow, but he has been able to look back beyond it, to put himself in touch, however tenuously, with old values and perceptions.

Chorus of the Newly Dead, on the other hand, completely omitted from the *Collected Poems*,

was made up of painful emotions which had been working like yeast inside him ever since those first five years in Glasgow when his father, his two brothers, his mother had died one after the other. . . . In the *Chorus of the Newly Dead* he was making his first poetic attempt to come to terms with Death by looking for a transcendental meaning in life.[5]

This poem, for all its scale and ambition, cannot be considered a success, and Muir himself was dissatisfied with it:

The idea greatly moved me, but my imaginative excitement never managed to communicate itself, or at best now and then, to the poem; the old disability which I had struggled with in Hellbrunn, a simple lack of skill, still held me up. In any case the theme was far too great for my powers. . . . [6]

The poem shows a collection of social misfits in an Idiot, a Beggar, a Coward, a Harlot, a Poet, a Hero and a Mystic — looking back over their life on earth. Linking each section is the Chorus, which questions and comments. Technically Muir tries to add interest by metrical variation. The Chorus sections use mainly pentameter lines in rhyming five, six or seven line stanzas, whereas the "characters" are presented in a variety of forms. The Idiot, for instance, speaks in two-foot lines, in *a b c b d b c b* stanza, reflecting, presumably, the chopped, gnomic utterance and the fragmented logic of the idiot. But the lines lack subtlety and variation and remain wooden and rhythmically stiff:

> They flung me out;
>   They broke my brain.
> Down beat the sun,
>   Down beat the rain.

39

They broke upon me:
　　All was vain.
The truth is hard,
　　The false is plain.

Clumsiness of syntax and metre characterizes this poem, though there are evident signs of the poet's desire to experiment. Dimeter, trimeter, tetrameter and pentameter lines are all used, and the section on the Hero is particularly interesting as a sustained exercise in feminine, falling rhyme.

The poem is noteworthy, too, for its creating of symbolic landscape. More than in *First Poems*, Muir is striving for magical, archaic feeling, a landscape where dream is relevant to his poetic purpose:

Those proud heraldic animals
　　Like pictures in a primal dream,
Holding unconscious festivals
　　Which past our primal darkness gleam!

That stationary country where
　　Achilles drives and Hector runs,
Making a movement in the air
　　Forever, under all the suns!

And that ghostly eternity
　　Cut by the bridge where journeys Christ
On endless arcs pacing the sea,
　　Time turning with his solar tryst!

It is significant that these lines, which stand out as somewhat different from the rest of the poem, should be the ones which Muir was most pleased with. These lines, he writes:

express my state at that time better than anything I could say now. . . . These lines surprise me afresh when I read them, and bring back the days when I walked in the pinewoods on the Sonntagberg. . . . We long most for the places in time where we were happy, and I was happy during these spring and summer months on the Sonntagberg, composing an abortive poem.[7]

Chorus of the Newly Dead might well be "abortive" and technically clumsy, but as a means of penetrating to the Fable it is important. In this poem "Time's deer is slain" and Muir is able to construct, to some extent, symbolic action in symbolic, timeless places:

Dark shapes stood
　　Near by us, and we found our way
Within Life's vast and glittering wood.

> On either side existence lay
> Unending.   When we sought to leave the track,
> The earth, awake or slumbering, turned us back.

Through imagination, Muir has set out on the road back to his roots and thence forward towards integration of opposites in himself. Already in this poem, Muir's imagination can range from the prostitute in "that one mean street" to "Forests and rivers of eternal Kings" and attempt to join them in one symbolic construct. As yet he is unable to do so successfully, but his war with time and place has now been firmly declared. The thing which has dragged him down will be countered with weapons which can transcend it and relegate it. In a letter written while he was working on this poem, Muir verifies that his search is for values and order. He is trying, he writes, for an atmosphere of "mystery and wonder at the life of the earth . . . an assumption of infinite and incalculable powers behind the visible drama."[8] It seems to me very doubtful that the poem transmits these things, and it is primarily a failure of technique which causes the immense gap between the conception and the actual result.

Variations on a Time Theme was not published until eight years after *Chorus of the Newly Dead*. Although it is grouped as ten sections under the one title, the poems were published separately and, according to Butter, were probably not written "with any idea of forming a sequence. He was preoccupied with time, and so the poems which came were related in theme; but they are ten poems, not an attempt at a single one."[9] The poems are based on the paradox, always central to Muir's thought, that men are immortal souls, who, once fallen from eternity, must travel in the restrictions of time. In these poems Muir introduces his symbols of Eden and the Fall, time and eternity, Troy, and the idea of eternal recurrence — the Fable of men, generation after generation, taking the same road across time. This journey is past, present and future; its components — human and animal and natural — are as permanent as heraldic devices. In Eden, in the unconscious, in dream, in imagination, there is no time, and we are always aware of this as we are thrown into time from eternity. This is a common enough idea, containing within it both Platonic and Christian elements, as well as elements of modern psychology. It is close to Bergson's idea that time is not the

41

linear sequence of separate events seen by the intellect, but the inter-penetration of past and present revealed to intuition. Muir would have agreed with Kierkegaard that "Time does not really exist without unrest; it does not exist for dumb animals who are absolutely without anxiety,"[10] and even more with Mircea Eliade[11] who postu-lates a strong distinction between "profane" time and "mythical" time which is very close to Muir's conception of time and eternity. The individual, Eliade argues, may project into "mythical" time only in certain ways, such as "on the occasion of rituals or of important acts." Time may be abolished "through the imitation of archetypes and the repetition of paradigmatic gestures." Interest-ingly, Eliade claims that primitive societies, removed from their "paradise of archetypes" regard the human condition "as a fall"; a fall into history or "profane" time. And Eliade's discussion of the Fall, the eternal return, time and eternity, are uncannily close to Muir's ideas as expressed in his poetry.

Muir, was not, of course, interested in formulating a philosophical constant or even a vocabulary about time. His approach was instinc-tive, intuitive and shaped not only by his own experience of the "Fall" from Orkney to Glasgow, from eternity to time, but by his ability or inability to formulate a poetic symbology which could absorb and integrate this experience. For him the penetration of time into a higher world of eternity, of vision, remained the vital thing, and this could only be contemplated by the use of symbol.

In terms of technical development and introduction of symbol, *Variations on a Time Theme* is most interesting. Muir now accepts, quite clearly, the possibility of removing his poetry from real land-scape and allowing it to construct its own postulates of time and place. The landscape is a wilderness, a desert, a wasteland over which generations travel. The focus shifts from "we" as mankind, to the tribes of heraldry, to the poet himself, who, for the first time, brings a deeply confessional element to the surface in Poem III:

> A child in Adam's field I dreamed away
> My one eternity and hourless day,
> Ere from my wrist Time's bird had learned to fly,
> Or I had robbed the Tree of which I die. . . .

and yet though this seems clearly personal, the "I" moves quickly outward into more general significance:

> I walked the shrunken hills and clouded plains
> Among my flocks, pleased with a shepherd's gains, . . .
> . . . now I walk the sand
> And search this rubble for the promised land.

Even more autobiographical and confessional is Poem IX, originally published as "The Dilemma," in which the presence of a blocking agent — here called Indifference — is clearly related to the later image of the Intercepter. Amoral, lacking human compassion of religious sense, the intruder is "Packed in my skin from head to toe," and is related here closely to Time: "If I could drive this demon out/ I'd put all Time's display to rout." Opposed to this intruder is the Soul, and the poem resolves itself around this conflict, which becomes a battle between time (Indifference) and eternity (Soul).

In terms of rhyme and metre, these poems show a great advance on the previous work. Muir has developed a more confident tone; a strange flat elegiac rhythm is heard throughout, completely appropriate to the primitive, endless landscape. Most of the poems are written in loose pentameters, some rhymed tightly like III and VIII in heroic couplets; some in blank verse. Poem VII is particularly interesting. Of the fifteen lines, twelve end in the word "Time," giving a heavy liturgical obsessive effect, like a ritual chant of despair. The other three lines end with the words "liberty," "free" and "Eternity" as if escaping from the prison of time. Muir uses rhyme highly expressively, making the desire to be free of time, and its tentative possibility, a property of the poem's sound as well as its sense. And, apart from poems VI and X, Muir has abandoned the tight regular rhyming stanzas of his first two books in favour of a looser verse paragraphing, much more effective in embodying the wide sweep of landscapes out of time and space, and the sheer magnitude of the symbolic Fall from Eden:

> Now these dead stones
> Among dead stones, where the late nomads pitch
> Their nightly tents, leaving a little refuse,
> The comfortless smell of casual habitation,
> Human or bestial — indistinguishable.
> These; and light and water casting back
> Our shallow masks to shame us.   Or at most
> The shades of our ancestors, lingering yet.
> Play in the ruins of their former house.
> Remembering the eyes once bent upon them
> That one day left them.

>   That is long ago;
> A memory of our fathers.   We have known
> Only this debris not yet overgrown.
> Never to be removed.
>   Dead and our own.

The Fall is here linked to time. Eden is a memory, almost a race-memory, and man's fallen condition is the journey through the wilderness. Muir's thought is hardening into a wider symbolic frame, with the problem of time linking the other symbols of Eden, the Fall, the Journey, which are presented more nakedly now and without superfluous explanation from the poet. But, compared with his later poems, there is a stiffness, a certain obscurity, an obsessiveness which denies the symbols the freedom to justify themselves and find their own significance. *Variations on a Time Theme* can by no means be regarded as a failure. Elizabeth Huberman's brilliant analysis of the sequence[12] demonstrates clearly the depth and richness to be found there. It is an ambitious work which extended, perhaps over-extended, the poet's technical abilities, but pointed him firmly in the direction of the symbolist mode.

The next stage in Edwin Muir's poetic development was to widen the scope of this rather baldly presented symbolism and to explore the potency and validity of the symbols by testing them in different contexts. *Journeys and Places* is, as its title suggests, built around the symbolic journey. Using a variety of verse-forms, the poet ranges over myth and history, finding correlations for his own private visions of experience and extending gradually the significance and range of his symbols. That he is still obsessed with problems of time and space is made clear in the Prefatory Note:

The Journeys and Places in this collection should be taken as having a rough-and-ready psychological connotation rather than a strict temporal or spatial one. The first deal more or less with movements in time, and the second with places reached and the character of such places; but I have also included in the latter division imaginary situations which by a licence of the fancy may perhaps pass as places, that is as pauses in time.[13]

The immediately striking thing about these poems is a new denseness of both texture and reference. No longer content to symbolize a general pattern, Muir enriches it by incorporating figures like Tristram, Hölderlin, a Trojan slave, Merlin, the Enchanted Knight,

44

Mary Stuart, and Ibsen, all of whom are incorporated as part of a symbolic pattern of movement or stasis.

"The Stationary Journey" develops the paradox in its title by presenting a vision of going back into time, past Charlemagne, St. Augustine and the Pharaohs, to the beginnings:

> And there in transmutation's blank
>   No mortal mind has ever read,
> Or told what soul and shape are, there,
>   Blue wave, red rose, and Plato's head.
>
> For there Immortal Being in
>   Solidity more pure than stone
> Sleeps through the circle, pillar, arch,
>   Spiral, cone, and pentagon.
>
> To the mind's eternity I turn,
>   With leaf, fruit, blossom on the spray,
> See the dead world grow green within
>   Imagination's one long day.

Once at this point, the poet can remake history, but the poem ends with an image of imprisonment:

> A dream!   the astronomic years
>   Patrolled by stars and planets bring
> Time led in chains from post to post
>   Of the all-conquering Zodiac ring.

The desire to transcend process and the inevitable dilemma this brings, are echoed in other poems like "The Mountains," "The Hill," and "The Road," where the road "cuts off the country of Again" and where time is confused and dislocated:

> And there within the womb,
> The cell of doom,
>
> The ancestral deed is thought and done,
>   And in a million Edens fall
> A million Adams drowned in darkness. . . .

This theme is expanded in "The Mythical Journey," a poem which successfully links the Story and the Fable, being both autobiographical and archetypal. The journey is from the starkness of "the North" to the "free summer isles." And then it closely images the move from Orkney to Glasgow:

> The towering walls of life and the great kingdom.
> Where long he wandered seeking that which sought
>   him
> Through all the little hills and shallow valleys.
> One whose form and features,
> Race and speech he did not know, shapeless,
>   tongueless,
> Known to him only by the impotent heart . . .

This leads to "the conclusion without fulfilment," and a great vision wider than any Muir had yet incarnated in symbol:

> And all the dead scattered
> Like fallen stars, clustered like leaves hanging
> From the sad boughs of the mountainous tree of Adam
> Planted far down in Eden.   And on the hills
> The gods reclined and conversed with each other
> From summit to summit.
>
>   Conclusion
> Without fulfilment.   Thence the dream rose upward,
> The living dream sprung from the dying vision,
> Overarching all.   Beneath its branches
> He builds in faith and doubt his shaking house.

The great landscape is now overlooked by vague gods — gods who will re-appear later in "The Labyrinth" — and there is an implied optimism in the last four lines. It is the country of the Fall and man is firmly in it and "unfulfilled," but there is a "living dream" and a building of a house in faith as well as in doubt. "The Mythical Journey" with its supple blank verse, is perhaps Muir's first fully successful poem and can be seen as a prototype for later work. It is on one hand a symbolic recreation of the poet's early experience and on the other a poem of the Fable, incarnating the myth, the journey of all fallen men seeking lost patterns and lost meanings.

In this volume, the Fall grows in importance as a symbolic concomitant of time and the journey. The Fall threw men into time, into the eternal journey. In this volume, too, the confusions and questionings of men are emphasized, as if, to Muir, the symbol is still being tested. In "The Fall" he asks:

> What shape had I before the Fall?
>   What hills and rivers did I seek?
> What were my thoughts then?   And of what
>   Forgotten histories did I speak

> To my companions?   Did our eyes
>   From their foredestined watching-place
> See Heaven and Earth one land, and range
>   Therein through all of Time and Space?

The visions and madness of Hölderlin offer no answers. At the end of "Hölderlin's Journey" the hero remains confused: "Dragging in pain a broken mind/ And giving thanks to God and men."

The two poems about Troy are equally concerned with the Fall. Troy becomes a symbol like Eden or Orkney and, when it is lost, time and chaos enter into it. "Troy," one of Muir's most powerful early poems, focuses on an old man left behind in the deserted ruined city, living like a modern refugee in the sewers with rats. Confused, disoriented, he cannot conceive of the change from myth to time, from the whole city to the fallen city. He is finally found by robbers and dragged to the surface:

> And there he saw Troy like a burial ground
> With tumbled walls for tombs, the smooth sward
>   wrinkled
> As Time's last wave had long since passed that way,
> The sky, the sea, Mount Ida and the islands,
> No sail from edge to edge, the Greeks clean gone.
> They stretched him on a rock and wrenched his limbs,
> Asking: 'Where is the treasure?' till he died.

The Fall implies here desolation, ruin, a change in human nature from the heroic madness of the old man to the cynical greedy cruelty of the casual robbers. There is a great pathos in this poem; a concern for the human spirit dragged out of its element and faced with animal savagery. In the world of the fallen, the world of time, where the old order lies in ruins, even casual misunderstandings can be terrible and wasteful and people removed from what makes man deeply human. The technical power of "Troy" shows Muir's increasing mastery of form. The metrical variations in the pentameters give the poem a dramatic quality. Take for example the lines

> Crying: 'Achilles, Ajax, turn and fight!
> Stop cowards!'   Till his cries, dazed and confounded,
> Flew back at him with: 'Coward, turn and fight!'
> And the wild Greeks yelled round him.
> Yet he withstood them, a brave, mad old man,
> And fought the rats for Troy.   The light was
>   rat-grey. . . .

which we may scan as follows:

47

```
/ x | x / | x / | x / | x / |
/ / | x / | x / | / x | x / | x
x / | x / | x / | x / | x / |
x x  / / | / / | x  |      |
x / | x / | x x | / / | x / |
x / | x / | x / | x / | x / | /
```

Only the third of these lines is regularly iambic; the other lines, playing against the chopped syntax and the reported speech, are subtly varied. The strange, short line, with its four consecutive stresses breaks the design; the two lines with extra syllables give a quiet change to the oral pattern. There is no sense in this poem that syntax and metre are incompatible, or that each is reducing the other to awkwardness.

The reality presented by "Troy" is the reality of evil after the Fall. It is, as Holloway notices, "A deeply disturbing reality. Not, if you like, the suave intricacies of daytime observation, but the poignant or frightening diagrams of dream or nightmare."[14] Troy has been assimilated into Muir's symbology without apparent effort. The Fall is a rich and complex symbol, capable of many presentations.

This volume contains two more poems of great interest and high quality. "Merlin" is Muir's first successful short lyric, as opposed to his longer, more meditative poetry. A singing treatment of the theme of time, it has an uncanny power, derived largely from its tone and its structure based on three consecutive questions:

> O Merlin in your crystal cave
> Deep in the diamond of the day,
> Will there ever be a singer
> Whose music will smooth away
> The furrow drawn by Adam's finger
> Across the meadow and the wave?
>
> Or a runner who'll outrun
> Man's long shadow driving on,
> Break through the gate of memory
> And hang the apple on the tree?
> Will your magic ever show
> The sleeping bride shut in her bower,
> The day wreathed in its mound of snow
> And Time locked in his tower?

The trappings of magic and legend add a luminous quality to the poem, which poses again the question of whether anything can undo the Fall and cut through time. The yearning to go back to a timeless reality echoes again here, though implied throughout, as an antidote to the bright magic of the language, is the dull certainty that there is no answer to the questions. But it seems over-dramatic and critically sentimental to burden this lovely lyric with the weight of interpretation that Daniel Hoffman puts upon it:

In his poem "Merlin", Muir tries to summon Druidic spells such as those that worked for Yeats and Graves — belief in the Celtic Otherworld, in the power of magic — as an alternative to Christian responsibility for sin in a world of change.[15]

It is the simple syntactical and tonal inevitability of the poem, together with its shining surface, that gives it its power. It is a lyrical, rather than philosophical, treatment of time and the Fall.

Another strangely effective lyric is "The Enchanted Knight," a re-writing of Keats' "La Belle Dame Sans Merci." Muir's knight lies still, his armour rusting, dreaming of old friends but unable to contact them. The poem concludes with an image of terror:

> But if a withered leaf should drift
> Across his face and rest, the dread drops start
> Chill on his forehead.   Now he tries to lift
> The insulting weight that stays and breaks his heart.

This nightmare image of fear and helplessness; the weight of the dead leaf representing, perhaps, the whole weight of time and death; the desperate heavy feeling of total paralysis, of death-in-life, makes one wonder if something of the poet's own experience of paralysis and breakdown lies behind this.

Willa Muir tells something of the pressures behind the poems in this volume. The Muirs, in St. Andrews, were deeply disturbed by events in Europe and by the cold, hostile philistinism of the town and its university:

None of the Journeys or the Places was a direct representation of raw personal experience. Feelings of bewilderment, of baffled loss, of mental trouble, of 'conclusion without fulfilment', are transmuted by his imagination into other strange, remote forms. Tristam goes mad and recovers: Hölderlin goes mad and does not recover, Troy appears as a 'sack-end' of history, the Enchanted Knight stricken in a field comes back again, the poet meditates on his life before the Fall and wanders through solitary private places. . . . [16]

It is true that there is much questioning, much realization of loss and of man's imprisonment in this volume. But there are simultaneously compensating factors; hints of faith and acceptance of the journey and the place; a growing knowledge and understanding of the nature of Eden and the Fall; and, above all, an expansion of the system of symbols through which the poet can transcend time and present a pattern of significance. Further, in this volume, Muir is developing his own voice — a firm meditative style, where the form is as loose or as tight as necessary and where the symbols take their place naturally and without strain. These poems fall short of his full mature technique but the technical progress he has made since *Chorus of the Newly Dead* is remarkable.

There is no such dramatic development between *Journeys and Places* and *The Narrow Place*, in which Muir collected the poems written between 1937 and 1942. In this period, when war had broken out, both Edwin and Willa Muir were sick and it was a period of great anxiety. Muir took a clerical job in the Food Office in Dundee, and in the evenings drilled with the local Home Guard until he overstrained his heart. In addition to the worry of circumstances and sickness, Muir was clearly feeling some inner strain, some spiritual lack which deeply concerned him. In a letter to a friend in 1940 he wrote:

I find with some dismay, after going over my life, that I have no philosophy — here am I, a middle-aged man and a professional writer, and I have no philosophy. . . . I believe that I am immortal, certainly, but that in a way makes it more difficult to interpret *this* life (in another way it makes it easier: I would be the last to deny that: if life were *only* this life, I would find it virtually impossible to find a meaning in it — moral or aesthetic). . . . I suppose what I mean when I say I have no philosophy is that I have no explanation, none whatever, of Time except as an unofficial part (?) of Eternity — no historical explanation of human life, for the problem of evil seems insoluble to me . . . there may be something more in faith that we can account for, a source of energy and reconciliation which philosophy cannot reach. I do not know: I wish my mind were more single and clear.[17]

And in another letter of the same year, he wrote to the poet William Soutar:

I believe in God, in the immortality of the soul, and that Christ is the greatest figure who ever appeared in the history of mankind. I believe in the Fall too, and the need for salvation. But the theological dogmas do not help me; I can't digest them for my good. . . .[18]

Spiritual satisfaction, for Muir, was to come later. His nature, as poet as well as man, could not respond to rational orthodoxy or sheer dogma; religion, to him, was exploration, the discovery of as many means as possible to gain access to a higher reality. However, the belief in immortality and eternity, so central to Muir's thought, provides no answer to the problem of evil in time. This is one reason why all his poetry up to *The Labyrinth* in 1949 must be regarded as only partially successful. With the 1949 volume, Muir began to be able to explore evil more directly, by releasing open conflicts of opposing symbols, thus discovering the potential and the significance of evil in terms of his other beliefs. In an interesting way, Edwin Muir seems to have sensed the necessity of doing this in 1940 when he wrote of the experience of the "mystical poet" who sees

a world in which both good and evil have their place legitimately; in which the king on his throne and the rebel raising his standard in the market place, the tyrant and the slave, the assassin and the victim, each plays a part in a supertemporal drama which at every moment, in its totality, issues in glory and meaning and fulfilment . . . it is the supreme vision of human life, because it reconciles all opposites; but it transcends our moral struggle, for in life we are ourselves the opposites and must act as best we can.[19]

This is a most important statement, as it describes the aesthetic to which all Muir's poetry aspires and, indirectly, points to the possible healing of division in the psyche, as good and evil, Story and Fable, are assumed into symbol and vision. However, this state was not to be achieved by Muir for several years, until, in fact, evil had overwhelmed him once again as a result of his experience in Czechoslovakia.

The Narrow Place has little unity as a collection. More than in the previous volume, the poems are linked to this world, to real places instead of to dream and vision. There is a good deal of insistence upon Platonism; the problem of war and evil is introduced, as is the theme of the sterility of contemporary Scotland; some of the poems go back to Muir's Orkney childhood, and there is the first love poem to his wife. It is difficult to find a single consistent tonal or symbolic element. The technical level is now generally high; the poet handling rhyming forms as well as blank and free verse with confidence.

"Scotland 1941" extends the symbolic fall to Scotland, whose once fabulous, creative identity has been drastically reduced by religious repression and materialism:

Here a dull drove of faces harsh and vexed,
We watch our cities burning in their pit,
To salve our souls grinding dull lucre out,
. . . .

Now smoke and death and money everywhere,
Mean heirlooms of each fainter generation,
And mummied housegods in their musty niches,
Burns and Scott, sham bards of a sham nation,
And spiritual defeat wrapped warm in riches. . . .

This may be compared with "Robert the Bruce," in which the old
hero: "outfaced three English kings/ And kept a people's faith."
The acknowledgement of Scotland's fall, written in bitterness, has its
counterpart in more symbolic poems like "The Grove," where the
landscape is again dream-like, and the symbol of the labyrinth is
introduced for the first time. "The smothering grove" contains "The
idol-crowded nightmare Space"; a great pageant of animal and
human. The poem ends with ambiguity. We "passed through it,"
and yet "We know/ there was no road except the smothering grove."
And there are further positive elements partially developed, almost
grasped, in poems like "The Trophy" and "The Annunciation,"
where, in Platonic terms, wholeness is seen as a possibility:

Whether the soul at first
This pilgrimage began,
Or the shy body leading
Conducted soul to soul
Who knows?   This is the most
That soul and body can,
To make us each for each
And in our spirit whole.

But wholeness of spirit cannot be found in this volume of poetry.
Time, war, evil remain undigested and too strong, although the old
gods are "bountiful and wise" displaying "vast compassion curving
like the skies . . . " and the soul is celebrated in "The Bird" "For its
strong-pinioned plunging and soaring and upward and upward
springing." In "The Guess," a dream releases a positive, Platonic
belief, and "The Day" — one long sentence of seventeen lines —
ends in a prayer for the regaining of eternity:

Oh give me clarity and love that now
The way I walk may truly trace again
The in eternity written and hidden way;

52

Make pure my heart and will, and me allow
The acceptance and revolt, the yea and nay,
The denial and the blessing that are my own.

The poetic triteness of these lines does nothing to disguise the urgency
of the plea. As yet, Muir can only find fulfilment occasionally, almost
by default. The Fall dominates Eden, and confusion precludes
clarity.

But one answer to the dilemma is discovered in "The Confirmation," which is a love poem address to "an actual, middle-aged,
much harassed wife."[20] Here the woman is symbolized as

> a place
> Of welcome suddenly amid the wrong
> Valleys and rocks and twisting roads.

There is no difficulty here in ascribing positive values. In his wife,
Muir has found a symbol which defeats confusion:

> Your open heart,
> Simple with giving, gives the primal deed,
> The first good world, the blossom, the blowing seed,
> The hearth, the steadfast land, the wandering sea. . . .

Similarly, in "The Commemoration," love is seen as an element
which can defeat time:

> This strand we weave into
> Our monologue of two,
> And time cannot undo
> That strong and subtle chain.

In "The Return of Odysseus," too, Muir concludes his first poem
about Penelope in terms of love, where faith can command time and
space:

> She wove and unwove and wove and did not know
> That even then Odysseus on the long
> And winding road of the world was on his way.

The confused journey of fallen man (through time) still dominates
Muir's symbolism. The images of Eden, of love, of eternity remain
gestures. He is pitting a tenuous faith against a terrible certainty and
the result is unbalanced. His thought and his symbolism have led
him into an *impasse* which cannot be escaped until he finds some
way of releasing the vision of Eden with sufficient strength and
significance to counteract the vision of time and blockage. Elizabeth

53

Huberman believes that in this collection, and especially in the poem "The Gate," Muir's pessimism is at its greatest, at "the central, lowest circle of Inferno."[21] This places more weight on the poem than it can bear. "The Gate" is more ambiguous in its treatment of evil than later poems; it is more general in focus and the poet seems further removed from its implications than he is in many of the poems in *The Labyrinth*, where hysteria and total loss of self seem checked only by the fragile resistance of the poetic form itself. Nor can I agree with Professor Huberman's claim that, in *The Narrow Place*, Muir "has arrived at an indisputable technical mastery."[22] This does not take into account the dramatic and highly significant movement, from *The Labyrinth* onwards, into the techniques of symbolism, which was to release resonances, complexities and a universality beyond anything he published before 1949. In *The Narrow Place*, the visions of good and evil are, for the most part, treated separately, in self-enclosed structures. They are not yet embodied in fully viable symbols; they do not meet and struggle in any strenuous and exploratory way; nor are their deepest potencies, containing both private and public experience, fully realized.

In 1942, the Muirs left St. Andrews for Edinburgh, where Edwin had been given a position in the British Council, organizing programmes and entertainment for foreign allies. This was a happier period in his life. He was "no longer turned in on himself"[23] and wrote more quickly. There is new evidence, too, of a more positive attitude in the volume *The Voyage* which contains most of the poetry written in these years in Edinburgh.

Introducing the poem "In Love for Long," the last poem of the collection, for a radio programme, Muir said: "I had an unmistakable warm feeling for the ground I was sitting on, as if I were in love with the earth itself, and the clouds, and the soft subdued light."[24] And the poem, a delicately shaped song in trimeter lines and rhyming six-line stanzas, celebrates this temporary feeling of universal love and communication. The poem admits the fragility of the state; its existence under sufferance, as it were:

> This happy happy love
> Is sieged with crying sorrows,
> Crushed beneath and above
> Between to-days and morrows;
> A little paradise
> Held in the world's vice.

But the final stanza develops this image in a startling way, assimilating the love and sorrows into a compassionate acceptance of design:

> This love a moment known
> For what I do not know
> And in a moment gone
> Is like a happy doe
> That keeps its perfect laws
> Between the tiger's paws
> And vindicates its cause.

The extra rhyming line of this final stanza gives a strong sense of emphasis and a patterned inevitability. This poem is grateful for what is, even if the sense of love and beauty is merely transitory .

Similarly, "A Birthday" turns on the joyful acceptance of the world:

> I never felt so much
> Since I have felt at all
> The tingling smell and touch
> Of dogrose and sweet briar,
> Nettles against the wall,
> All sours and sweets that grow
> Together or apart
> In hedge or marsh or ditch.
> I gather to my heart
> Beast, insect, flower, earth, water, fire,
> In absolute desire. . . .

In his elegy for a dead girl — "For Ann Scott-Moncrieff" — Muir celebrates her being exactly herself, "entirely Ann." Although deeply human and caught, like all of us, by the Fall, she remains a positive force of hope and of acceptance. And in wider, more philosophical terms, the sonnet "The Transmutation" posits an eternity more certain than Muir has yet allowed. The tone of the poem is one of awe and wonder, of a strange certainty:

> That all should change to ghost and glance and gleam,
> And so transmuted stand beyond all change,
> And we be poised between the unmoving dream
> And the sole moving moment — this is strange
>
> Past all contrivance, word, or image, or sound,
> Or silence, to express, that we who fall
> Through time's long ruin should weave this phantom
>   ground
> And in its ghostly borders gather all.

55

In this collection, time is treated with less fear. It still impinges strongly upon experience, modifying attitudes and shaping imagination, but can be accepted now for what it is, as in "Time Held in Time's Despite":

> The hours that melt like snowflakes one by one
> Leave us this residue, this virgin ground
> For ever fresh, this firmament and this sun.
>
> Then let us lay unasking hand in hand,
> And take our way, thus led, into our land.

Pattern and acceptance are, for the first time in Muir's poetry, possible even within the prison of time. These few poems at the end of *The Voyage* are evidence of a felt experience of wholeness, a new dimension in Muir's thought.

Elsewhere in the collection, however, are poems of blockage similar to those of *The Narrow Place*, where

> The endless trap lay everywhere
>   And all the roads ran in a maze
> Hither and thither, like a web
>   To catch the careless days.   ("The Escape")

And "Moses," a meditation of the fate of the Jews, includes a new thickness of feeling as the horrors of the 1939-1945 war are introduced:

> Nor, did we see, beyond, the ghetto rising,
> Toledo, Cracow, Vienna, Budapesth,
> Nor, had we seen would we have known our people
> In the wild disguises of fantastic time,
> Packed in dense cities, wandering countless roads,
> And not a road in the world to lead them home.

The meaninglessness of war is shown vividly in "Reading in Wartime" a brilliantly constructed poem of thirty-nine rhymed lines written in just one sentence:

> Boswell's turbulent friend
> And his deafening verbal strife,
> Ivan Ilych's death
> Tell me more about life,
> The meaning and the end
> Of our familiar breath,
> Both being personal,
> Than all the carnage can. . . .

"The Return of the Greeks" again deals with the business of war;[25] the imagery and terminology of modern war are used in "The Escape," a meditative poem about time and place; "The Rider Victory" turns the victorious warrior into a frozen piece of statuary in an empty landscape. But the difference now is in the attitude Muir adopts to evil, suffering and time. Where he was previously content to describe its powers of thwarting and repressing experience, he now attempts a compromise. In "Sorrow," he writes:

> I cannot have it so
> Unless I frankly make
> A pact with sorrow
> For joy and sorrow's sake,
> And wring from sorrow's pay
> Wealth joy would toss away —
> Till both are balanced, so or so,
> And even go.

The beautiful autobiographical poem "The Myth" traces the poet's own journey:

> My childhood all a myth
> Enacted in a distant isle;
> Time with his hourglass and his scythe
> Stood dreaming on the dial,
> And did not move the whole day long. . . .

And, after the "tragi-comedy" of youth and the "reverie" of manhood, the poet concludes that today the same "faithful watchers" who guarded his timeless childhood are still present, and the journey has been good.

The newly apprehended harmony in these poems is imaged in the preponderance of three- and four-foot lines — short, singing, light forms which lack the meditative weight of Muir's more usual pentameter verse. In twenty years of writing, he has learned the craft of poetry and has found ways of recreating and exploring in verse the symbolic constructs of his developing thought. He has located and isolated and examined his symbols of time, the journey and the Fall, and come, finally, to a partial compromise of time and eternity, Story and Fable. But the negative aspects of his symbology were not to be sidestepped so easily and painlessly. After his years in Edinburgh, Muir was sent to Prague, right into the heart of a Europe still shattered by war, and was to stay there until after the horrors of the Russian "Putsch" in 1948. These events undid the shyly woven harmonies of *The Voyage* and plunged Edwin Muir back into neurosis, seemingly overwhelmed by evil and, as he had been in Glasgow and London, lost from his Fable. It is only after this second fracturing of his world that he was forced into a new poetic technique in order to explore and shape the new experiences of terror. In one sense, he had to start all over on the journey towards the value of the transcendent symbol. He had to learn techniques he had not yet discovered — techniques which would simultaneously free both positive and negative symbols and place them in opposition. In particular, he had to learn to use the symbolist techniques of time/space dislocation, syntactical mis-functioning, the self-analysis of language by itself. With *The Labyrinth, One Foot in Eden* and the last uncollected poems, Muir achieved his greatest work. Under the insistent pressure of his own personal search for balance, his poetry took on an urgency it had previously lacked, and building on the tentative symbology of his previous volumes, Muir unconsciously found himself using new techniques in order to encompass the vicious opposites of post-war European experience, and his own tenacious belief in immortality.

CHAPTER FOUR

The Labyrinth

The poems in *The Labyrinth* (1949) were written in Czechoslovakia between 1945 and 1948, when Edwin Muir was Director of the British Institute in Prague. These were dramatic and tragic years for Muir; so much so that on his return to England in 1948 he suffered a breakdown and withdrew into a state of despairing apathy, "a dead pocket of life,"[1] for several months. On his arrival in Prague, after a journey through countries scarred and altered from the war, Muir had been horrified by stories of Nazi atrocities during the recent occupation and the effect this had had on the Czech people, but even more disturbing was the ferment of political intrigue, culminating in the "Putsch" of 1948 when Russia effectively and brutally took over the country. This sudden *coup* was reinforced by a sinister and pervasive apparatus of secret police, informers, censorship, and personal and artistic repression and, in this climate of fear and suspicion, Muir found it almost impossible to function.

Willa Muir writes of these years that "the unrest, the flurries from pessimism to optimism which ravaged the country ravaged Edwin and me as well,"[2] and many of the poems in *The Labyrinth* exhibit the poet's shocked awareness of how great political machines can dehumanize and brutalize individual lives. The problem of evil and suppression obsesses him, and in no other volume of his poetry do we sense so sharply what M. L. Rosenthal calls his "infinite sadness, and the repressed hysteria that underlies it."[3] Here the redemptive possibilities of Eden and eternity, towards which his symbology had been moving, become swamped and almost negated by an overwhelming sense of man caught in time, in social and political necessity. The shadow of the labyrinth broods over this collection, manifesting itself as an agent of blockage, interrupting and disorientating man on his journey back to Eden. Poems like "The Combat," "The Interceptor," "The Interrogation," "The Helmet," "The Good

59

Town," "The Usurpers" are informed with a barely controlled violence of feeling and a political awareness new in Muir's work, even though the negative experience itself was by no means new to him, being a parallel in many ways to the violent sense of threat and disorientation he had experienced as a boy when he moved from Orkney to the industrial squalor of Glasgow. At that time he felt he had moved into time from eternity, into disintegration from wholeness and unity, and the "fearful shape of our modern inhumanity"[4] which impinged so sickeningly on him in Prague became a further manifestation of that symbolic Fall, the loss of Eden, he had experienced in the labyrinth of Glasgow's slums some forty years previously. The recurrence of this destructive ghost, released from a place in his mind he had thought sealed, must have been terrible.

A sense of distortion and loss is clearly seen in the first poem of the collection, the sonnet "Too Much," and the title poem of *The Labyrinth* dramatically embodies this same sense of terror and loss of certainty. Not only is "The Labyrinth" interesting in terms of its desperate tone of nightmare, its sense of the lost self and its obsessive concern with psychological blockage, but it illustrates fully, for the first time, Muir's use of symbolist techniques. It is as if the new urgency of the content, the violence of the conflict of positive and negative potencies, has forced him into dramatic technical experiment, and, instinctively it seems, he uses classic symbolist devices. In this poem, and frequently in his poetry from this volume on, Muir employs a non-logical structure, dislocating tenses and confusing dream and reality in an attempt to free his symbols from the restrictions of time and space. And this deliberate movement in and out of time and reality is reinforced by a highly expressive use of syntax and metre.

In a broadcast, Muir described the genesis of "The Labyrinth":

Thinking there of the old story of the labyrinth of Knossos and the journey of Theseus through it and out of it, I felt that this was an image of human life with its errors and ignorance and endless intricacy. In the poem I made the labyrinth stand for all this. But I wanted also to give an image of the life of the gods, to whom all that is confusion down here is clear and harmonious as seen eternally.[5]

This account makes clear the central strategy of the poem — the juxtaposition of the images of confused man and harmonious gods, of the Fall and Eden — but the result is, in fact, far richer than Muir intimates here.

"The Labyrinth" is a highly complex poem. It draws together all Muir's great symbols — Eden, the Fall, time, the journey, the labyrinth — into a coherent and fully realized structure which resolves itself perfectly while remaining accessible to many levels of interpretation and response. The poem starts with the hero looking back at the labyrinth:

> Since I emerged from the labyrinth,
> Dazed with the tall and echoing passages,
> The swift recoils, so many I almost feared
> I'd meet myself returning at some smooth corner,
> Myself or my ghost, for all there was unreal
> After the straw ceased rustling and the bull
> Lay dead upon the straw and I remained,
> Blood-splashed, if dead or alive I could not tell
> In the twilight nothingness (I might have been
> A spirit seeking his body through the roads
> Of intricate Hades)....

We are immediately presented with a vision of chaos; the protagonist (Theseus/Muir/Everyman) dazed and lost, splashed with blood, not knowing whether he is dead or alive. The labyrinth is deliberately likened to Hades, as a symbol of anti-Eden or anti-Heaven. It is the country of fallen man, removed from his beginnings and diverted from his true journey. But Muir immediately opposes this opening symbol with a compensatory vision of Eden:

> ... ever since I came out
> To the world, the still fields swift with flowers, the trees
> All bright with blossom, the little green hills, the sea,
> The sky and all in movement under it,
> Shepherds and flocks and birds and the young and old,
> (I stared in wonder at the young and the old,
> For in the maze time had not been with me....

This vision of growth, of archetypal simplicity, with everything untroubled and in its place, heightens the effect of the labyrinth by contrasting emblematic pastoral colours with the "twilight nothingness," and the full potentiality of life and growth with the sterile half-life of the fallen condition. Through the device of the line "For in the maze time had not been with me," Muir now switches tenses, taking us back into the labyrinth with an evocation of bewilderment and helplessness:

I had strayed, it seemed, past sun and season and
        change,
Past rest and motion, for I could not tell
At last if I moved or stayed; the maze itself
Revolved around me on its hidden axis
And swept me smoothly to its enemy,
The lovely world)....

This is close to Kafka's nightmare world of disoriented man confronted with vast hostile organizations which lead him to doubt the
authenticity and validity of his existence. The labyrinth undermines
the self. Unlocated in time and space, the struggle for individual
survival is made desperate by the absence of fixed points by which
the self can find balance and perspective.

Up to this point, Muir has distanced this vision of chaos and
insanity by placing it firmly in the past as a memory of the now safe
traveller. Now he takes even that prop away by bringing the labyrinth into the present, continuing the Kafka-like images of helpless
disorientation of perception:

... since I came out that day,
There have been times when I have heard my
        footsteps
Still echoing in the maze, and all the roads
That run through the noisy world, deceiving streets
That meet and part and meet, and rooms that open
Into each other — and never a final room —
Stairways and corridors and antechambers
That vacantly wait for some great audience,
The smooth sea-tracks that open and close again,
Tracks undiscoverable, indecipherable,
Paths on the earth and tunnels underground,
And bird-tracks in the air — all seemed a part
Of the great labyrinth.   And then I'd stumble
In sudden blindness, hasten, almost run,
As if the maze itself were after me
And soon must catch me up.

The protagonist is not free from the experience of terror. The self
remains threatened and paranoid as the past presses into the present.
The Eden-vision is undermined and becomes fragile in face of this
reassertion of terror. The labyrinth is no longer a myth of time past
but a massive reality reaching into the hoped-for stability of the
present. The hero remains confused, uncertain of his actuality, split
into the labyrinth-man and the religious visionary:

> But taking thought,
> I'd tell myself, 'You need not hurry.   This
> Is the firm good earth.   All roads lie free before you'.
> But my bad spirit would sneer, 'No, do not hurry.
> No need to hurry.   Haste and delay are equal
> In this one world, for there's no exit, none,
> No place to come to, and you'll end where you are,
> Deep in the centre of the endless maze.'

Here the opposing symbols of the poem converge and move into direct confrontation. But just as the voice from the labyrinth, "my bad spirit," seems triumphant, Muir brings us back to the vision of Eden and the life of the gods, almost desperately invoking another world, which, by its transcendent properties, can perhaps defeat the chaos which threatens to overwhelm the protagonist:

> I could not live if this were not illusion.
> It is a world, perhaps; but there's another.
> For once in a dream or trance I saw the gods
> Each sitting on the top of his mountain-isle,
> While down below the little ships sailed by.
> Toy multitudes swarmed in the harbours, shepherds
>   drove
> Their tiny flocks to the pastures, marriage feasts
> Went on below, small birthdays and holidays,
> Ploughing and harvesting and life and death,
> And all permissible, all acceptable,
> Clear and secure as in a limpid dream. . . .

This great vision of the gods is an expansion of the lines in the early poem "The Mythical Journey":

> And on the hills
> The gods reclined and conversed with each other
> From summit to summit.

but in the symbolic structure of "The Labyrinth" the vision takes on a much wider significance. In this world everything is permissible and without tension. The gods preside over a place of harmony, "Where all these things were woven," and the labyrinth, in comparison, becomes small and inconsequential. The problem of time, however, is further confused here by the poet, for the vision of harmony occurred "once in a dream or trance." The world of the gods is a dream-reality, unconnected to the time-place of the labyrinth, and expressed with all the precise vagueness of a dream. The scene on which the gods look down is filled with "toy multitudes" and

63

"tiny flocks"; the ships are "little," birthdays and holidays are "small," giving simultaneously an impression of unreality, of a toy landscape, and the sense of the striking new perspective from the high world of the gods. The gods themselves remain unconcrete, symbolized as insubstantial voices, creating only a vast music over the human landscape.

The next six lines defiantly celebrate the redemptive authenticity of this vision:

> That was the real world; I have touched it once,
> And now shall know it always.   But the lie,
> The maze, the wild-wood waste of falsehoods, roads
> That run and run and never reach an end,
> Embowered in error — I'd be prisoned there
> But that my soul has birdwings to fly free.

The conflicting symbols of the maze and Eden are temporarily reconciled here by the insistence upon a fortifying, Platonic reality, by which the pressures of actuality can be transcended. The tense is present once more, with the hero looking back on his vision while still conscious of the "wild-wood waste of falsehoods" — the labyrinth — pulling at his feet.

But the poem cannot end here. Once again, Muir deliberately confuses the tenses, modifies the conclusion, and reaches for the ambiguity of the symbolic conflict:

> Oh these deceits are strong almost as life.
> Last night I dreamt I was in the labyrinth,
> And woke far on.   I did not know the place.

We are left to decide whether last night's dream is the same as the early experience in the labyrinth, or whether it is a further vision of the former reality. Certainly we have been led back into the world of vision, having moved in and out of time and actuality throughout the poem, and the last line, because it leaves us stranded outside the safety of the concrete world of here and now, is charged with a vague menace. "I did not know the place" demonstrates once more the dislocation of time and space around which the structure of this poem is built. Ending in this way with a return to disorientation, Muir leaves us not with the vision of the gods but with the knowledge of nightmare, threat, bewilderment. The gestures towards a healing unity are proved to be no more than tentative, and the gap between human and divine reality, between time and eternity, falsehood and truth, remains strongly implicit.

This summary of the structure of "The Labyrinth" permits us to look more closely at the details of the symbolist method employed by Muir. We have seen how the poet works with two opposing symbols — the labyrinth and Eden — to create tension and meaning. I have deliberately avoided trying to interpret these symbols more widely, but it is clear that they are extremely rich and resonant, generating both personal and universal meaning. "The Labyrinth" is a strongly symbolistic poem — non-rational, non-conceptual, non-allegorical — where the symbols, as we have seen, do not stay located in time or space, but are endlessly shifting between past and present, actuality and vision. In this way they become centres of many overlapping circles of meaning, where oppositions are emphasized and resolved in a completely non-logical manner. There is no either/or in the symbolist imagination as there is in the logical process. In this poem, the labyrinth does not represent either the Fall of man or insanity, say; it encompasses the Fall and emotional blockage, loss of control, the political terror in Prague, the sour and squalid tenements of Glasgow, the labyrinth of the original Greek myth, the awareness of death, the soul's dark night, the sterile technological world of secondary objects and Muir's experience of Kafka's stories. And yet the symbol is more than all of these. Similarly, the world of the gods in the poem embraces Eden and Orkney, the harmonious relationship with the animals, pre-industrial life, positive religious experience, a celebration of poetic creation and a healing return from madness and confusion. In addition, we must remember that the poem tells us that both of these symbols derive from dreams or trances. The poem moves imperceptibly from level to level, place to place, tense to tense; from the world of myth to the real world of Prague; from Orkney to Glasgow; from sanity to madness. All this is achieved by the use of the two symbols, which Muir leaves next to each other to mean what they can. This is the essence of the symbolist method, and the essence of Muir's art. Time is not process; symbol is not tied to concept, as in allegory; inner and outer worlds become inseparable. The poet makes just one act of perception, through the symbols, which transcends analytic thought; the symbols are not reminders of meaning as much as sources of meaning, striving to define themselves. In this poem, the dark vision of the labyrinth is threaded by the bright symbol of rebirth and harmony, the conflicting symbols acting as generating elements in an undifferentiated stream of thoughts, feelings, perceptions and associations.

Writing about Whitman's great elegy for Lincoln, Charles Feidelson describes the symbolist act of creation:

The act of poetizing and the context in which it takes place have continuity in time and space but no particular existence. Both are 'ever-returning'; the tenses shift; the poet is in different places at once; and at the end this whole phase of creation is moving inexorably forward. Within this framework the symbols behave like characters in a drama, the plot of which is the achievement of a poetic utterance.[6]

"The Labyrinth" is not *about* a labyrinth, nor *about* Muir's personal experience; rather it *enacts* the symbolic journey through the dark in terms of the vision of light. It is a perfect example of how the successful symbolist poem actually embodies what it is about by its use of symbol, syntax and prosody, and this poem clearly gives the lie to those who play down Muir's technical abilities.

For instance, J. C. Hall has claimed that "in this poem 'The Labyrinth' Muir sustains the first sentence for thirty-five lines without metrical support."[7] This is demonstrably not so. "The Labyrinth" is written in regular metre, often loose, but with a five-foot line throughout. The syntax and metre are complex, and they are vital to the poem's effect and to the presentation of the symbolism.

The first sentence does, indeed, go on for thirty-five lines, enacting in its tenuous, uncertain, broken syntax the stumbling journey through the labyrinth. The pentameter lines use many foot-substitutions to enhance the syntactical re-enactment of the theme, letting the language speed up or fall away in flat despair. Let us consider lines 8-15:

```
        /      / |  x  / | x x / |x  /  |x    / |
8     Blood-splashed, if dead or alive I could not tell
      x x   / |x     / |x    / | x  /  | x    / |
      In the twilight nothingness (I might have been
      x  /|x / |x   x  / |x    /    | x  /  |
10    A spirit seeking his body through the roads
      x /  | x x    / |x     /|x  / | x x   / |
      Of intricate Hades) — ever since I came out
      x x    /  | x  / |/     / | x / | x  x / |
12    To the world, the still fields swift with flowers, the trees
       /   /  | x  / |x   x /|x  x    / | x / |
      All bright with blossom, the little green hills, the sea,
```

```
x   /│x  /│x  /  x    /│x  /│
The sky and all in movement under it,
 /   x │x  /  │x  /│x  x   / │x  /│
Shepherds and flocks and birds and the young and old
```

15

Here we seen only one line of regular iambic pentameter. Of the forty feet in the eight lines, there are no fewer than fourteen non-iambic substitutions, occurring not only in the usual first but in all of the five positions. This is a highly patterned poetry, but rhythmically extremely flexible. In these lines, too, we can see the labyrinthine effect of the syntax: the paranthesis introducing a new image and followed immediately by the change of tense and location; the run-on lines; the switch in tempo (and stress pattern) in line 12 to indicate the sudden emergence into the world of Eden; the many monosyllabic words, arranged in a simple catalogue form, in lines 12-15, which contrast formally with the much more tortured description of the labyrinth itself.

This order of technical complexity continues through the whole poem, performing a vital expressive function. After the long first sentence, the syntax and metrical pattern alter perceptibly. Short sentences, appropriate to the dialogue between the good and bad spirit, as well as imaging the desperate haste to leave the maze behind, are suddenly given a strikingly regular metrical base:

```
x  /  │x  /  │ x  /│x /│ x  / │
In sudden blindness, hasten, almost run,
x /│x    /│x /│ x   /│x /│
As if the maze itself were after me
x     /  │ x    /  │ x /│ x /│ x      /│
And soon must catch me up. But taking thought,
x   /│ x /│ x   / │x  /│x    /│
I'd tell myself, 'You need not hurry.   This
```

These lines, dealing with actuality, are perfectly regular, but with the great vision of the gods we return to the earlier pattern of long sentences and many non-iambic feet, giving an immediate effect of non-reality, of dream. Of seventeen lines describing the vision of the gods, only three are regular iambic pentameter and there are only two sentences. But again, emerging from this dream of the gods, the syntax and metre bring us back to reality, moving forcefully and purposefully back into regularity to conclude the poem:

```
 /   x │x  /│ /    /│ x   /  │ x / │
That was the real world;   I have touched it once,
```

```
     x  /  |  x     /  |x /  | x    /   |x  /|
And now shall know it always.    But the lie
     x   /  | x  /  | x     /  | x   /| x     /  |
The maze, the wild-wood waste of falsehood, roads
     x   /  | x    /| x /  |x  /  | x  /  |
That run and run and never reach an end,
     x   /  |x x  / |x    /  | x  /| x      /  |
Embowered in error — I'd be prisoned there
     /   /|  x /  | x   /  | x x /   /  |
But that my soul has birdwings to fly free.
     x  /  | x /  | x    /   | / /  / | x  / |
Oh these deceits are strong almost as life.
     x    /  |x   /  | x x / |x  /|x  /  |
Last night I dreamt I was in the labyrinth,
     x   /  | x   /| x /  | x    /  | x   /  |
And woke far on.    I did not know the place.
```

Here the metrical resolution endorses the poem's conclusion. The iambic pulse now dominates so strongly that the earlier irregularities have been absorbed. The syntax, culminating in the last short sentence, is strong and tight, giving force to the poem's ending. Thus we can see that the prosody of the poem is highly expressive, itself symbolizing dream and the time-space dislocation through irregularity, and actuality through insistent regularity. Throughout "The Labyrinth," metre and syntax are, in this way, an organic part of the poem's movement in and out of actuality and dream. The shifting of tenses, the slackening and tightening of the metre, the negative and positive uses of syntax, all combine with the richness of the symbols to embody the poem's many levels of meaning. In this way, the experience of "The Labyrinth" is rendered not only by the symbols but by the movement of the lines, as the processes of frustration, stasis, growth and fruition are expressed and embodied in the poem's sound. In sound, as in the conflict of symbols, when one tension is resolved another begins, thus creating a formal complexity which perfectly embodies the psychological complexity which lies behind the maze/Eden conflict.

Before leaving this poem, it is worth turning briefly to Kafka in relation to the symbol of the labyrinth. In particular, Muir's critical writing on Kafka helps to clarify the relationship between the hero and the two opposing symbols, which lies at the heart of this poem. In an essay on Kafka, Muir writes:

The image of a road comes into our minds when we think of his stories, for in spite of all the confusions and contradictions in which he was involved he held that life was a way, not a chaos, that the right way exists and can be found by a supreme and exhausting effort, and that whatever happens every human being in fact follows some way, right or wrong. . . . He looks ahead and sees, perhaps on a distant hill, a shape which he has often seen before in his journey, but always far away, and apparently inaccessible; that shape is justice, grace, truth, final reconciliation, father, God. As he gazes at it he wonders whether he is moving towards it while it is receding from him, or flying from it while it is pursuing him. He is tormented by this question, for it is insoluble by human reasoning . . . the right turn may easily chance to be the wrong, and the wrong the right.[8]

And later in the same essay, Muir refers to "the frustration of the hero . . . caused by what in theological language is known as the irreconcilability of the divine and the human law; a subtle yet immeasurable disparity."[9]

These remarks are remarkably relevant to Muir's own work and to "The Labyrinth" in particular. The central symbol of the journey; the "supreme and exhausting effort" to find the right way; the distant goal, apparently inaccessible, which is "final reconciliation"; the frustrated, tormented self; the "irreconciliability of the divine and the human law" — these are strongly present in "The Labyrinth," embodied by the two symbols. Ultimately, the fallen hero — as much Everyman in Muir as in Kafka — struggling towards the grace and fulfilment of a transfigured reality is at the centre of Muir's imaginative vision. We know that translating Kafka had affected Edwin Muir and his wife deeply. He records that "At one stage the stories continued themselves in our dreams, unfolding into slow serpentine nightmares, immovably reasonable."[10] The labyrinth of this poem reflects this serpentine nightmare perfectly and we must agree with Elgin Mellown that "many of Muir's poems . . . inevitably remind one of Kafka's stories; and certainly Kafka, even if he did not directly influence Muir, strengthened the poet's faith in his own ideas."[11]

"The Labyrinth," for all its vision of the gods, is one of Muir's most serious explorations of frustration, evil and terror. He is struggling to acquire a negative capability; to find a means of preserving the self and the vision of harmony and joy in a world seemingly bent on destroying them. He pits an imaginative reality against the forces of darkness, refusing to meet despair on its own terms, but translating the battle into a symbolic conflict which escapes from time and place, but which still can move towards integration and resolution. As a result, this is not a poem of defeat, but one more stage on the journey towards truth. At the age of sixty, Muir is only now able to treat, through symbol, his knowledge of the hideous gap between human reality and the world of the gods. In "The Labyrinth" he peers over the abyss of insanity and despair, but does not go over. There is a defiance embodied in the positive symbols which precludes their annihilation by the negative. Although balance has been lost, and the values of imagination, love, individuality, freedom are almost extinguished, the possibilities of integration and rescue remain implicit, unkillable. The thread leading out of the maze is there in this poem, elusively and weightlessly beckoning as it floats in dream and hope. It is a thread which will eventually lead Muir out into the positive landscape of *One Foot in Eden* (1956), where the labyrinth shrinks under the confidently asserted pressure of symbols of growth and regeneration.

The problem of evil continues to obsess Muir in the poems of this volume. Time after time he returns to the theme of blockage and diversion, as the maze of necessity intrudes between man and the longed for source at the end of the journey. In these years in Czechoslovakia, it obviously became difficult for him to keep in touch with the Fable, and yet the longing, at sixty years, for an escape from the pressures of actuality became more and more desperate. Those critics like Allott, who finds that Muir's poems do not "explode into meaning," have surely missed the shock and the terror of this volume. At times, one feels that only Muir's already established use of language and symbol stop these poems from disintegrating completely under the fierce pressure of feelings. The triumph for the poetry and the man himself is that the symbols, the structures and the techniques manage to preserve at least some form and coherence in this desperate situation, although we know from Willa Muir's description[12] that the poet did, in fact, break down tragically when they returned to England from Prague. Until then, and these poems are the proof, Muir fought his despair and managed to preserve himself.

"The Return" contains some of Muir's finest lines. Not as ambitious as "The Labyrinth," its method, nevertheless, is similar as it weaves two symbols together in opposition — the house and the labyrinth — and suspends the poem between the past, the present and the future; between real and imaginary perception; between personal and universal experience.

There is a weight of elegy in this poem, manifesting itself largely in the rhythms, and one senses a diminished energy in the language. The dominant tone is one of terrible regret and cruelly frustrated desire. The sharpness and flux of the opposing symbols in "The Labyrinth" has been muted here into a slow merging and a deeply moving, sustained utterance of loss and time passing.

The poet projects the hero/traveller into the future:

> I see myself sometimes, an old old man
> Who has walked so long with time as time's true
>   servant,
> That he's grown strange to me — who was once
>   myself —
> Almost as strange as time, and yet familiar
> With old man's staff and legendary cloak,
> For see, it is I, it is I.   And I return
> So altered, so adopted, to the house
> Of my own life.

The key word in this poem is "old." The processes of life, the eternal desire to return to the lost Eden, dim the perception of the self, alter and adapt the personality. The old man imagines his lost home, out of time, where

> . . . welcome waits, and not a room but is
> My own, beloved and longed for.   And the voices,
> Sweeter than any sound dreamt of or known,
> Call me, recall me.

The Eden symbol is much less lofty here, imagined as it is in terms of domesticity and simple welcome, but it is as much the archetypal source as the place of the gods. The return home is described poignantly:

> I draw near at last,
> An old man, and scan the ancient walls
> Rounded and softened by the compassionate years,
> The old and heavy and long-leaved trees that watch
> This my inheritance in a friendly darkness.

This moving scene of recognition is given its power by the subtle variations in the loose penameter lines and the utter purity of the vision. As they often do, Muir's greatest effects derive from simplicity, even understatement, and from the accumulated effect not only of the poem's expression of its own archetype but of a recollection of the same archetype in other poems.

But this vision of near fulfilment is destroyed in the last five lines of the poem. The intensely realized homecoming cannot take place. The labyrinth intrudes once again. Evil "rises against me" and deflects the traveller from the door. We are left with the quiet, but still terrible, image of the continuing road and a knowledge of tragedy completely dominating the low-toned language and rhythm. The symbol of darkness, for all the desperate imagining of its opposite, concludes the poem. In the vision of Eden the years are compassionate and the darkness is friendly. Outside that vision time and the forces of darkness are in control. "The Return" is a poem of great beauty and one of the finest examples of sustained elegiac tone in all of Muir's work. After "The Labyrinth," it acts as a kind of epilogue, musing quietly and plangently over the tragic outcome of the earlier poem, and by this quiet re-enactment, emphasizing terribly the plight of man in his search for permanence and grace.

Surprisingly, I have found no reference to "The West" in the work of any critic of Muir's poetry. It is not one of his best poems, but it has a twofold importance. Firstly it is a poem of acceptance and modified triumph among many poems bordering on despair, and secondly it is one of the clearest poetic utterances Muir makes about the Fable and its relation to the Story. It is a much less taut poem than most in *The Labyrinth*, lacking the barely submerged hysteria and deep sorrow so typical of Muir's response to the experience of evil, and as a result it is more steady and detached. The "I" of the first four poems in the volume has become "we," the technique is more reflective than dramatic and the poet has managed to attain a certain detachment.

The poem concerns one of his favourite themes, that of the recurring ancestral pattern into which all men are assumed from birth. The symbol used is that of a landscape or country across which mankind is constantly moving towards the west. Muir's presentation of this landscape comes through five lines, remarkably unspecific, describing the death and burial in the west of people who were close to them: "We followed them into the west/And left them there, and said good-bye." It is not clear whether this is a reference to parents who take us part of the way or to some other real or imaginary funeral, but Muir's image develops so quickly that we do not need to know. Already we are in the landscape and timescape of symbol.

Beyond the grave "another west ran on/A west beyond the west. . . . " The protagonists return home only to be confronted by people moving westward. The image is rich with allusions; one thinks of the sun setting; the American myth of the promised land in the west; perhaps, above all, knowing Muir's obsession with Odysseus, of Tennyson's Ulysses:

> . . . for my purpose holds
> To sail beyond the sunset, and the paths
> Of all the western stars, until I die.

The symbol receives no explanation from Muir, and surely needs none.

The poem states the poet's idea of the Fable:

> . . . and that migration
> Has been from the beginning, it is said,
> And long before man's memory it was woven
> Into the tranquil pattern of our lives.

The woven pattern of life, so central to the Eden-symbol, is the equivalent here of the gods' dialogue in "The Labyrinth": the two elements of peace and weaving together lie at the heart of Muir's vision of fulfilment. His dismay with the real world of the twentieth century stemmed largely from war and from old patterns breaking up, so the weaving of Penelope, say, in "Telemachos Remembers," the chords of harmony in the song of the gods, the woven pattern of our lives, can be seen to be a direct antidote to despair and the fallen, time-locked world. The vision of the Fable in "The West" is remarkable for its tranquillity, which the poet emphasises by language and rhythm. The pattern of life is:

> . . . like a quiet river,
> Which always flowing yet is always the same,
> Begets a stillness.   So that when we look
> Out at our life we see a changeless landscape,
> And all disposed there in its due proportion,
> The young and old, the good and bad, the wise and
>   foolish,
> All these are there as if they had been for ever,
> And motionless as statues, prototypes
> Set beyond time, for whom the sun stands still.

This poem achieves, through its symbol, a very curious effect. We have the great surging movement of all mankind across the panoramic landscape, which becomes transformed, suddenly, into a frozen vision, almost emblematic, of mankind as static. The moving picture becomes a frieze as Muir's symbol takes us out of the flux of time/space into the "changeless landscape" of symbol where men are prototypes and the sun stands still. The canvas changes effortlessly from Brueghel to Nolan; from teeming life to statuary within a landscape. This superb effect is created partly by the sudden weighted shape of the line "The young and old, the good and bad, the wise and foolish," which has, apart from its two massive caesuras, six stresses in a poem which, apart from the opening tetrameter, is written in five stress lines. It is also created by Muir's sudden switch of place, only possible by this particular symbolist technique, whereby the "we" who are participants, suddenly become observers and "look/Out at our Life." The Story and the Fable are thereby mixed and shown to be inseparable. The poem returns to the strange burial of the first lines, having assumed the individual story into the universal pattern of human life and death. Men, Muir wrote in *The Estate of Poetry*, "will pass through the ancestral pattern, from birth to childhood and youth and manhood and age and death."[13] This poem is a celebration and acknowledgement of that pattern, and the poem ends with two lines of acceptance. Because of the Fable, the great recurring undercurrent of all life, we can and must accept the here and now. The Fable is incomplete as a theory; it must become concrete through the Story. So, for the first time in this volume so full of the heavy knowledge of evil, Muir has succeeded in concluding with an acceptance of life where the intercepting power of the maze has not intruded into the transcendental pattern. This positive attitude is not long sustained, however, and we feel that it is only achieved by retreating from the immediate battleground of the symbols and becoming detached to a certain degree. The problems are still with the poet.

This can be clearly seen in the longest poem of the collection "The Journey Back" — a sequence in seven sections, in some ways reminiscent of the technique of *Variations on a Time Theme* — with each section having its own individual tone and form which modifies the others.

This poem has received surprisingly little critical attention, in spite of the praise it has elicited from Kathleen Raine ("Muir's greatest poem"[14]) and Elizabeth Jennings ("Muir's finest poem."[15]). Only Elizabeth Huberman has given the poem a more than cursory treatment, coming to a less positive conclusion on the grounds that "The mystery . . . is perhaps a little too easily achieved and sustained here, as if it were the result more of technical devices than of imaginative insight."[16]

I think it is by no means Muir's finest poem, but it is certainly of intense interest, particularly as it adds something to our understanding of Muir's symbol of the journey and the evil which diverts man from his true road. It is technically interesting in its handling of forms and tones, and it contains some remarkable passages of a rare directness concerning the realities of the mid-twentieth century.

The theme, once more, as hinted in the title, is the journey towards Eden. In this poem, however, Muir makes it explicit that it is a journey in more than one direction. J. C. Hall makes this point clear:

For Muir the journey is not only forward on the inexorable stream of time, but backwards also to the source of that innocence and clear-sightedness which we lost so long ago in the "smothering grove."[17]

We move backwards as well as forward to find our Eden, for the journey is a circle. As Eliot put it:

> We shall not cease from exploration
> And the end of all our exploring
> Will be to arrive where we started
> And know the place for the first time.[18]

This attitude towards innocence and grace, with its strong belief in the unfallen state of the child, is close to both Romantic and Christian thought, although Muir's exploration of the idea, presented through non-assertive and freely moving symbols, is completely flexible and undoctrinaire. There are traces of the influences of *Four Quartets* in Muir's late poetry, notably in the treatment of time, the image of the rose and the obsession with grace and redemption, but Eliot's poem is worked out in much more formal and explicitly Christian terms than Muir ever used. Muir's Christianity never excluded other archetypes or solutions; his symbolic frame of reference remained wider than Eliot's more committed use of Christian symbol. It is perhaps possible to see, too, in "The Journey Back," Eliot's formal influence, — a symbolic structure with various movements differentiated by verse-form and tone — although, as we have seen, Muir had already used this technique in *Variations on a Time Theme* fifteen years earlier.

"The Journey Back" is in one sense a very personal poem. The generalized "we" of "The West" becomes "I" once again, and although the poem deals just as urgently with collective experience, the cycles and returns and renewals of the whole human race, we are never in any doubt about the authenticity of the individual experience.

The first eight lines present us with images of drought and water. The past is dead, but the lives of the dead run as water through the living, just as our lives will turn into a "myriad tributaries" in our successors. The poem continues with the story of a journey:

> So I set out on this calm summer evening
> From this my house and my father's.   Looking back
> I see that all behind is pined and shrunken
> The great trees small again, the good walls gone,
> The road grown narrow and poor, wild heath and
>   thorn
> Where comfortable houses spread their gardens.

This vision of a wasteland is also a vision of the wrecked garden. Time is typically dislocated as Muir presents the start of his journey, so obviously Orkney/Eden, in the present tense. The first part of the journey is safe and quiet; the boy is secure, trusting; the way, at first, friendly. We notice that, in spite of the title, the poem is working in terms of a journey forwards and not back, adding a further diversion to the treatment of time and place here. The rhythms are loose, almost prosy, with the sound, at this stage, embodying the lack of tension in the journey.

We now move immediately from Eden to the world outside the walls, from Orkney to Glasgow, from the "friendly station" on the quiet road to the labyrinth. The language tightens, becomes harder; the rhythms become more savage and congested; the syntax is forced:

> I must in other lives with many a leap
> Blindfold, must lodge in dark and narrow skulls
> With a few thoughts that pad from wall to wall
> And never get out, must moulder in dusty hearts,
> Inhabit many a dark or a sunny room,
> Be in all things.   And now I'm locked inside
> The savage keep, the grim rectangular tower
> From which the fanatic neighbour-hater scowls;
> There all is emptiness and dirt and envy,
> Dry rubbish of a life in anguish guarded
> By mad and watchful eyes.

76

This is another description of the labyrinth where man is imprisoned, blindfolded, locked in small rooms, surrounded by hostile forces. It is a description of the poet's physical and mental life in Glasgow, and in the ghastly bone factory at Greenock. The ruined garden has given way to a place of spiritual sterility where the self is threatened "by mad and watchful eyes" lurking in the urban wilderness. The poem continues with language and rhythms of unusual vehemence and concreteness for Muir:

From which I fall
To gasp and choke in the cramped miser's body
That winds its tightening winch to squeeze the soul
In a dry wooden box with slits for eyes.
And when I'm strangling there I flutter out
To drift like gossamer on the sunny wind,
A golden thistledown fool blown here and there,
Who for a lifetime scarcely knows a grief. . . .
Perhaps a murderer next, I watch those hands
That shall be always with me, serve my ends,
Button, unbutton for my body's needs,
Are intimate with me, the officious tools
That wash my face, push food into my mouth,
Loathed servants fed from my averted heart.

This is the record of a deep existential crisis of identity. The self is disgusted by its parts and the body usurps the soul, which has been squeezed out of shape and almost blind. Identity goes, self becomes insubstantial, blown by the circumstances of physical existence. Life is loathsome without the vision of the soul, or the knowledge of the early state of grace. This passage describes "the absurd" of Camus where human beings become aware, often suddenly, of living without a God, in the void, without any support. It also anticipates the streets of hell in his later poem "Milton," and it is not difficult to connect this passage with the mental breakdown and latent schizophrenia of his pre-analysis days, nor to see the refugees and displaced persons of war-torn Europe existing in the ruins of their lives.

The idea of derangement, of the fragmented self, is emphasized by the next paragraph:

So I usurp, grown avid for the end,
Body on body, am both father and child
Causer and actor, spoiler and despoiled,
Robbing myself, myself, grinding the face
Of the poor, I poorest, who am both rich and poor,
Victor and victim, hapless Many in One.

77

The labyrinthine, broken syntax of this one complex sentence suggests as much as the confused conceptual meaning of the language a broken mind. The metre is rough, too, with the iambic pattern almost submerged under the weight of substitutions. The passage recalls his years in Glasgow, when inwardly divided and deeply repressed, he was obsessed by Nietzsche, trying to survive his cruel experience of separation by becoming hard and pitiless. This period of his life, when he was active in politics, unhappy in his jobs, having casual affairs with women, was obviously a time when he tried to recreate himself, as a self protective measure, and to become what he was not. But the false-selves cannot work, and the poem goes on:

> In all these lives I have lodged, and each a prison.
> I fly this prison to seek this other prison,
> Impatient for the end — or the beginning
> Before the walls were raised, the thick doors fastened,
> And there was nothing but the breathing air,
> Sun and soft grass, and sweet and vacant ease.

The end is the beginning. Here Muir again projects us back to the creation, this time, seemingly, to the world even before Eden. As Kathleen Raine says:

... the story of the Journey goes back long before men. ... *The Journey Back* ... traces the long travelling through the animals, the earth itself, to the stars and the first stuff of the material world.[19]

But this vision of created innocence is not a practical escape, for the cycles and patterns of human life remain inexorable, and here, finally, Muir has realized that only he can work out his journey, however "random" the self. The image of the good man, the Christ or Adam he knows he will meet, is not simply a reference to Christ, but a humanized symbol of the joined circle, the escape from time, the return to the restored Eden.

The second part of the poem consists of six six-line stanzas, rhymed *a a b c c b*, and extremely formal in technique. The poem is written in exact accentual-syllabics; each stanza consisting of trimeter/trimeter/dimeter/trimeter/trimeter/dimeter, where the trimeter couplets rhyme and the two two-foot lines rhyme. The result is a song-like formalism, contrasting sharply with the loose accentual pentameters of the long first section. As is sometimes the case when he is using extremely tight rhyming forms, Muir's language tends towards over-simplicity and a high proportion of the words are monosyllabic. At this stage, he seems not quite at ease in a form as tight as this, and is forced by the exigencies of rhyme into clumsy syntax and redundant adjectives to fill the formal pattern:

> Through countless wanderings,
> Hastenings, lingerings,
> From far I come,
> And pass from place to place
> In a sleep-wandering pace
> To seek my home.

In these lines, "From far I come" and "a sleep-wandering pace" seem devoid of genuine poetic energy, while "Forgotten long" in the second stanza, by its weak rhyme-forced inversion and lack of activity, weakens the stanza. Muir, at this stage, seems to need the flexibility and space of a looser form to do justice to his ideas.

This section, recounting the journey from the beginning of creation, is a dream landscape, full of dying stars, dragons, mysterious forests, and strange places. The theme is clear in general as man journeys "To find the secret place/Where is my home," but the mystical apparatus here seems to be dragged in to no real purpose. Nothing is added to the first section, and a tonal break, without a further thematic dimension being added, is hardly adequate. The short third section is much more successful. We are taken immediately into a vision of pre-history, where

> ... the poor child of man, leaving the sun,
> Walks out into the sun and goes his way,
> Not knowing the resurrection and the life. . . .

A strange vision of the self watching the self bury the self in an age-old ritual turns into an image of death without resurrection. The human tragedy is that of "not knowing the resurrection and the life," as man lives enclosed with earth and all its things, obsessed with the trivial pattern of every day. Outside the selfish circle of man, destinies fall; love, like the seasons, blossoms and dies, and man, without these, is as dead as if he were in the iron-age barrow of the first lines. We are reminded of the first section of the poem, where the poet insits that each man is responsible for breaking out of death. In this section, a specifically Christian image of resurrection is used as an antidote to the life of earth.

Section four builds on this section. Like section three it is rhymed, the pentameter being interrupted by short lines, giving a control by the use of sound pattern and an odd elusive timing. This section, released even further from the time pattern of the pentameter norm, has a correspondingly increased release from time in the content. It is a mystical section, warning at the start that "fed flesh, or colour, or sense, or shape" must not be trusted. The poem dissolves here into a vague symbol of transcendence, where "child and woman and flower/Invisibly fall through the air on the living ground." The power and the forms of spiritual wholeness, out of time and not of the earth, descend in the air about us, as the poem draws our attention to the mystical reality we have lost.

Section five is a curiously constructed poem of fifteen lines. It is written in loose tetrameters with a final five-foot line, and rhymes *a b a b c d d c e e f g g h h* — almost as if the poem were a sonnet with an extra line. In addition to the odd rhyme scheme and the looseness of the metrics, the word "blessing" appears five times in the last seven lines. And yet, for all this, the poem does not seem clumsy or unbalanced, mainly because the content is so strong and the emotion so densely and strongly developed.

There are two clearly defined areas of this section. The first seven lines are strikingly specific:

> I have stood and watched where many have stood
> And seen the calamities of an age
> Where good seemed evil and evil good
> And half the world ran mad to wage
> War with an eager heart for the wrong,
> War with a bitter heart for the right,
> And many, many killed in the fight.

This specificity serves as a powerful antidote to the dissolving mysticism of section four. We are as close, in these lines, to hearing Muir's direct, personal comment on the 1939-45 war and the political terrors of Europe as anywhere in his poetry. The tone of savage elegy is most impressive; the strength of the feeling unmistakable. The second paragraph moves outward from the local experience and again we see one of Muir's characteristic techniques as he changes in mid-poem from "I" to "we" as his symbol enlarges itself and moves around in time and place. The personal Story is almost always, in Muir's imagination, modified and expanded into the universal Fable:

> In those days was heard a song:
> Blessing upon this time and place,
> Blessing upon the disfigured face
> And on the cracked and withered tongue
> That mouthing a blessing cannot bless,
> Blessing upon our helplessness
> That, wild for prophecy, is dumb.
> Without the blessing cannot the kingdom come.

The song here is as vague as the whispers in the air of section four. It is the word of a larger reality than mankind's. The insistence upon the religious act of blessing in order to bring "the kingdom" shows further evidence of Muir's shifting towards Christian symbolism. But this poem is wider than a Christian polemic. The need for blessing is as universal as was the Ancient Mariner's blessing of the sea-creatures; it is an attitude of spirit towards creation, without which we are dumb and helpless and only through which grace and healing of some sort can come. Man fallen as far as in this poem, as in Auschwitz and Belsen, must somehow break out into the world beyond evil.

The penultimate poem of this sequence again breaks the tone through formal devices. It is written in *terza rima*, that most formal and shaped of forms, and is both highly lyrical and strongly ritualistic. The vision is again that of Eden — the place to which we are trying to journey back. This time it is a place of light and silence, a mountain-land with "music underground":

> An ever-winding and unwinding air
> That moves their feet though they in silence go,
> For music's self itself has buried there.
>
> And all its tongues in silence overflow
> That movement only should be melody.

The walkers on this land are the ones who have had the blessing. They remain undefined. They are not gods specifically, looking down; nor men in an afterlife or before birth. They are all of these things, and we do not need to link symbol to concept. The important thing for Muir is that

> All we have seen it;   while we look we are
> There truly, and even now in memory,
>
> Here on this road, following a falling star.

It is the longed-for place and also the remembered place, but we are on a different road, following not the tranquil planet of Eden, but a falling star. This beautiful lyric distils its meanings out of sound, shape, image and rhyme. It is one of Muir's purest poems.

"The Journey Back" concludes with a return to the style of the opening section. Loose, blank-verse pentameters carry the thought and the symbol, the syntax and rhythms reinforce and comment on the meaning, and we are switched from vision to reality with ease. The poem starts with a sentence of twenty-four lines, recreating the journey it postulates, using syntax as a strongly expressive function. The poet is musing about the journey:

> Yet in this journey back
> If I should reach the end, if end there was
> Before the ever-running roads began
> And race and track and runner all were there
> Suddenly, always, the great revolving way
> Deep in its trance; — if there was ever a place
> Where one might say, 'Here is the starting-point,' ...

This journey cannot be made, except by the calling into play of symbol. The Fable cannot be dissociated from the Story:

> If I should reach that place, how could I come
> To where I am but by that deafening road,
> Life-wide, world-wide, by which all come to all....

Muir is asserting, once again, that the pattern of the journey must include the Fall, the dark night, the striving to overcome and to survive, before the "blessing" can come. The poem postulates a more Christian interpretation of man's life than we have previously seen, and the final fusion of Platonism with Christianity ties the poem's symbolism in a great vision of the recurring journeys of men in an unreal world, while the timeless world of Eden and fulfilment manifests itself unmistakably, though stubbornly out of reach. Elizabeth Jennings considers the poem's ending as "a vision of triumph won through striving and also through arduous surrender. It is a Christian vision...."[20] This is true up to a point, although I feel that the symbolic pattern here, seen as part of Muir's developing symbolism, is more than Christian. It is true that the vision of Eden has become more specifically Christian, but it remains something wider than Christianity *per se*.

"The Journey Back" is certainly an impressive poem, but one is conscious of weakness in the poem, primarily in the use of symbol.

In Muir's greatest work the tensions are generated by the movement of symbols around each other, touching, merging, conflicting, springing apart, creating a pattern of both local and universal meaning. In "The Journey Back," this tension is not always evident. Instead, one is sometimes aware of an over-conscious craftsmanship, of the poet's attempts to achieve tension through the variations of tone and technique in the various sections of the poem. It is in this area that the weaknesses lie. The connections between the poem's parts are not always mutually energizing and enlivening, nor is there enough cross-reference of image and symbol to enable a fertile development to take place. The whole poem is contained in the first and last sections and even the frequent felicities of the mystical and lyrical sections in the poem's centre do not fully justify them. The symbolic pattern of the poem is not as sharp or meaningful as in his best work, and there is a slight uneasiness about the unprepared Christian imagery lying next to the familiar images of the road and Eden. He has not yet, I think, assimilated it adequately into his mythology. "The Journey Back" contains some of his greatest writing — sections one, five and seven especially — but as an organically satisfying whole there are signs of clumsy stitching and loss of focus.

The shorter poems which follow "The Journey Back" do not display any great confidence in the ultimate triumph of good over evil. In spite of the ending of "The Journey Back," we are plunged into a world of nightmare and political evil, where the vision of Eden subsides temporarily under the pressure of the experience of terror.

"The Bridge of Dread" has all the quality of a nightmare. Here again, Muir uses physical, bodily imagery to convey some undefined terror impinging upon the individual and threatening his survival. It is a poem of unlocated, undefined crisis as the traveller tries to cross the symbolic bridge — an image reminiscent of that in the earlier "The Rider Victory." In the earlier poem, however, the image is treated in heraldic terms very different from the concrete yet imprecise horror of "The Bridge of Dread," where the stagnant air "breaks in rings about your feet/Like dirty suds." In the penultimate stanza the hysteria merges into an apocalyptic vision:

> Until you see a burning wire
> Shoot from the ground.   As in a dream
> You'll wonder at that flower of fire,
> That weed caught in a burning beam.

We are told no more. The fire seems to be both physical danger and a purifying agent, freeing the traveller from the previous crisis, for the poem concludes with a kind of escape:

> And you are past.   Remember then,
> Fix deep within your dreaming head
> Year, hour or endless moment when
> You reached and crossed the Bridge of Dread.

The "dreaming head" calls into question the reality of the experience but the point is clear. Man can survive crisis and threat to his survival, but only at the cost of being born into experience. The crossing of the bridge must be acknowledged and remembered. Crisis alters us and if we are to survive we must come to terms with the ultimate terror and live in its knowledge. The symbol is rich, incorporating mental and physical horror, both personal and universal, and showing again how, at this time, Muir was desperately trying to understand and conquer his obsession with evil. He is trying to allow the survival of self by transmuting it into symbol. By this means, he can see his own crisis in terms of the experience of all human beings and impose a pattern on it.

The nightmare quality of this poem is further emphasized by the simplicity and formalism of the rhyming tetrameter stanzas, which understate by their apparent lightness and ease the swelling hysteria they transmit, thus exaggerating it and making it seem obscene and unnatural. With this sort of theme, so obsessively presented, a tight form is necessary if the content is not to burst out into incoherence or overstatement. The form here is controlling the evil as well as emphasizing it, by imposing its pattern of short stanzas, full-rhyme and short sentences.

"The Helmet" is a study of the dehumanizing effect of war, in the shape of a soldier who has become so brutalized that he is merely an instrument or machine. The form is again tight — rhyming four-line trimeter stanzas — and again there is evidence of the padding and rhyme-forcing which is sometimes apparent when Muir uses short-lined, rhymed structures. But here it is at a minimum and the poem succeeds in spite of it. The poem opens confidently, stating its theme directly and strongly:

> The helmet on his head
> Has melted flesh and bone
> And forged a mask instead
> That always is alone.

84

The face has become a mask, blank and ruined as a bombed city. Personality has gone. Faced with this automaton, with man turned by war into machine, all we can do, Muir suggests, is to wait until our real selves emerge. But the poem ends without hope, showing us the terror and nightmare behind the blank mask:

> But he can never come home,
> Nor I get to the place
> Where, tame, the terrors roam
> Whose shadows fill his face.

The soldier has become a wider symbol of fallen man, displaced from his home, racked with terrors which have become tame through the familiarity of long acquaintance. The hard-won semi-affirmation of "The Journey Back" has again been swamped by the pervasiveness and strength of evil.

"The Child Dying" is quite different, and a poem unlike any other Muir wrote. A dramatic monologue, it is spoken by a child at the moment of death. In July 1946, he sent the poem to a friend, Joseph Chiari, telling him that this was the first poem he had written in Czechoslovakia.[21] That it was written first perhaps explains its unexpected appearance in the middle of his group of poems on the nature of evil, although I feel it might have been placed more advantageously at the start of the volume. In the same letter to Chiari, Muir wrote:

I've been trying for some time to write poetry that was both simple and unexpected; and if this poem is good — I can hardly tell whether it is or not — I think I have succeeded. But where it came from I simply can't tell.

The last sentence implies that this is a poem about universal and not about a specific experience, and it certainly succeeds in being both simple and unexpected. It is moving, serious and masterful, with a perfectly sustained tone and a sense of grief and dissolution which is well controlled and modulated. The danger with this sort of highly charged subject is that of sentimentality. I think the poem manges to avoid it, but at times comes very close with its very simple, repetitive, Gentle-Jesus-like language.

The poem is addressed to the child's father, who has been, presumably, discussing the impending death with the child. The theme is the nature of death and the ensuing liberation from time and space, though here this liberation is never treated, as in the vision of

85

Eden, as perfection of innocence. In this poem the apprehension, fear and regret of the dying child constantly serve as reminders of the earthly business of death as the world begins to dissolve. Death may be a release, as in the first stanza, or an escape from necessity and time, when "I shall be out of all your day" with the ability to remember from the after-life grass, light, sun and sea, but "the world is out," nevertheless, and the child is afraid:

> Father, father, I dread this air
> Blown from the far side of despair,
> The cold cold corner.   What house, what hold,
> What hand is there?   I look and see
> Nothing-filled eternity,
> And the great round world grows weak and old.

We can see in this stanza how Muir has used metrical variation to recreate in the sound pattern the awful solemnity of the child's realization and the beginnings of the process of death. We may scan the stanza as follows:

```
/  x  | /  x  | x  /  | x  /  |
/  x  | x  /  | /  x  | x  /  |
x  /  | /  /  | xx /  | /  /  |
x  /  | x  /  | x  /  | x  /  |
   /  | x  /  | x  /  | x  /  |
xx /  | /  /  | x  /  | x  /  |
```

The great weight of spondees, with a slow piling up of adjacent stresses, emphasized by the extremely active syntax, expresses exactly the blank and huge experience of the child, especially as it follows much lighter sounding stanzas. The final stanza completes the process:

> Hold my hand, oh hold it fast —
> I am changing! — until at last
> My hand in yours no more will change,
> Though yours change on.   You here, I there,
> So hand in hand, twin-leafed despair —
> I did not know death was so strange.

Here the first five lines are in broken syntax as the experience is forced into utterance by the child. As the world breaks up, so does the language, until the final statement of the last line, where the substitution of a trochee in the third foot places all the weight on the word "death" as the child dies. These last two stanzas show how Muir's craftsmanship can, at this stage of his development, serve a vital function in the poem's strategy. The rhythm moves as the mind moves and as the feeling develops. Through metrical variation in stanza four and syntactical manipulation in the final stanza, a whole dimension has been added to the experience of the poem, and form and content are totally inseparable. "The Child Dying" does not use the symbolist method of other poems in *The Labyrinth*; it exists alone, as a strange and deeply moving expression of human death, in which Muir has been able to escape his personal preoccupations with evil by putting himself into another person and another voice.

"The Combat" has probably received more critical attention than any other of Muir's poems. This is primarily because, up to now, Muir's critics have concentrated on showing connections between the life and the work rather than on detailed textual criticism and "The Combat" is very amenable to this approach. The poem derives from a dream, described in detail in *An Autobiography*, about two animals fighting. It is also probably connected with another dream about a boxing-match and two actual experiences of witnessing one-sided physical violence in Glasgow. Both the dreams and the real fights follow a pattern. In every case the struggle is between a person or animal of great strength, size and ferocity and one much smaller, more timid and helpless. It is a blank vision of needless cruelty and senseless physical violence, but Helen Gardner is right when she says that, in these dreams and experiences,

the particular horror of *The Combat* is missing. For the awful and nightmarish element in the poem is the idea of endlessness. The battle of the heraldic and the shabby beast goes on outside Time. The proud beast will always win, the shabby beast will always lose; but nothing is settled. All is to be fought over again, abominably and eternally.[22]

That "The Combat" is a crystallization of these memories and dreams has been noticed by Hoffman, Gardner and Butter. What has not been mentioned is the possibility that this obsessive dream is derived from an old Orkney legend, which Edwin Muir almost certainly knew as a child. There are several versions of this legend, which is known as "The Tale of the Everlasting Battle." The first known reference to the tale occurred in the ninth century, but there is evidence to suggest that it was even then a well-known story. In this tale two kings, Hogin and Hedin fight over Hogin's daughter, Hild. Marwick recounts the legend as follows:

87

The two kings landed in Hoy and prepared for battle. Hedin again, however, proposed peace and offered much gold as compensation for his act, but Hogin answered: 'It is too late; I have already drawn my sword Dainsleif which was forged in the smithy of the Dwarfs. Each time it is bared some man must die. Its stroke can never be parried and its wound never heals'. Hedin replied: 'You boast of your sword, but that does not mean you shall boast of victory. That sword is best which fails not its owner at need'.

Thereupon the battle began. After fighting all day they retired to their ships at night. Afterwards Hild went out and by her magic restored the fallen warriors to life, and next day the battle was renewed, and so on each day thereafter, and will continue to rage until Ragn arok — the 'twilight of the gods'.[23]

According to Marwick, this legend, or versions of it, was repeatedly mentioned in Old Norse literature and was discovered as a ballad in 1774. It is not unlikely that Muir had heard a version of the story, which, buried in his unconscious, helped to shape the dreams which inspired "The Combat."

Although the poem is remarkable for its closeness to the dream, Muir adds a moral attitude. He writes, in stanza two: " . . . I accuse/The crested animal in his pride," and in the ninth stanza he comments on the shabby animal: "And yet I never saw/A beast so helpless and so brave." What emerges most strongly from the poem is the sheer horror of this unequal and eternal battle, as the small beast refuses to give in:

> One would have said beyond a doubt
> This was the very end of the bout,
> But that the creature would not die.

Finally, like the big boxer in the dream, the proud beast is frustrated as the battle drags on:

> The killing beast that cannot kill
> Swells and swells in his fury till
> You'd almost think it was despair.

"The Combat," by its very subject-matter, implies a direct confrontation of symbol. There is no place here for modulated and interweaving symbolic development, as the symbol of pride, cruelty and strength attacks the symbol of helplessness, defiance and courage. We are far from the vision of Eden here. The poem is drenched with the knowledge of evil and oppression and its theme is survival itself. The symbols float freely out of time and in a locale "somewhere beneath the sodden skies." They are uttterly non-concrete and non-referential and we would be misunderstanding the symbolic method if we attempted to destribe the poem as the eternal battle between Christ and Satan; between the war-machine and the individual; between Nazi Germany and Czechoslovakia; between the crucifiers and Christ. The poem perhaps contains these things somewhere in its structure of meaning, but ultimately it belongs to the unconscious whence it came. All we can be safe in saying is that it shows, symbolically and in non-concrete, non-rational terms, the possibilities of evil, cruelty and casual, endless oppression. It enacts a crisis where there "was no place/Or time for chivalry or for grace." The battle is unequal and yet the thing which opposes evil so hopelessly and endlessly never dies, and although "It was not meant for human eyes" this battle, and this poem, with their naked portrayal of evil, fit perfectly into the heart of *The Labyrinth*, where the problem of evil, approached from many directions, is the theme of so many of the poems. The animals are in the labyrinth, and part of it.

"The Combat" shows Muir's ability to abstract his material without losing dramatic energy. The poem records, in Rosenthal's words "the essential discovery of life's cruelty ... which cuts at us like a sword slash in the face."[24] That there remains some hope, however, is clear from the survival of the shabby beast. Muir himself said a few words about the poem at Harvard in 1955, which Butter has transcribed from tape as follows:

Helpless ... little animal ... might be a ... or stand for something in humanity that can be killed — that, that cannot be killed, actually — that is always attacked, that is in a very vulnerable position. It is very valuable ... that after it has ... been ... beaten or vanquished, it does return again. It's in a way, it's a ... rather horrible (way?) but it's an expression of hope at the same time, at the end. I take it to be something like that. Or it might be taken as humanity and all the enormous forces, particularly nowadays, ranged against humanity in every way.[25]

This is interesting for its complete preoccupation with the victim of the attack, and for Muir's obvious inability to explain his symbols any further than "something in humanity" that is attacked by "enormous forces." The symbolist method of this poem, because it is so completely non-referential, illustrates perfectly the essential non-allegorical technique of Muir, who leaves the symbols to generate their own significance and create their own terms of reference.

The conflict has no location in time or space, the combatants have no motives, the combat has no result. And yet the nightmare quality of the feeling, the desperate response to mortal threat and the urgency of the need to survive, emerge from this poem incredibly strongly.

It is worth noting, again, that possible hysteria is countered by strict formalism. The tetrameter lines and the five-line stanzas rhymed *a b a c b*, give the poem a necessary tighness and control, preventing any unshaped escape of the desperate content.

"The Combat" can be seen as the key expression of Muir's pre-occupation of evil at this troubled time in his life. Willa Muir recalls the time when the poem was written:

There were days when my heart withered up and I felt a *scunner* at the Czechs, mere grumblers at a *fait accompli*; there were other days when I was filled with remorse, especially when my friend Jirina, who was being threatened with the loss of her small widow's pension if she did not join the Party, said one must never lose faith, never give up hope. Edwin then produced his poem; 'The Combat,' which steadied both of us with its reminder that the armoured Killing Beast could not kill humanity, humble and battered as that may be.[26]

"The Intercepter" continues the obsessive exploration of evil and the forces which thwart "the blessing," this time in more personal terms. It is a disturbing poem, hinting at some deep, neurotic, even schizophrenic blockage in the poet's apprehension of the world. The Intercepter, a dramatically personified symbol, is ultimately the same as the labyrinth — something which diverts, intercepts, dominates, frustrates and threatens man as he attempts to journey towards grace and integration. Again the obsession is so great that the vision of Eden cannot come through.

The prototype of this poem is section IX of *Variations on a Time Theme* concerning Indifference: "Packed in my skin from head to toe/Is one I know and do not know." These lines are echoed by the ending of "The Intercepter": "The Intercepter frowns at me/With my own frowning face," with its insistence that the Intercepter is part of himself — a personality which, by becoming dominant, negates his existence, "and to my 'Yes' says 'No'." The poem is about a man haunted by evil, powerless to throw off the shackles of his other self. The most terrible image is that in the third stanza where: "The Intercepter lifts his hand/And closes up my side." It closes up the power to dream and to escape into imagination, but beneath this is the image of the crucified Christ, whose side is gashed and bleeding to redeem the world and fallen man. The blocking of the side thus implies a blocking of the redeeming blood, recalling the earlier lines about Indifference, who "Can stare at beauty's bosom coldly/And at Christ's crucifixion boldly." Contrasted to this indifference in the next paragraph of *Variations on a Time Theme* is "The unending open wound in Jesus's side," suggesting that the poet, consciously or unconsciously was rewriting the same experience here, or at least returning to the same obsession of the imprisonment of the real self within a false or evil self.

Willa Muir, discussing Muir's breakdown when they escaped from Czechoslovakia, makes much of this poem and its symbol in her discussion of her husband's state of mind. The Intercepter seemed to her to be a re-appearance of "the influence that had led him in earlier years to shut doors so often on his feelings."[27]

What appeared to have been a completed process of integration had been changed by the political events in Czechoslovakia into a withdrawal, which, when the Muirs had returned to Cambridge, led him to vanish "into a remoteness further away, more unreachable than ever before."[28] Willa Muir, looking back, thinks that "my homespun friend Indifference," a demon inside him, had never really left him:

The Intercepter cutting Edwin off from natural feeling was his own defence against the doctrine of Original Sin. . . . It was the Fall of Man and the consequent inherited guilt of the whole human race that kept haunting his imagination, and, I suspected, at times had paralyzed him like his own Enchanted Knight.[29]

She goes on to link this with the Calvinistic imagination of Scotland which "must have taken root in his unconscious at an early very impressionable age" combined with the death of his brother Johnnie, and Muir's subsequent self-protection through the Nietzschean rejection of sympathy. Looking back at the poems in *The Labyrinth*, Willa Muir believes that in "The Journey Back" Edwin was approaching Christianity, but "it looked as if the Intercepter had broken into and temporarily stopped a process already under way."[30]

This poem, then, as well as continuing the exploration of the evil which haunts and blocks man, demonstrates the psychological effect of an awareness of this fact. It is a disturbing poem, with its simple regular, rhyming form, emphasizing, like "The Combat," the vulnerability of man. But now it is more than a physical combat; it is a struggle for survival for spiritual and psychological balance, as the forces of evil and hope move their battleground into the poet's mind. The dark secret-sharer threatens our integrity and the battle is for nothing less than survival itself.

The little *terza rima* poem "Head and Heart" also continues the idea of the divided self, and the following four poems return strongly to the problem of evil, expressed in political terms. "The Interrogation" attempts fairly successfully to weld overt social and political reality to a wider statement about the situation of the threatened individual. The poem is obviously, on one level, a treatment of what was happening in Europe:

> We could have crossed the road but hesitated,
> And then came the patrol;
> The leader conscientious and intent,
> The men surly, indifferent.
> While we stood by and waited
> The interrogation began.

There are echoes here of "The Helmet" in the surly indifference of the men, professionally dehumanized and merely instruments of oppression and system impinging upon the helpless individual. There are echoes, too, of the one-sided battle in "The Combat" and the all-pervasive knowingness of "The Intercepter." The preoccupations of these poems remain constant, dominated by the persistence of evil, the helplessness of suffering humanity and the desperate need to survive. Endless, almost casual, suffering is approached by Muir, both directly and indirectly, by the means of free-moving symbols, self-analysis or political events. In each case the breaking-point is near and hysteria is barely controlled.

The menacing but casual beginning of "The Interrogation" is continued by adding the further image of the lovers across the road, "Hand linked in hand, wandering another star/So near we could shout to them." The lovers, removed from the brutal scene of the interrogation, present another reality and the possibility of freedom. Far less powerful than the Eden-vision in earlier poems, this reality nevertheless serves the same function of heightening the negative image by its presence. The love of political power, of totalitarian intrusion and abuse, cannot be everything, even though the tortured human-beings are far removed from the freedom of the lovers in their field.

The poem ends with three most moving and personal lines which encapsulate Muir's 1948 experience with a terrible clarity:

> We are on the very edge,
> Endurance almost done,
> And still the interrogation is going on.

The interrogation keeps going on, just like the eternal combat, just like the constantly reappearing Intercepter, and political oppression in Europe.

Formally the poem is written in free verse, although we can scan ten of the twenty-one lines as pentameter, as if Muir could not really break away from the line he so often uses. The result is particularly interesting, except that, in this poem, the tone is important and the flat, almost prosy, non-musical pattern helps to create that tone. There is oddly no anger in this poem, no protest, merely a sense of weary inevitability and of compassion for the lovers across the road. The whole poem is understated which adds to the sense of terror and helplessness; even the tone and form seem to have given in to the power of evil, unable to raise their voices in defiance.

This poem is a striking fusion of political matter with Muir's wider mythology. His method, it is now clear, does not rely exclusively on the disconnected reality of free symbols in fusion or opposition, but can also absorb concrete social contexts. "The Interrogation" is certainly a political poem, but simultaneously it is a poem about the necessity of man's having to answer questions about the meaning of his existence and how he lives in moments of crisis. The compulsion to integrate and unify disparate experience, so central to Muir's imagination, manifests itself in many ways, and his poetic method is now equal to the fierce demands he makes upon it.

In a broadcast, Muir gives us a glimpse of the imaginative process leading to his major poem "The Good Town":

A little after writing 'The Labyrinth' . . . I had an idea for two poems about towns, one to be called 'The Good Town', and the other 'The Bad Town'; and I intended the towns to stand as symbols of two ways of life. But as things were then shaping in Prague, I saw that the only way to treat the theme was to describe a good town turning into a bad one. Yet the poem is not really about Prague or any other place, but about something that was happening in Europe. Stories of what was occurring in other countries to whole families, whole communities, became absorbed into the poem, which I tried to make into a symbolical picture of a vast change.[31]

This passage gives an insight not only into the poem described, but into the poetic method which is coming to its maturity in this collection. The "idea" which came to Muir was that of two opposing symbols, "two ways of life," which at first he saw as two separate poems. As the instinctive symbolizing and synthesizing process of his imagination worked on the symbols, modified strongly by what he saw happening in Prague and "something that was happening in Europe," the two symbols become united in one creative act. The act, the poetic utterance, would not be concerned merely with one town, but would "absorb" the European reality, with all its suffering, and emerge finally as "a symbolic picture of a vast change."

Muir originally intended to call this volume of poetry

"Symbols," or something of that kind, for they all deal with symbolical human situations and types; and I hope this will give the volume a sort of unity, and at the same time that won't cause the contents to be monotonous.[32]

Certainly we have seen this technique of evoking universal situations through symbol in the poems of this volume. The symbolist imagination, seizing reality by means of wide-ranging symbol, is constantly trying to reconcile opposites in order to reach towards the numinous. The eternal combat between these forces, expressed symbolically in the poetry, is a matter of desperate importance to Muir. And this struggle, in all its urgency, gives the lie to Frederick Grubb's comment that "his mind became passive under the bombardment of myths, dreams and symbols, propending reality."[33] Even less convincing is Edwin Morgan's criticism of Muir's method, based so obviously on a conception of poetry as directly expressed experience, in which he writes:

... when Muir does want to comment on contemporary life he may be rather at a loss, wanting to mythologize but being too timid to euphemerize. Muir's chief weakness, indeed, is that he came to use Good and Evil as flags of convenience.[34]

Those "flags of convenience" took Muir to the brink of insanity. Morgan seems to miss the terror in Muir's life and poetry, and shows a certain misunderstanding of symbolist technique. There is more than one way of dealing with contemporary reality, and Muir's use of symbols, while certainly not *merely* concrete, contains a frightening amount of mid twentieth-century reality absorbed into something wider which enhances and examines that reality. His poems are not, as Mr. Morgan suggests, "abstract, allegorical landscapes."[35] On the contrary, they are symbolic landscapes, incorporating direct experience, but refusing to remain on a local conceptual level. It is a critical irrelevance to describe the poetic symbol as "abstract" or indirect or a "flag of convenience." The symbol generates and controls its own reality, looking backwards and forwards, drawing into its orbits many strands of experience and many modes of existence.

And "The Good Town" does present us with a potent symbol. Morgan claims that:

One simply doesn't accept the "universalizing" black-and-white opposition between the Danny Kaye "streets of friendly neighbours" where lock and key were "quaint antiquities fit for museums" while ivy trailed "across the prison door" and their later metamorphosis into a place where

> if you see a man
> Who smiles good-day or waves a lordly greeting
> Be sure he's a policeman or a spy.[36]

On the contrary, I think we are forced to accept it if we are not reading the poem simply as narrative or basic realism. The symbols of the good town and the bad town, or before and now, by their opposition and development in this poem, create an imaginative pattern which is, *in the terms of its symbols*, true and justified. I do not feel that "The Good Town" shows Muir's method at its best, but it is certainly neither fair nor helpful to criticize it as if it were a literal, historical summary of events in Prague in 1948.

The persona of the poem is an old citizen who has experienced all the changes. The town, when good, was subservient only to the law of time, and the first paragraph is Muir's Eden-vision, modified to include both natural time and urban reality. The prisons were empty, grass and flowers grew, life continued in mutual trust. This idea of supreme tranquility, the happy mingling of youth and age, and the knowledge of harmony and exact pattern, is very similar to previous expressions of the Eden-vision, both linguistically and imaginatively. In spite of this being an urban setting, it is contained in the same vision of prelapsarian unity which so obsessed Muir throughout his life. The "streets of friendly neighbours," far from being "Danny Kaye," are strongly reminiscent of the pattern of Orkney life in which Muir grew up.

95

This first section, the necessary prologue to the concentration of chance and event which constitute the rest of the poem, cleverly introduces the key images of lock and key, prisons, houses, grass and flowers, all of which become transformed when the town falls. We may notice, too, the stately movement of the verse, as always in the vision of Eden, where the slow, deep harmony the poet evokes becomes echoed and emphasized by the clear open-worked tone of the texture. The form is loose pentameter blank-verse, in Muir's mature style, and the variations in feet and syntactical pattern create variety without losing the strength of the metrical pulse. The language, in this first section, is gentle, using assonance and alliteration to create the required harmony:

> . . . the ivy grew
> From post to post across the prison door.
> The yard behind was sweet with grass and flowers,
> A place where grave philosophers loved to walk.

Here the subtle patterning of the vowels is effective in slowing the pace and emphasizing a quiet but positive harmony.

In the blank space between the first and second paragraphs, the Fall occurs and time has moved to the present. The mood of harmony is shattered, the metrical pattern of the verse is coarsened, the diction becomes harsher:

> Look well.   These mounds of rubble
> And shattered piers, half-windows, broken arches
> And groping arms were once inwoven in walls
> Covered with saints and angels, bore the roof,
> Shot up the towering spire.   These gaping bridges
> Once spanned the quiet river which you see
> Beyond that patch of raw and angry earth
> Where the new concrete houses sit and stare.

The earlier reality has been torn apart, just as Hamburg, Dresden, Coventry were altered overnight from bombing. These lines are an elegy for a broken Europe and a lost harmony. The people are also changed, having become displaced, strangers, in direct opposition to the harmonious family and community life of the poem's first lines. Evil intrudes into the town like the serpent into the garden:

> In our houses
> Invaders speak their foreign tongues, informers
> Appear and disappear, chance whores, officials
> Humble or high, frightened, obsequious,
> Sit carefully in corners.   My old friends

96

> (Friends ere these great disasters) are dispersed
> In parties, armies, camps, conspiracies.
> We avoid each other.   If you see a man
> Who smiles good-day or waves a lordly greeting
> Be sure he's a policeman or a spy.
> We know them by their free and candid air.

From the autobiographies of both Edwin and Willa Muir we can see how close this is to the political reality of Prague just before and after the "Putsch." It is also reminiscent of Muir's reaction to Glasgow and its "foreign" hostile people; it is also, poetically, a transformation of the images of human harmony into a sub-human chaos, which tears away all that men ideally live by.

These first two sections represent the two symbols of "the good town" and "the bad town." The second half of the poem is a reflection on the relationship of the two symbols and an inquiry into the causes of destruction and evil.

Firstly, and directly, the old man states:

> It was not time that brought these things upon us,
> But these two wars that trampled on us twice,
> Advancing and withdrawing, like a herd
> Of clumsy-footed beasts on a stupid errand
> Unknown to them or us.   Pure chance, pure malice,
> Or so it seemed.

It is the mentality of "The Helmet," of men becoming impersonal agents of destruction, that has caused the chaos. As Rosenthal says of this poem, "our century has beaten the humanity out of modern man."[37] The tranquillity of life has become a procession of crippled citizens, "changed in body or in mind"; a hideously altered landscape where "The roads ran crooked and the light fell wrong" and, finally:

> . . . the fine new prison,
> The house-doors shut and barred, the frightened faces
> Peeping round corners, secret police, informers,
> And all afraid of all.

But this explanation is insufficient:

> 'Could it have come from us?   Was our peace peace?
> Our goodness goodness?   That old life was easy
> And kind and comfortable; but evil is restless
> And gives no rest to the cruel or the kind.
> How could our town grow wicked in a moment?
> What is the answer?

97

The old citizens wonder if the old order did not in fact produce the evil; that it came from within as well as from without. We all ape those who dominate us and ordinary man, "poor ordinary neutral stuff," is swayed and influenced by conflicting forces. Again we have Muir's basic vision of reality — the dual forces warring through men and landscapes, capable of sustaining but also of eroding and destroying. The poem goes on:

> No: when evil comes
> All things turn adverse, and we must begin
> At the beginning, heave the groaning world
> Back in its place again, and clamp it there.
> Then all is hard and hazardous.

The patterns of conflict are recurring and eternal. With each fall, and by now the fall of the town has been firmly linked to the Fall of man, the process of the journey and the labyrinth begins once more, as we attempt to rediscover and recreate the spoiled garden. As the poem ends evil again seems dominant, and the people are left, "walking among our ruins." Thus Muir has expanded his two simple images of the good town and the bad town into a poem which not only describes the process of ruin, and speculates on its cause, but which grows to include his all-inclusive mythology of Eden, the Fall, and the journey. It is ultimately irrelevant whether we see the town as Prague or Troy or Glasgow, or even as Muir himself, or the garden of Eden. The symbolic structure embodies the undermining and destruction of potential security and good, from within and without, and, although the vision of good here is perhaps not as impressively realized as in other poems, the poem affirms Muir's view of life as conflicting forces. The local contemporary detail is strong in "The Good Town," but the symbols penetrate far beyond this context, showing once more something of the struggle Muir was going through before his breakdown.

One of the most concentrated descriptions of evil in this volume is "The Usurpers," which, as Rosenthal puts it, "stares into the blank face of a world 'liberated' from every old concern and value and finds no answer but 'black in its blackness'."[38] We are taken from the thoughts of the victims in "The Good Town" to the thoughts of the vanquishers, and the poem deals with one of Muir's pre-occupations — the tragic consequences of man's seeing himself as completely caught in time, and living by a belief in the historical process. It is a theme he also treats with great intensity in prose, especially in his essay on Spengler,[39] where he condemns Carlyle, Nietzsche and Spengler as belonging to "a special class of writer: the pseudo-man of action" who romanticizes brutality. The belief in life as "a play of forces, in which one factor, and one factor alone is decisive: power" is rejected by Muir in favour of a view of life "as a progress from the cradle to the grave, not as the growth, fruition, decline and downfall of civilizations," starting from the individual but reaching the universal, "since individuality is the universal form in which human life manifests itself." Man, Muir believes, is also "an immortal soul, whose essence could never be seized and contained by history." Mortality and individuality, together with the search for "immortality," are denied by the historical view, and these are exactly the qualities which make us human. Muir sums this up:

... the historical sense must always be revising its conception of history in accordance with the contemporary growth of history. It has no hold on any other reality, and without a hold on some other reality, it is impossible to have a true conception of human existence.

"The Usurpers" is a poetic utterance of this view. The conflicting symbols are those of the will and those of the imagination — men who live entirely within time and reject any other significance — and those who can, at least in the imagination, escape from the necessity of history by embracing a higher reality. It is a poem about the inhuman and the human, not just about the Fascist or Communist mentality.

In *An Autobiography*, Muir writes of a friend's showing him a photograph of some local Gestapo men:

The young men were ranged in two rows in their neat uniforms, but they stared out at us with professionally measuring but unhappy eyes. ... She (Vera, Muir's friend) pointed at one young man and said without expression: 'That is the one who strangled my husband'. But it might have been any of the others. They stared out from the photograph with the confidence of the worthless who find power left in their hands like a tip hastily dropped by a frightened world. ... I could not believe that the Gestapo men in the photograph were enjoying the summer light and the country air, and thought that the light itself must have come to them twisted and splintered as they lived out their daily waking nightmare. ... [40]

These tortured yet blindly criminal men are talking in the poem. Hitler and the Gestapo, the Czech and Russian secret police, the

99

Nietszchean Superman, the strong beast in "The Combat," the masked soldier of "The Helmet," the all-pervasive Intercepter — all these are present in this symbolic embodiment of the forces of blind will and the subhuman lust for power over life. For these men the "ancestral voices," the "old garrulous ghosts" of the gods, eternity and Eden have been conquered. In their place is the present, the reliance of self and the will. Beyond that, nothing. This perverse misinterpretation of humanism is one which specifically denies a wider reality or meaning:

> When night comes
> We drop like stones plumb to its ocean ground,
> While dreams stream past us upward to the place
> Where light meets darkness, places of images,
> Forests of ghosts, thicket of muttering voices.
> We never seek that place. . . .

The "place of images" is the unconscious and the imagination — the symbol of human things which cannot be measured or controlled with will but which haunt each one of us and are deeply part of being human. The usurpers close themselves to experience of this sort out of fear, but they admit to remembering and to being troubled, when "the day itself sometimes works spells upon us." Like Muir himself in Glasgow, they are not letting themselves be fully open to experience. Some of the most powerful lines Muir wrote conclude this poem:

> We have thought sometimes the rocks looked strangely
>   on us,
> Have fancied that the waves were angry with us,
> Heard dark runes murmuring in the autumn wind,
> Muttering and murmuring like old toothless women
> That prophesied against us in ancient tongues.

> These are imaginations.   We are free.

The climactic irony of this last line is successful. They are discussing, or trying to discuss as irrelevant and restrictive, the very things that would make them really free. As it is, they are free only of being fully human. Appropriately, it is the natural world — rocks, waves, wind — which disturbs the usurpers, as well as the old foolishnesses of prophesies and runes; the sort of mystic superstition they have tried to escape from. The texture and rhythms of the lines are a central part of their effect. The repetition of "murmuring," combined with "muttering" and "toothless" creates a striking sound-pattern which echoes the sense; the extra foot in the second of the two lines and the two opening spondees in the first recreate the insistence and strangeness of the voices which haunt the soulless men. These men, who live as instruments of will, strive to forget eternity, so deeply are they immersed in time and process, but eternity still makes itself known to them, even though they reject its intimations.

The poem is reasserting, however desperately and obliquely, that man is more than his small temporal story. Muir's two conflicting symbols, though one is somewhat repressed here, form the basis of "The Usurpers." They have usurped not just a town or country but their own humanity. To be human we must explore the "place of images" and listen to the voice of the numinous, through the "ancestral voices" and our "fluttering dreams." The poem, then, strongly rejects the mode of life it ironically presents, but again we feel that the knowledge of evil emerges more strongly than the implications of hope. "The Usurpers" adds strong irony and a new approach — through the mouth of "the enemy" — to the presentation of evil so strongly dominant in this collection.

"Oedipus" is a psychological study which broadens into a discussion of guilt and evil in the relationship between man and the gods. Probably the most prosy of his blank verse pentameter poems, "Oedipus" is perhaps too long for what it has to say and the protagonist, as symbol of guilty, suffering man, fails to become as rich and significant as Muir obviously wanted.

It is not, perhaps, very surprising that Muir should bring the figure of Oedipus into his symbolic vision. Like Ulysses or Theseus, Oedipus is on a journey, plagued with difficulties, trying to reconcile the evil of his temporal life with the will of the gods. He is Muir's archetypal wanderer, who, symbolically, develops into a universal representative of man. He, like Muir, Theseus and fallen man, is struggling in the labyrinth:

> I am one
> Who as in innocent play sought out his guilt,
> And now through guilt seeks other innocence,
> Beset by evil thoughts, led by the gods.

If the gods are good, the protagonist asks, why have I been led into the trap of guilt?

In the most highly charged section of the poem, the language strongly evokes the labyrinth:

And when in memory now,
Women of light and darkness, a stifling web,
I call her back, dear, dreaded, who lay with me,
I see guilt, only guilt, my nostrils choke
With the smell of guilt, and I can scarcely breathe
Here in the guiltless guilt-evoking sun.

Oedipus accepts his destiny and the action of the gods and through his suffering and questioning learns "to see with something of their sight." He finally realizes that the gods themselves are not exempt from the evil consequences of the Fall. It is "their guilt and mine,/ For I've but acted out this fable." There is no easy consolation in submitting to the gods. The poem ends with a subdued, but real vision of the weight of evil which cannot be evaded. Again in this poem the seemingly affirmative vision is severly modified by the pressure of tragic knowledge implied in its presentation. Oedipus accepts his lot, but this ultimately seems no more than a somewhat reluctant acquiescence in a principle of evil the gods themselves cannot escape. The poem is another symbolic treatment of the Fall and man's difficult journey subsequent to it.

The next poems in *The Labyrinth* are the three short love poems, "Circle and Square," "Love's Remorse," and "Love in Time's Despite," which leave, temporarily, the preoccupations of evil and guilt. Not in themselves significant in terms of the symbolist method, these poems, and their placement in his work, are nevertheless important because they show the start of a tentative affirmation and a restoring of balance. After these poems the power of evil and the symbol of the labyrinth never have quite the same strength again. From this point, we feel that personally, imaginatively and symbolically, Muir has passed the deepest crisis and is moving towards the inclusive celebration of *One Foot in Eden*. In terms of the journey, the echoes and reminders of the labyrinth become fainter and more distant.

This new assurance is also exemplified by the new technical assurance these poems demonstrate in the handling of short lines and tight, rhymed forms. Helen Gardner claims that " 'Circle and Square' has more right to be called metaphysical, in both senses, than many a witty modern poem modelled on Donne."[41] The poem is written in traditional question and answer form and the dialogue between the two lovers is concerned with whether one can give the whole of oneself to the loved one (symbolized by a circle), or whether one can give only half of oneself (symbolized by a square), thus retaining the precious value of each lover's individuality. The poem affirms the latter, giving its reasons firmly but tenderly in its last two stanzas:

> 'And let the circle run
> Its dull and fevered race.
> You, my dear, are one;
> Show your soul in your face;
> Maintain your place.'

> 'Give, but have something to give.
> No man can want you all.
> Live, and learn to live.
> When all the barriers fall
> You are nothing at all.'

As we have seen, Muir's short-line poems are sometimes marred by metrical rigidity, clumsy inversion, rhyme-forcing and unvaried, line-and-stanza-stopped sentence structure. This is not true of "Circle and Square," which exhibits something of the variety possible even with short lines. Here the five-line stanza, rhymed *a b a b b*, consists of four trimeter lines followed by a dimeter. If we scan the poem, we see that, even in a form as tight and seemingly inflexible as this, there is considerable metrical variety, giving the poem tonal life and modulating the tone. The last three stanzas may be scanned as follows:

```
x  /  | x  /  | x  /  |  (x)
/  x  | x  /  | x  /  |
x  /  | x  /  | x  /  |  (x)
x  /  | x  /  | xx /  |
/     | x  /  |

x  /  | x  /  | x  /  |
x  /  | x  /  | x  /  |
/     | x  /  | x  /  |
/     | x  /  | xx /  |
/  /  | x  /  |

/  x  | x  /  | xx /  |
/  /  | x  /  | x  /  |
/     | x  /  | x  /  |
x  /  | x  /  | xx /  |
xx /  | xx /  |
```

We can see immediately that there are a considerable number of trochaic, spondaic and anapestic substitutions in all positions in the three-foot lines, as well as pyrrhic feet and missing first syllables. So confident is the metrical system that Muir can end the poem with three anapests without doing any violence to the sound organization. In lines as short as this, this sort of variation is not easy, especially when the rhymes are close together, but Muir works the form with ease. He varies the sentence length, uses more enjambement than usual, but retains strong exact rhyming throughout. The language, compared with his longer-line poems, is more spare; there are few adjectives and no signs of extra words used to fill a pre-determined metrical pattern. Altogether, we can see that as well as perfecting his symbolistic method in this volume, he is learning to handle forms with a greater ease and to use tight metrical and stanzaic structure in a way that does not brutalise his subject.

"Love's Remorse," a Shakespearean sonnet, celebrates the renewing powers of eternity, as opposed to time, but here the concept of eternity is humanized by being anchored in the concrete knowledge of human love. "Love in Time's Despite" treats the traditional love-time theme in much the same way, suggesting that, through love, access to the world outside time is possible.

These three love poems are surprisingly positive coming after the despairing fight against nihilism in the earlier poems of *The Labyrinth*. But there is also a poignancy built in to them — a falling cadence, a sadness implicit in the very sound and tone, a grave measured beauty, full of knowledge and humility, yet marvellously simple. Muir writes, as Helen Gardner says, "as one who knows the strength of love and the strength of grief."[42] For all the tenderness, one feels that these love poems are informed with the tragic knowledge of experience. They have something of the feel of Hardy's admittedly more obviously elegaic love poems, written after he had travelled through the landscape of tragedy in his novels. As with Hardy's, Muir's poems seem to gain a seriousness and a dimension for having this knowledge somewhere behind them; the longing, in Hardy's case, for the ability to recall love from death and, for Muir, the urgent search for the means to escape time and go past it. And yet, in Muir's case, there is a new strength in these poems, however traditional their resolution of man's dilemma.

With "Soliloquy" Muir returns to the technique of using symbol to explore reality and to free his imagination from time and space.

The speaker is the hero/wanderer, vaguely defined as a seventy-year-old man living in a country house in Greece. The poem is a meditation on the meaning of experience and the way men use it. The all-seeing narrator looks at human experience:

> I have seen Alexandria, imperial Rome,
> And the sultry backlanes of Jerusalem
> One late spring evening thirty years ago
> Trouble me still.   It was a holy day:
> The inns and taverns packed to the very door,
> Goods, cattle, families, fellowships, clans;
> And some time after a man was crucified,
> So it is said, who died for love of the world.
> Strange deeds, strange scenes.   I have passed through
> war and peace. . . .

The immediate reference to the crucifixion is modified by the casual ignorance of the narrator, and this is Muir's method throughout the poem, confusing events and attitudes by introducing the narrator's own biography — the Story — and his own sometimes confused throught-processes, and mixing this with significant events — the Fable — and the poet's own judgments on both. The narrator has seen refugees, migrations, battles, madmen, and is trying to make sense of the random flux of experience; to find an underlying pattern and a creative clarification. He has found among the chaos of his life, one truth which is "scarecly to be borne":

> That there's a watershed in human life,
> A natural mountain which we have to scale;
> And once at the top, our journey all lies downward,
> Down the long slope to age and sleep and the end.

He has found that he is caught in time and involved in an inevitable process. The poem then switches back to memory from the present, as the narrator tells of Troy, now ruined and grown over by time and of curious temples he has seen of some old sun-worshipping religion. His comment on these is simply "Past reading." He is becoming more and more interested in his own conclusions and drags us straight back to the present with an urgent appeal to use experience wisely:

> Select, select: make an anthology
> Of what's been given you by bold casual time.
> Revise, omit;   keep what's significant.

> Fill, fill deserted time.   Oh there's no comfort
> In the wastes of empty time.   Provide for age.
> Life must be lived;   then live. . . .

This desperate pleading is reflected cleverly by the irregularity and breathlessness of syntax and metre. Then again, as memory and reflection take over, we revert to quieter, more regular sound patterns. The next lines could come straight from Muir's mouth:

> And so I turn
> To past experience, watch it being shaped,
> But never to its own true shape.   However,
> I have fitted this or that into the pattern,
> Caught sight sometimes of the original
> That is myself — should rather be myself —
> The soul past price bartered at any price
> The moment bids, cheap as the cheapest moment.
> I have had such glimpses, made such tentative
> Essays to shape my life, have had successes,
> Whether real or apparent time may tell,
> Though there's no bargain you can drive with time.
> All this is insufficient.

The last, thrown-away line emphasises the impossibility of an adequate pattern being imposed simply by an analysis of one's past. The soul is only caught sight of some times and then bartered. Time remains in control.

We return to specific memories or visions in the next section; fleets, disasters, crucifixions, wrecks and a lack of pattern; and the poem ends with two rather ambiguous sections, where hope and tragic resignation seem awkwardly balanced:

> I have thought of death,
> And followed Plato to eternity,
> Walked in his radiant world;

This radiant world, Plato's other world, is the Eden-vision which is intermittently visible, and these lines suggest that, fortified with glimpses of eternity, man can withstand the terrible random suffering, the great defeats and movements in history and in time.

The last lines of the poem form a tremendous climax of prayer, addressed to unspecified gods, full of the knowledge of man's sin and inadequacy but confident of the greater reality which can bring salvation:

Set up the bleak worn day to show our sins,
Old and still ageing, like a flat squat herd
Crawling like sun on wall to the rim of time,
Up the long slope for ever.

　　　　　　　Light and praise,
Love and atonement, harmony and peace,
Touch me, assail me;　break and make my heart.

This conclusion is quite unlike those of the earlier poems in this volume, not only in its specifically religious language, but in its implication of a new receptiveness and openness. The poem is a reflection on human history and myth, with the emphasis on randomness and meaninglessness, but it postulates the eternity of Plato and the existence of a higher place of appeal very forcibly. The device of the old Greek narrator is arbitrary. Muir is here reflecting once again on the possibility of breaking out of the labyrinth of time into the "radiant world" that insists on teasing the experience of every man's life. The speaker starts by saying "I have seen more than I know" but the poem ends with the realization that we know more than we have seen.

"The Absent" again links man's present, worldly life with a higher reality, but this time in terms of those who are not with us. These absent ones are never explained, but exist as powerful presences modifying our lives. Muir is again using a conflict of symbols as the basis of his technique, but in this poem, instead of calling them Eden and the labyrinth, he calls them we, representing this limited life of the Story, and They, who belong to the timeless world of the Fable. The absent ones exist somewhere out of time, beyond the reach of the Fall; we exist as their inheritors, yet also as "usurpers claiming/ The sun and the kingdom of the sun." We have no right to this claim. All we can hope for, the poem concludes, is that, through the power of the knowledge of the absent ones, "sorrow/And loneliness might bring a blessing upon us."

This most tangential and remote use of symbol, even further removed from referential reality than usual, is parallelled by the poem's structure and sound values. Ostensibly the poem is in free verse, although the many pentameter lines and the rhyming give an oddly formal sound. The poem reads like a liturgy, using alternating long and short lines and repeated syntactical and linguistic figures in a ritualistic way. The most interesting formal device, however, is the rhyming. Of the poem's twenty-four lines, seven end with the word "us" and a further eight rhyme, or half rhyme with "us." This intensive patterning is reinforced by the other eleven line endings of "sun," "love," "love," "air," 'wander," "air," "absence," "sorrow," "memory," "claiming" and "sorrow," where the air-love pattern and the repeated "sorrow" add to the effect of ritual. This intensity of rhyming, combined with the flat, repeated phrases like "we are the Others," "For they are not here," "Since They are not here," "For we are the Others," gives a tone of remoteness; a ceremonial, formal flatness which embodies perfectly the remote, released symbols.

It is further interesting to note that, like the poem before it, "The Absent" ends on a note of religious possibility, however tentative or desperately prayed for, as if the labyrinth symbol has shrunk and the Eden symbol has gained strength. Both are still acknowledged and used to create conflict, but the fear of being overwhelmed has now gone, together with the tone of desperate, even shrill hysteria.

"The Transfiguration" is a great symbolic and psychological step forward, and anticipates the religious celebration of many of the poems in the next volume, with their new and more specifically Christian symbolism. It is a poem of light and radiance, of sight being "rinsed and cleansed," of the return to the "unfallen world." It is a vision of the material world re-shaped and transformed. In a broadcast, Muir said:

I had always been deeply struck by the story of the Transfiguration in the Gospels, and I had felt that perhaps at the moment of Christ's Transfiguration everything was transfigured, mankind, and the animals, and the simplest natural objects. After the poem appeared I had a letter from a lady who had made a long study of the subject, and to my surprise I found that the idea which I had imagined in my own mind possessed a whole literature, and that in some of the Russian churches it was often represented pictorially. Perhaps in the imagination of mankind the Transfiguration has become a powerful symbol, standing for many things, and among them those transformations of reality which the imagination itself creates.[43]

This is a perfect subject for Muir's symbolist technique, giving him an actual event, or myth, with which to evoke the "transformations of reality" with which his poetry and life are concerned. The theology of the Transfiguration is complex and, as Professor Butter goes into this in some detail, I shall not deal with that aspect, except to refer to a letter Muir wrote to Maisie Spens, the lady referred to in the broadcast. Muir wrote:

I know nothing of the literature of the Transfiguration, and in writing the poem did not see where it was leading me. On the other hand I have always had a particular feeling for that transmutation of life which is found occasionally in poetry, and in the literature of prophecy, and sometimes in one's own thoughts when they are still. This, I think, is one of the things which have always been with me, or more exactly, which have persistently recurred to me. . . . [44]

This last sentence is significant because of the time he wrote "The Transfiguration," after his battle, personal and poetic, with the forces of despair and evil, when visions like this were blocked and unable to pierce the obsessions with the labyrinth and the Fall. The recurrence of this vision shows the final emergence from hell and breakdown into a landscape of light and silence. It is, perhaps, more useful to examine the poem in terms of the more general "transmutation of life" Muir refers to in the letter, than to see it purely in terms of Christianity, as Butter does when he takes the "we" of the poem to be just the disciples. Muir's symbols are not this closely linked to concept, and, although the poem specifically embodies the Christian transfiguration, the symbols move more widely in time and space than this. Willa Muir sees this depth of accumulated meaning clearly when, interpreting the poem as an attempted antidote to the power of the Intercepter, she writes:

In Prague he had composed a much better poem, a lovely poem . . . "The Transfiguration", in which he journeyed back through Time undoing human aberrations to reach a primal innocence transfiguring the whole world. That was an attempt to rid himself of something which had apparently long troubled him; one would have said a successful attempt, driving his demon out.[45]

It is in terms of his developing symbolism of time, the journey, the labyrinth and Eden that we must see "The Transfiguration"; the new, explicit Christian references merely add to the clustered meanings of the symbols without changing them. Here Christ and the biblical myth act as energizing and releasing agents for the symbols. They are not new symbols, for, as I have said, Muir's symbolistic technique cannot work as an alternative, either/or system, but is accumulative, growing in dimension but not changing its form. This poem is a triumph of that technique, mingling dream with myth; imaginative reality with actuality, time past, present and future with imagined timelessness, the pain of frustrated man trapped in his life with intimations of freedom in eternity. It is thus of a certain symbolic density and complexity; much more, I believe, than "an examination, made entirely in lucid imagery, of an event from the New Testament. . . . "[46]

As well as from its Biblical source, "The Transfiguration" derives from both dream and personal experience. Muir records his first May Day demonstration in Glasgow, where he saw the crowds of rich and poor, healthy and crippled, and had "the feeling that all distinction had fallen away like a burden carried in some other place, and that all substance had been transmuted."[47] He also records a dream:

I dreamt that there had been great rains, and from a high peak I was looking down on a new crystal river flowing through some pleasant, green, undulating country: I thought it was France. All along the river, whose course I could follow for hundreds of miles, the children crowded to the water and eagerly flung themselves in. Then the older people came, until the very old men and women were there, bathing in the river. . . . [48]

The dream continues with a warning that harlots are bathing further up the river:

At this I felt alarmed, for I thought that the prostitutes would infect the river; but then I knew that these waters could easily wash away every impurity and still remain pure.

The description of the dream concludes with an assertion of total transmutation and purity:

The undulating country itself looked somewhat like a map, but through it flowed that great river of water, so living, so deep and pure, that an actual river would have appeared artificial beside it, as though it alone contained the original idea and essence of pure and cleansing and ever-flowing water.

"The Transfiguration" distils Muir's waking and dreaming experience of universal purification, tying it symbolically to the mythology he had developed.

The first forty lines, among the most luminous and most intensely lyrical he ever wrote, present a vision of the transfigured life:

> So from the ground we felt that virtue branch
> Through all our veins till we were whole, our wrists
> As fresh and pure as water from a well,
> Our hands made new to handle holy things,
> The source of all our seeing rinsed and cleansed
> Till earth and light and water entering there
> Gave back to us the clear unfallen world.

The purification by water and light is a mystical baptism, making men "whole" and restoring the prelapsarian harmony of the world.

This radiant vision is interrupted by three questions, which call for a verification of the reality of the opening affirmation:

> Was it a vision?
> Or did we see that day the unseeable
> One glory of the everlasting world
> Perpetually at work, though never seen
> Since Eden locked the gate that's everywhere
> And nowhere?   Was the change in us alone,
> And the enormous earth still left forlorn,
> An exile or a prisoner?

Apart from linking the symbol of the transfiguration directly to Eden and the timeless world before the Fall, Muir here is freeing his symbolism from being anchored or over-specific. Symbolic perception works at all levels, mingling conscious and unconscious, actuality and vision, and this tactic of questioning the validity of the perception has the effect of universalizing the described experience, and simultaneously justifying the symbolist technique. The creative confusion of time/space is further heightened by the next sentence:

> Yet the world
> We saw that day made this unreal, for all
> Was in its place.

The experience of transformation has clarified the unreality of the tangible world. The world of Eden is once more characterized by Muir's constant imaginative description of all being "in its place." The poem continues with a long celebration of the perfection of the "real" world of eternity, which is closely developed from previous poems:

> The painted animals
> Assembled there in gentle congregations,
> Or sought apart their leafy oratories,
> Or walked in peace, the wild and tame together,
> As if, also for them, the day had come.
> The shepherds' hovels shone, for underneath
> The soot we saw the stone clean at the heart
> As on the starting-day.   The refuse heaps
> Were grained with that fine dust that made the
>   world. . . .

The transfiguration has purified the animal world and the inanimate world, as well as the human world, turning refuse into the "fine dust that made the world" as the symbolism penetrates back through time to "the starting-day."

This general treatment becomes more refined with the first direct reference to Christ as he walks with the people through the town and the "lurkers" and murderers stepped from the shadows to join them. They "came/Out of themselves" in their transfigured state; out of the prison of the self. This is a reversal of the image in "The Usurpers," where the townsfolk were forced inside themselves through fear. Now those obsessive entanglements are left behind:

> And those who hide within the labyrinth
> Of their own loneliness and greatness came,
> And those entangled in their own devices,
> The silent and the garrulous liars, all
> Stepped out of their dungeons and were free.

This all-inclusive vision of harmony and wholeness directly asserts its triumph over the labyrinth and the forces of evil. But in a typical shift of tense, from past to present, Muir brings in the opposing symbol:

> If it had lasted but another moment
> It might have held for ever!   But the world
> Rolled back into its place, and we are here,
> And all that radiant kingdom lies forlorn,
> As if it had never stirred;   no human voice
> Is heard among its meadows, but it speaks
> To itself alone, alone it flowers and shines
> And blossoms for itself while time runs on.

The vision fades, defeated by the weight of time and necessity. The regret, the sense of a near breakthrough, is strong here, as is the dull tragic awareness of the world of unreality — this world rolling back and reasserting itself. And yet, in a further confusion of tenses, the visionary world of eternity is not now evoked in past tense, but as an active agent in the present. It is, of course, timeless, and although the humans are caught in time and have been pulled back by time from their experience of transmutation, the "real" world, almost mockingly," speaks/To itself alone."

The cruel disappointment of being snatched away from this state of perception has been somewhat compensated for by an insistence upon the eternal validity of the timeless state. It now becomes symbolically further confirmed by the last paragraph, where the tense switches first to the future and then, finally, to eternity once more. The vision will be restored again, not through the active participation of Christ alone, but when

> ... all things,
> Beasts of the field, and woods, and rocks, and seas,
> And all mankind from end to end of the earth
> Will call him with one voice.   In our own time,
> Some say, or at a time when time is ripe.

The Eden-vision is released here by the symbol of Christ, but the apocalypse is more than Christian; the speakers more than the disciples:

> Then he will come, Christ the uncrucified,
> Christ the discrucified, his death undone,
> His agony unmade, his cross dismantled —
> Glad to be so — and the tormented wood
> Will cure its hurt and grow into a tree
> In a green springing corner of young Eden. ...

Time future merges into the journey back, into "young Eden." The process of transmutation will take things back to first sources, and just as the clothes early in the poem revert to being flowers and sheep, so does the Cross — symbol of murder and betrayal — revert to being a tree in Eden. The betrayer will regain total innocence and the labyrinth of time and evil will be forgotten.

A luminous vision of harmony and mystical perception, "The Transfiguration" does not escape from or evade the knowledge of evil, but the energy of the positive symbolism relegates evil and defeats it, just as earlier in this volume, evil was blocking the vision of transmutation and wholeness. The local imagery and tone are part of the poem's expressiveness, being informed with both an upsurging energy and a massive tranquillity, which is reinforced by the gentle patterning of the pentameter blank verse and easy syntax. The poem is full of radiance and light, its language expressing the "rinsed and cleansed" perception which is presented.

Elsewhere, Muir wrote:

I realized that immortality is not an idea or belief, but a state of being in which man keeps alive in himself, his perception of that boundless vision and freedom, which he can faintly apprehend in time, though its consummation lies beyond time.[49]

This idea of "a state of being," rather than "an idea or belief" is why this poem is more than Christian. "The Transfiguration" uses some Christian symbolism, but only as part of its wider symbolic structure. Its real value is that it not only expresses but embodies that state of being, with all its consummation and limitation. The poem embodies, in fact, the "transformations of reality which the imagination itself creates" that he had described in his broadcast and which are also dealt with in "The Transmutation." If we regard the original transfiguration as a symbolic event, we can see the complexity of Muir's symbolic embodiment of that symbolic event. And yet, in spite of this complexity, the poem is simple, lyrical and easily accessible, once we let the symbols assert their own life and pattern. There is no distinction possible between the inner and the outer world in a symbolist poem. We are given one act of perception through the symbolic structure, and within that act, time and space, dream and reality, revolve freely, held only by the strength of the symbols.

The vision of harmony continues in the last three poems of *The Labyrinth*, though not with the same intensity as it is grasped in "The Transfiguration." "The Debtor" is a short meditative poem of acceptance of things as they are, where tensions between the Story and the Fable have disappeared. The first-person narrator celebrates the sustaining power of the understood pattern, where the dead, natural processes, prayers, history, all bring blessings and support. The knowledge of Eden and eternity is strongly present. This is again a vision of harmony, where "victor and vanquished" become one, and all strife and terror and fear have become obsolete. Cleansed by ancient springs, life becomes not only tolerable, but something sacred and whole.

"Song" takes us back to the tone of the love poems earlier in this volume. Intensely lyrical, positive in theme, it has a strong undertone of sadness and compassion — the tone of the songs in *Twelfth Night*, *The Tempest* and other Shakespeare plays.

The poem affirms the power of love while simultaneously acknowledging, and accepting, the divisions and tragedies of human life. The slow, elegiac, lyric awareness of inevitability and sadness, as well as the beauty, implied in the passing of time, develops into a simple and formal statement about the human condition:

> Sunset ends the day
> The years shift their place,
> Under the sun's sway
> Time from times fall;

> Mind fighting mind
> The secret cords unwind
> No power can replace:
> Love gathers all.

There is no doubt that Muir has come through the crisis of evil and the labyrinth, but equally there is no doubt that crisis has left him with a knowledge that haunts him, even when he knows he can defeat his fear of it. This poem, in fact, apart from the refrain line "Love gathers all" is full of details of division. The direct reference to the labyrinth in stanza two and the deliberate images of loss and separation act in opposition to the assertion of the refrain and the serenity of the tone:

> Father at odds with son
> Breeds ageless enmity,
> Friendships undone
> Build up a topless wall;
> Achilles and Hector slain
> Fight, fight and fight again
> In measureless memory:
> Love gathers all.

The odd, rather grave formalism of the lyric is heightened by the fact that the sense goes in pairs of two lines, and the syntax, which really demand sentences to end within the stanza, winds strangely along, making each stanza a complete sentence.

The last stanza, referring to the things which have so preoccupied and frightened Muir in previous poems, makes clear the triumph and acceptance; the Fall is part of a greater pattern which absorbs it:

> The quarrel from the start,
> Long past and never past,
> The war of mind and heart,
> The great war and the small
> That tumbles the hovel down
> And topples town on town
> Come to one place at last:
> Love gathers all.

It is not difficult to see Glasgow, Prague or Troy here, but the strain has gone, and the squalor, misery, barbarism and evil are dissolved away by the lyric into a formal but moving realization of the pattern of the Fable and the power of love. The effect is gained largely through control of tone, which, in its turn is influenced by the metrical qualities. In this poem Muir confirms his technical assurance and maturity by again handling the short trimeter and dimeter lines with variation and control. The metrical subtlety of the first few lines, for example, establishes the tone as well as the sound-pattern, and the single sentence stanzas move in parallel with each other towards the clinching sound, sense and rhythm of the refrain line, which anchors the poem's structure and meaning and draws them together.

The final poem in this collection is "The Toy Horse," a short poem of five tetrameter quatrains, fully rhymed, which is interesting for the way it moves outward from local concrete observation into the timeless world. The toy horse, the "Dumb wooden idol" with a "lifted foot" is transformed into a heraldic symbol which links time to eternity; a piece of statuary which leads man on his fabled journey:

> His lifted foot commands the West,
> And, lingering, halts the turning sun;
> Endless departure, endless rest,
> End and beginning here are one.

The horse symbolizes what Eliot called "The still point of the turning world"; the motionless centre of the ever recurring pattern of human lives as man moves across the fabulous landscape towards eternity:

> Dumb wooden idol, you have led
> Millions on your calm pilgrimage
> Between the living and the dead,
> And shine yet in your golden age.

The Labyrinth ends, then, on a note of affirmation, more muted than in "The Transfiguration," but no less certain that it is possible to overcome chaos.

The poems in this volume represent the flowering of Muir's technical skill and the perfecting of his symbolist method. In these Prague poems we are at the very centre of his struggle between evil and good; *The Labyrinth* being a journey from the lowest depths of despair and disintegration to a tentative celebratory acceptance of the triumph of good. Almost every poem here revolves around the symbolic confrontation of good and evil, of Eden and the labyrinth, and we are taken by the developing symbols deep into both.

The terrible experiences of Prague took Muir to the edge of total disintegration. Many of these poems, apart from their symbolic

qualities, are fine political studies, presenting with a terrible awareness the psychological impact on both individuals and the community
of war and political terrorism. The values of imagination, love,
individuality, freedom are almost extinguished by the impersonal
power of the will, and the struggle is for the survival of the self
against these forces. Only by perfecting his use of symbol, whereby
it could range freely and untethered over time and space, could Muir
cope with the intensity of concrete reality in terms of some wider
reality so important if men are to survive and remain stable and
whole.

The Labyrinth shows Muir's slow struggle with the forces of evil,
played out through the combat of symbols. As we have seen, he
manages to overcome the threat of annihilation, so frighteningly
imagined in poems like "The Combat" and "The Intercepter," in
terms of symbol, but the personal price was high. Once out of
Czechoslovakia and back in England, at Cambridge, Muir "was
hardly recognizable as the same man."[50] Willa Muir describes his
state as "inert," and he seemed to go into complete withdrawal:

He seemed almost dumb and although neither deaf nor blind heard and
saw things without attaching meaning to them. His eyes went to and
fro following, as if by compulsion, any small movement within range, a
tortoise walking along a garden path or a golf ball being putted across
a lawn, but they might as well have been camera eyes; he watched these
movements with the vacant stare of a shell-shock case after a modern
war. . . . Left to himself he merely sat and stared.[51]

This state lasted three months. It was as if the long struggle to
conquer the dark forces symbolically in the poetry had left him
drained and empty. In a way he was "a shell-shock case," for The
Labyrinth is the record of a war, symbolic and psychological, but as
desperately important and painful as any physical conflict. The
process he had triumphantly completed in his poetry seemed only
half over in his "other" life; as if he were still struggling, endlessly,
with the proud beast or meeting the Intercepter at every turn. His
wife felt that "he might be in a state of despair about the whole
human race, since his conflicts had vanished beyond reach."[52] She
recalls how E. M. Forster came to visit Muir "and gently tried to
talk to Edwin but could get no response; after a little while he went
quietly away." Muir himself describes these months:

As soon as I arrived (in Cambridge) I had a breakdown, and fell plumb
into a dead pocket of life which I had never guessed at before. . . . I

awoke each morning feeling that I had lost or mislaid something which I was accustomed to but could not name. . . . Memories of Prague now and then shivered the surface of my mind, but never sank deep into it.[53]

It is easy to see comparisons between this state of dejection and his earlier Glasgow and London experience. Both are a form of compensatory withdrawal after violence and evil have seemed to triumph over the intimations of eternity and spiritual and psychological balance.

Muir's breakdown shows that, however remote and impersonal his poetry sometimes seems, it is a deeply involved, though symbolic, penetration of very real personal experience. *The Labyrinth* is a record of a human-being moving sluggishly in the darkness of his own spiritual crisis. That it is also a universal statement of man's relationship with evil and his instinctive, insistent craving for the numinous is a tribute not just to Muir's wisdom and knowledge of human beings, but to his poetic method, which enabled him to link personal and the particular with the universal in a way that is wholly his own. As well as being a tortured, deeply unhappy human being, Muir became, with this volume, a major poet at the height of his power.

CHAPTER FIVE

One Foot in Eden

Muir sent the manuscript of *One Foot in Eden* to T. S. Eliot at Faber and Faber early in 1955. The poems were written in Rome, where he was Director of the British Institute from the beginning of 1949 to its closure in the summer of 1950, and at Newbattle Abbey College in Scotland, of which Muir was Warden from 1950 to 1955. The time in Rome was a particularly satisfying one for Muir, releasing him from his withdrawn state and enriching his vision of reality. In *An Autobiography*, he describes the change:

I saw in Czechoslovakia a whole people lost by one of the cruel turns of history, and exiled from themselves in the heart of their own country. I discovered in Italy that Christ had walked on the earth, and also that things truly made preserve themselves through time in the first freshness of their nature.[1]

As he puts it, "Rome made my wife well again and let me forget Prague."[2] He describes the Institute as "a sort of talkative Eden," which was "the most friendly, kind, busy place imaginable,"[3] and his wife describes him as:

. . . joyously released from imprisonment. He was able to come out of himself spontaneously again and meet the spontaneous Italians around him with a positive affection which they returned more than generously.[4]

Muir was visited by travelling writers and began to write again:

Sitting at ease on our roof top Edwin was moved to write occasional poems. Conversations there with visitors were gay and free. Wystan Auden, for instance, turned up one evening and over litres of *vino aperto* (seven litres, Hilde swore; she kept bringing them like a sorcerer's apprentice) argued the case for the resurrection of the body while Edwin argued for the immortality of the soul, in a happy antiphony that went on for hours. The rooftop was a liberating place.[5]

The significance of Rome for Muir's poetry and his constantly developing symbolism lies primarily in his new awareness of the Incarnation, by the statues and paintings:

That the images should appear everywhere, reminding everyone of the Incarnation, seemed to me natural and right, just as it was right that my Italian friends should step out frankly into life. This open declaration was to me the very mark of Christianity, distinguishing it from the older religions. For although the pagan gods had visited the earth and conversed with men, they did not assume the burden of our flesh, live our life and die our death, but after their interventions withdrew into their inpenetrable privacy.[6]

This new awareness of the physical actuality of Christ helped to strengthen Muir's belief that the world of men and time can and must be brought into relationship with the eternal, timeless world. His comments on the old pagan gods help to elucidate a poem like "Oedipus" where, as we have seen, the god-man relationship is shown as real, but in the last analysis, curiously imperfect. His time in Rome strengthened and deepened his beliefs about man in time and men's relationship with the timeless. Just as in his Orkney childhood legend and history seemed magically real and ever-present, so in Italy he felt again in touch with the timeless:

The grass in the courtyard of the Temple of the Vestals seemed to be drenched in peace down to the very root, and it was easy to imagine gods and men still in friendly talk together there.[7]

In a letter to Chiari in December 1949, Muir developed this perception:

I'm much struck with Rome, and all its wealth of associations: you feel the gods (including the last and greatest of them) have all been here, are still present in a sense in the places where they once were. It has brought very palpably to my mind the theme of Incarnation and I feel that probably I shall write a few poems about that high and difficult theme sometime: I hope so.

... I'm rather afraid of writing on such a theme and though it occupies my mind whenever my mind is free from daily affairs, I feel nothing is ready yet to be written down.[8]

Butter rightly points out that Muir refers here to Incarnation and not *the* Incarnation. It is also interesting that Muir describes Christ as "The last and greatest" of the gods, suggesting perhaps no difference in kind and no exclusiveness. Muir's religion, dominated always by his receiving and pondering symbol and archetype, could never be narrowly Christian. As Kathleen Raine has written:

If he was a Christian poet he was so by convergence of symbol not (as for example T. S. Eliot) by subscription to doctrine. His view could never be measured in any pinpoint of orthodoxy; for in revealing in part the mystery, he leaves it still a mystery. The most certain thing he knew of it was that it is unknowable. He did in fact increasingly use a traditional symbolism as he discovered that his vision itself placed him within age-old traditions; that what he had glimpsed in dreams had been man's theme for countless centuries.[9]

Muir's religion derived from his symbols and embraced dream, myth, history, Christianity, the old gods and his own personal view of time and immortality. The knowledge of the Incarnation in Rome added to this symbolism and gave him new approaches and energies with which to release his symbols, but Christ could not exclude the Greeks and the old gods. Muir's symbolism is accumulative, and believing in Christ as God in no way alters its range. It is interesting that in the *Collected Poems*, Muir leaves out five of the most obviously Christian poems from *One Foot in Eden*, partly because they are less successful as poems, but partly, one suspects, to ensure that "unfelt" or possibly doctrinal symbolism should not unbalance the revealed structure of symbol which so dominated his poetry and his imagination. This symbolism is ultimately wider than Christianity, just as it includes more than any one experience, event, idea, place or time.

The first poem in *One Foot in Eden*, the sonnet "Milton," reveals in its fourteen lines a complex drawing together of idea and symbol. At one level the poem is a remarkable distillation of Milton's life and work. The blind poet, dealing, like Muir, in symbols of the Fall and eternity, creates in his greatest work the terror and crisis of Hell, imagined through noise in his blindness, before emerging with real sight into the world of eternity and Paradise. The attainment of Paradise is through physical and spiritual suffering; the darkness and desolation of blindness and the experience of Dante's Hell. In J. R. Watson's words: "Pity requires suffering and evil for its existence; pity is a divine attribute so that through suffering one attains to Paradise."[10]

But this poem moves out beyond the ostensible subject of Milton. The symbolism of the man journeying towards paradise, being plunged into chaos and darkness and finally managing to emerge purified and "unblinded" is familiar to us. The poem, in fact, embodies the symbolism of the journey and the labyrinth; Milton becomes Muir and all men, and the description of hell becomes more than a reference to *Paradise Lost* or to Dante's *Inferno*. In his brilliant analysis of this poem, John Holloway shows unmistakably how "Milton," through its symbolism and technique, forces us to see our own world through the semi-transparent landscape of the poet's imagination: "If we are to imagine the noise in Muir's Hell as a 'steely clamour known too well on Saturday nights in every street', we know where we are."[11] This is indeed true, for we move out of the imaginative world of *Paradise Lost* and *The Divine Comedy*, through the symbolic labyrinth, right into the ugly brutality of drunken brawls in Glasgow and of Nazi atrocities and Communist oppression in Czechoslovakia. We move, as well, into a man's mind at a time of breakdown. Holloway goes on to develop this point:

To wander in this imaginary landscape, to experience its strangeness and terror, is to re-enter our own real landscape by an unexpected and revelatory gate. If Hell is like that, we are forced to say ... "Why this is Hell, nor am I out of it". *There*, the poet's imaginary and created world, has illuminated *here*, our real one.[12]

I have made this same point many times. The symbol incorporates both "worlds," using each to illuminate and refine the other, moving freely backwards and forwards between *there* and *here*, until they are inseparably woven together. Shut in this mental, spiritual and physical darkness, assailed by destructive powers, tempted to despair, man is still only "a footstep" away from the world of eternity. The opposing symbols are strongly contrasted in this poem. The anti-vision of hell incorporates darkness, noise, flame and blackened stone, while the Eden symbol consists of light, "unblinded eyes" and wide fields.

The sonnet form enables Muir to juxtapose his symbols more intensely and compactly than usual, with great energy and concreteness. The three quatrains each contain a separate, yet organic development of the theme, and the final couplet releases the poem's tension with its visionary finality. This finality is enhanced by the fact that the rhyme-word "Paradise" is also the rhyme-word of the first line and the poem has thus come full circle from the abortive attempt to achieve Paradise to the completed process of fulfilment.

"Milton" is a highly charged, compressed re-enactment of the process Muir so painstakingly describes in *The Labyrinth*. The final achievement of Paradise becomes possible only through a painful, necessary redemptive descent into hell and almost total deprivation of vision. The pressures of hell, so strongly imaged in this poem by the concrete language and evocation of chaotic noise, almost blind the man who voyages towards light but simultaneously show the strength and courage of the man who can survive such an experience:

> Shut in his darkness, these he could not see,
> But heard the steely clamour known too well
> On Saturday nights in every street in Hell.
> Where, past the devilish din, could Paradise be?
> A footstep more, and his unblinded eyes
> Saw far and near the fields of Paradise.

"Milton" is, on any terms, a fine poem, but it becomes even more powerful and moving when we bring to it the knowledge of Muir's own struggle, both personal and poetic, to stop the powers of darkness from blinding his vision. It is highly appropriate that the last line and a half of his poem should be inscribed on Muir's gravestone because the words "far and near" illustrate perfectly Muir's ability to bring that wider reality into a symbolic and meaningful union with man's temporal experience. In this poem, and in all his best poems, he created "a single unshakeable unity, with the memorableness, the burning insistence, of an icon."[13]

The next three poems "The Animals," "The Days" and "Adam's Dream," were all written in Italy before most of the other poems in this volume. They all deal with Eden and the creation of life, but, as we might expect, develop meaning beyond their ostensible themes. "The Animals" is a clear, melodic lyric where Muir's craftsmanship is clearly shown in the metrical patterning and subtle modulations of tone. The surface texture is so subdued that the poem's final irony is greatly heightened. As we have seen, Muir's vision of Eden has always been closely linked to his vision of everything being in its right place. This almost always includes animals, as well as man and the gods. In "The Animals" Muir celebrates the animal kingdom by contrasting its simplicity with man's dubious sophistication. Animals, above all, are without language as we know it, and as language makes our reality they are not part of it:

> They do not live in the world,
> Are not in time and space.
> From birth to death hurled
> No word do they have, not one
> To plant a foot upon,
> Were never in any place.

For with names the world was called
Out of the empty air. . . .

This strategy of pretended pity for the animals, who are unable to conceptualize their existence, is made clear in the next paragraph, where the general reflection becomes located at the fifth day of creation, when God created the animals:

But these have never trod
Twice the familiar track,
Never never turned back
Into the memoried day.
All is new and near
In the unchanging Here
On the fifth great day of God,
That shall remain the same,
Never shall pass away.

On the sixth day we came.

Free from our preoccupation with memory, or analysis of experience, the animals are pictured in an "unchanging Here," in a world of clarity and harmony which is eternal. Without sin, or the trap of the labyrinth, the animal world is one of harmony which "Never shall pass away." Following this line we can feel the sharp irony of the poem's last line, emphasized by its being visually separated. In the blank space between the two lines, we move from perfect harmony to the sudden advent of the creature who disrupted that harmony; the creature who pities the non-conceptualizing animals but who is much more to be pitied. The irony is strong. Man's knowledge is nothing compared with the original created harmony and, as we shall see in "The Horses," the animals — or rather what they represent symbolically in terms of innocence and eternal order — intimate the very thing man has lost and is desperately looking for. M. L. Rosenthal, who sees Muir as "a tragic spokesman for his (European man's) foiled humanist idealism,"[14] considers this poem "heartbreaking" because of its fierce awareness of primal innocence turned into ashes. For, Rosenthal writes, "what Muir implies is a cosmic sadness that once again the stars have 'thrown down their spears' and 'watered heaven with their tears'."[15] But although I agree that a huge, almost inconsolable sense of loss pervades Muir's work, I would have thought that "The Animals," largely because of the strong irony and the implied celebration, is not the best example of this.

The poem's technique is remarkable. The diction is simple throughout and the syntax unstrained, but the poem carries a measured burden of feeling, expressed largely through metre and symbol. The poem develops on an iambic trimeter base and is fully rhymed, but the metre here is tighter and more expressive than in many of Muir's poems. Harvey Gross has remarked on the use of the monosyllabic foot to give "a sense of powerful feeling, held in check"[16] in such lines as

<pre>
  x   / | x / | / |
From birth to death hurled
</pre>

and

<pre>
 / |x / | x / |
All is new and near
</pre>

There are many metrical variations throughout the poem, which create a teasing, half-strange music:

<pre>
  x   / | x / |x / |
But these have never trod
</pre>

<pre>
  /   x | x /|xx / |
Twice the familiar track,
</pre>

<pre>
 / x| / x |/   / |
Never never turned back
</pre>

<pre>
 / x|x / | x x   / |
Into the memoried day.
</pre>

<pre>
 / |x / |x / |
All is new and near
</pre>

<pre>
 / x |x   / | x / |
In the unchanging Here
</pre>

<pre>
 x   x / |/   / |x /|
Of the fifth great day of God
</pre>

<pre>
 x   / |x   / | x   / |
That shall remain the same,
</pre>

<pre>
 /   x|x / |x /|
Never shall pass away.
</pre>

<pre>
 x   x /   /| x   / |
On the sixth day we came.
</pre>

No two of these ten lines are metrically the same, and yet the poem stays close enough to its basic pattern for the variations to be recorded in the ear and played against the norm. Particularly effective is the line "Never never turned back" where the metre in fact *does* turn back and the sound of the line becomes as slow and reluctant as the sense; and the last line with its successful use of dipody followed by the strong final iamb (or spondee, if we wish to stress the irony of "we"), which is further emphasized by its being rhymed with a line well separated by stanza break and full-stop.

The treatment of time is also interesting. Muir once again dislocates the time sequence, thus making the poem about the creation but not exclusively. From the last line we gather that man has not yet arrived, yet the first section of the poem is man's critical judgment of the animals. The second section looks back on the creation; the third implies a long knowledge of man's destiny and weakness; and then we are taken to "the unchanging Here" of the creation of the animals by God. This technique helps Muir's irony by reflecting it structurally, allowing man his criticism, then showing its inadequacy before man has been created. "The Animals," modest thought it is, shows a perfectly assured dovetailing of music, meaning and tone. The vision, or experience, may be as simple as a child's, but the art used to embody that vision is complex and hard-won.

"The Days" continues the theme of the creation, presenting successive images of the start of the world and ending with an adumbration of man's life merging into an apocalyptic celebration of eternity. The poem is more mystical and visionary than most of Muir's work, taking us into the forming universe with strange, powerful images of perception:

> And the first long days
> A hard and rocky spring,
> Inhuman burgeoning,
> And nothing there for claw or hand. . . .

After the inhuman hardness comes

> The forest's green shadow
> Softly over the water driven,
> As if the earth's green wonder, endless meadow
> Floated and sank within its own green light.

where existence becomes distilled into colour and liquid in a mysterious perpetual movement. The animals are created and then man, with his naming of his environment, until the creation is over.

Up to this point, the form has echoed the content. The free verse lines vary a great deal in length, suggesting the vast ebb and flow of matter in motion. Rhymes are irregular, sometimes missing, and the sentence-structure points and contains each stage in the process.

The final twenty-three lines contain a long vision of life as it evolves from the moment of creation, expressed in just one slowly accumulating sentence of increasing intensity. Muir evokes a great world of mountains, rivers, cattle, people at peace, hunters and fishermen — an almost Eden-like world of harmony except for

> The hungry swords crossed in the cross of warning,
> The lion set
> High on the banner, leaping into the sky. . . .

with its intimations, however softened by the heraldic image, of war and bloodshed. The poem concludes with a strongly realized vision of ultimate harmony, and returns to its beginning with "the clear eternal weather" and the reference to "Things and their names." The prayer is for the ultimate transformation of the "fragmentary day" of this life into the timeless world of eternity.

Less clearly formed around the opposition of two symbols, "The Days" moves from an impressionistic, past-tense description through images of the stanzas of creation into a meditation on man's developing temporal life in the present-tense, until finally we are given a vision of a future apocalypse which will combine all tenses and gather time into eternity. The symbol of the creation is built upon and not opposed; evil is not symbolized or embodied in the poem's structure.

Muir's most direct treatment of the biblical myth of Eden is "Adam's Dream," where he uses the symbolic situation of Adam in the garden to generate a wider treatment of man's fallen state. Behind this poem is a reversal of Adam's dream recounted in Book VIII of *Paradise Lost*, where he dreams of Eden and then wakes to find himself there, exactly as in the dream. In Muir's poem, Adam, now fallen, dreams of his future descendants and the whole fallen, confused state of mankind, and then wakes to find it true. Adam's vision of fallen man is here Muir's vision, symbolically but concretely described. We are reminded of Keats' statement that "The Imagination may be compared to Adam's dream — he awoke and found it truth."[17] Muir's imaginative, symbolic vision of man in Adam's dream shows us the reality of our lives. Fallen, we are confused and caught in time, and Muir's Adam, only recently ejected from Eden, retains enough knowledge of the unfallen state to see what is in terms of what he knows could be. The poem describes the Story in terms of the felt and known Fable.

"Adam's Dream" is one of Muir's most successful poems. The pentameter blank-verse is handled with assurance and flexibility; the vision is intense, yet gravely lyrical and filled with a wistful knowledge of loss which modifies the beauty of the sound.

The poem starts after Adam's "agelong daydream in the Garden" as he dreams with "The gates shut fast behind him." He lives

> Fallen in Eve's fallen arms, his terror drowned
> In her engulfing terror, in the abyss
> Whence there's no further fall, and comfort is —

After this introduction we are taken straight into Adam's dream; from the symbolic past to the future/present of dream time expressed in the past tense. Again the poem's ostensible subject becomes no more than a springboard for a much wider symbolic treatment, possible because of the transcendental power of the poetic symbol which contains all time and all space. Adam's dream of the future becomes our present reality and our past and future.

In the dream, Adam stands on a mountain and looks over a huge plain, on which he sees mankind running and falling in disorder, though "tense with purpose." The Fall is imagined here as total, formless confusion; as man reproduces and multiplies the chaos grows:

> the plain was filling
> As by *an alien arithmetical magic*
> Unknown in Eden, a mechanical
> Addition *without meaning*, joining only
> Number to number in *no mode or order*,
> *Weaving no pattern.* For these creatures moved
> Towards *no fixed mark* even when in growing bands
> They clashed against each other and clashing fell
> In mounds of bodies.
>
> (my italics)

This emphasizes the lack of pattern in man's history, the chaos which leads to confusion and war, and the lack of a "fixed mark" or wider vision. The poem continues with an image very close to that of "The Combat," followed by a reference to the labyrinth and the narrow place:

> For they rose again,
> Identical and interchangeable,
> And went their way that was not like a way;
> Some back and forward, back and forward, some
> In a closed circle, wide or narrow, others
> In zigzags on the sand.

It is a picture of man's desperate struggle to survive. Confused, blocked, always at war, man appears to have no compensatory knowledge, only temporary relationships which are fleeting and ultimately of no use. The line "They ran awhile" is the only line in the poem which is not of five stresses and shows Muir's expressive, imitative use of metre. The missing feet, the disrupted truncated pattern of expectancy, illustrate clearly the next line: "They parted and again were single." The metre of the poem breaks apart, just as the lovers do, emphasizing the impossibility of harmony and lasting pattern.

Adam calls to the people and hears only an echo. The Fall is further illustrated by the next lines:

> The animals had withdrawn and from the caves
> And woods stared out in fear or condemnation,
> Like outlaws or like judges.

We remember Muir's idea of Eden with man and beast living in perfect harmony and the "friendly tribes of trees and animals" Adam had known in the garden before the Fall. "This is time," Adam realizes, and moves, with this sudden insight, closer to the people on the plain, seeing them more clearly "about some business strange to him." This close to fallen man

> Adam longed
> For more, not this mere moving pattern, not
> This illustrated storybook of mankind
> Always a-making, improvised on nothing.

The poem concludes with Adam's moving right into the figures, recognizing them and knowing himself.

> At that he was among them, and saw each face
> Was like his face, so that we would have hailed them
> As sons of God but that something restrained him.

And he remembered all, Eden, the Fall,
The Promise, and his place, and took their hands
That were his hands, his and his children's hands,
Cried out and was at peace, and turned again
In love and grief in Eve's encircling arms.

With the total identification comes the full knowledge of the Fall and also acceptance. The acceptance of human life, however full of grief, releases in him love and reconciliation as he joins with Eve and his descendants in a sad but conclusive harmony. The beauty of the language and the sound, the human joining together for love and protection, give a positive emotional climax. Once accepted, the Fall and its consequences are somehow free of the "engulfing terror."

At no point in this poem does Muir make moral judgments. There is no condemnation of Adam for his sin which lost eternity for all men, nor is there any horror in Adam when he finally realizes what has happened. Instead, the poem is filled with a great elegiac compassion for mankind, who, although undermined and doomed by the Fall, can find a certain peace and a knowledge of love which is meaningful, if temporary. Muir can now accept tragic experience in a way he was unable to do in the Prague poems. "Adam's Dream" proposes tragedy, but it is beyond tragedy, for all its knowledge. An elegy for fallen man, it becomes transmuted into a celebration of the "love and grief" of human experience, which is, in its own terms, of great value. This affirmation, the sense of a trust finally reposed in man, takes Muir's treatment of the Fall and lost innocence an important step forward.

This step is confirmed by the less successful "Outside Eden," which symbolizes fallen man as a simple, peasant tribe living outside Eden, but still able to see the glory of Eden in the distance. Man lives in the shadow of eternity, but is for ever removed from it.

In July 1952, T. S. Eliot asked Muir for a poem to be included in Faber's series of "Ariel" poems. Muir sent "Prometheus," with a letter in which he wrote: "I outstayed my time, and still have produced nothing that seems satisfactory. I send the result, but am not pleased with it."[18] Eliot liked the poem but suggested that Muir add a few lines to explain that Prometheus still lived on in Christian times. Muir added the fourteen-line third section which, as Professor Butter rightly says, "contains some fine writing"[19] but which also damages the poem by separating the rhetorical questions of the second section from the answers given in the last section.

Prometheus' agony will only be ended with "the end of all things." Around him is change. Nature, the animals and man perform their ordained changes as he watches:

> But pilgrim man
> Travels foreknowing to his stopping place,
> Awareness on his lips, which have tasted sorrow,
> Foretasted death.

Man's happiness lies in the fact that his unhappiness ends; Prometheus looks forward only to when time stops and the gods "bid me come/Again among them. . . . " The old gods, he thinks, will treat his knowledge of worldly agony as gossip, at best. What, he asks, will his reception back in heaven be?

The third section, the one added at Eliot's request, gives a picture of the world becoming godless. Olympus, he thinks, might be vacant as he has learned that the mysteries are dying and a new breed of hard, literal, peevish and spiteful men are destroying not only themselves, but faith and the gods. To whom then will he tell his story at "the world's end"?

And the poem's final answer to the "heedless" old gods and the fallen state of man is that

> A god came down, they say, from another heaven
> Not in rebellion but in pity and love,
> Was born a son of woman, lived and died,
> And rose again with all the spoils of time
> Back to his home, where now they are transmuted
> Into bright toys and various frames of glory;
> And time itself is there a world of marvels.
> If I could find that god, he would hear and answer.

Prometheus' agony, the old gods, unspiritual man, the endless pain of time are redeemed by Christ, though only tentatively. Prometheus has not found Christ, he simply asserts the superiority of the new myth over the old; the new God over the old.

Muir was right, I think, to be a little dissatisfied with "Prometheus." The focus is never clear, especially as the inserted section draws the attention away from Prometheus' agony and the shortcomings of the old vindictive gods and on to fallen man. Prometheus, as a symbol, is not permitted to gather much associated meaning. The poem seems either too long or too short and there are too many lines which lack a strong impulse and add little to the structure or meaning. The distinction between the old gods' lack of concern for man and Christ's desire and ability to weld man and God together does not emerge sharply enough to be as successful as Muir's best clashes of opposing values through symbol.

The much shorter "The Grave of Prometheus," on the other hand, is vital, buoyant and tightly constructed. The attempted resolution at the end of "Prometheus" is pointedly and poignantly rejected in the white space between these two poems. Now Prometheus is dead, on earth, having lost all contact with man, Christ and Olympus. The long agony ends in total silence and desertion. The gods have left Olympus, the vultures have gone and the fire is out. Now the hero turns into soil and the heroism and the agony are forgotten "in a breath," as time and the processes of earthly change transform him and dissolve him into ordinariness. Yet something noble remains as nature works on him to create a strange and restful memorial:

> Yet there you still may see a tongue of stone,
> Shaped like a calloused hand where no hand
>   should be,
> Extended from the sward as if for alms,
> Its palm all licked and blackened as with fire.
> A mineral change made cool his fiery bed,
> And made his burning body a quiet mound,
> And his great face a vacant ring of daisies.

These lines show the complete and final identification with nature as the man is absorbed into the earth. He is lost and pathetic, but also heroic, defiant and challenging. Saturating the poem are the silence, coolness and release Prometheus longed for in the previous poem. With the disappearance of the gods and his death, he has escaped time, but it has not ended, for the great process of dissolution continues around him and through him as the earth assumes him further into itself, defeating the flames and the agony with the cold yet fertile inevitability of grass and flowers. His grave exists out of time and out of space, as a symbol of release from pressure and an illustration of the way time stops or modifies experience. Muir gives us a monument to the inadequate old order and simultaneously a structured, deeply felt pity for individual experience subjected to the workings of time. The poem's method succeeds; indeed the release of Prometheus, so right and inevitable, seems here more hopeful and positive than the more tentative overt Christian symbolism which concludes "Prometheus."

"Orpheus' Dream" is one of Muir's best short lyrics. Here Orpheus does not lose Eurydice, but takes her out of Hades, leaving only her ghost behind. This reversal of the ending of the myth is in line with the deep sense of peace and fulfilment which characterizes so much of the poetry in this volume, where an undisturbed serenity rises higher and more insistently than the knowledge of loss and tragedy. And yet we are told that this is Orpheus' *dream* — not the reality — and we may suppose it to be dreamed after his losing Eurydice. This immediately has the effect of confusing dream and reality as we follow the poem, especially as stanza two is a dream-image within a dream. There is a further non-logical technique used when we realize that the first stanza is written in the third person, the second stanza moves into the second person and the poem ends with a marvellously contrived mixture of the two. The tense is past throughout, but the fact that the poem is a dream adds still further to the possibilities of time/space confusion. This supra-rational structure enables Muir to embody an experience far wider than if he had merely retold the myth (itself, of course, an embodiment of layered, collective experience). As we read the simple narrative, the many dimensions of significance work constantly upon us and we are led, as Holloway points out, "into a condition where these things, and the emotions which attend them, are felt with the force of an intuition."[20]

The poem's structure is in three parts. The first stanza, with considerable economy, presents a powerful image, full of wonder and deeply felt fulfilment:

> And she was there.   The little boat
> Coasting the perilous isles of sleep,
> Zones of oblivion and despair,
> Stopped, for Eurydice was there.
> The foundering skiff could scarcely keep
> All that felicity afloat.

The sense of fulfilment is strongly emphasized here by the very precariousness of the journey. "The perilous isles of sleep," "oblivion," "despair," "the foundering skiff" — all these show dramatically how the powers of darkness only just fail to stop the meeting. The strength of Orpheus' feeling is emphasized too by the repetition of "for Eurydice was there" and the great superlative of the stanza's last line. The image is quiet yet charged with vibrant feeling.

The second stanza explains the ecstasy of the meeting in Platonic terms. Here the physical details of the escape from the underworld are mirrored by abstract ideas of escape from this world to the original state of the soul. The concrete language and tone of stanza one move into these Platonic abstractions without any disruption of the poem's movement, as the poem is widened here to express a vision of perfect love outside time.

The last stanza starts with a summing-up of the abstract state of fulfilment: — "forgiveness, truth, atonement, all/Our love at once" — which is a vision of complete relationship on all levels. The poem concludes by retiring, loosely, to the myth-narrative, now that the lovers have achieved a strength from beyond human experience:

> till we could dare
> At last to turn our heads and see
> The poor ghost of Eurydice
> Still sitting in her silver chair,
> Alone in Hades' empty hall.

There is a vast pathos in these lines; a slackening emotion which balances the triumph of the departing couple. The confusion of dream and reality makes the ending ambiguous. Is Muir retelling the myth, and allowing his lovers the power to alter the story they themselves are acting in?[21] Or are we to accept that Orpheus really does fail to bring Eurydice up with him, but is contented to have the vision of their timeless love as far superior to her actual presence? The tone of triumph is informed with pathos in the poem's tone and metre and I doubt if we need to accept either alternative as the true "meaning." What matters is that we are forced to acknowledge "something which matters in life itself," which Muir has recorded in "the mirror, a diminishing and yet a magnifying glass, of a poem."[22]

"Orpheus' Dream" speaks of the deepest experience of love, the vital potentialities within human experience which can conquer the underworld and escape from time. In this timeless reality, all that Hades can retain is a ghost for the world of sense and of suffering can be transcended and left behind. The integrity, simplicity and utter beauty of this vision of human destiny is contained in a poem of flawless lyricism and, as we have seen, considerable symbolic complexity. The subtlety of the metre and syntax and the typical late-Muir tone of falling, elegiac affirmation anticipate closely the other three great tetrameter lyrics "Telemachos Remembers," "The Annunciation" and "One Foot in Eden." In these poems especially, through the intensity of charged symbol and perfected technique, Muir is able to pass beyond the good and evil which have haunted him and incorporate them into an assured and convincing synthesis.

In his earlier poem "Oedipus," Muir is concerned with the workings of guilt in the psyche and how far this could be legitimately externalized. Now he returns to the figure of Oedipus in quite a different way. "The Other Oedipus" has left guilt and evil behind and walks the land in a state of visionary other-worldliness, perhaps even madness, which makes irrelevant his guilt and knowledge of evil. Whereas, in the earlier poem, he is described as "I, Oedipus, the club-foot, made to stumble,/Who long in the light have walked the world in darkness," he is now "white-headed and light-hearted," and all around is "A brightness laid like a blue lake."

Oedipus, accompanied by his "serving-boy and his concubine," has gone outside "The last stroke of time" into a world of vision, into the Fable.

In this poem, Muir reverts to pentameter blank-verse with considerable success. The lyric tension of the rhymed four-stress lines disappears, but there is an increase in flexibility and varied stress patterns which succeed in altering the poem's speed and creating strong emphasis. In lines like

$$/ \quad /\ |\ x\ x\ /\quad /\ |\ x\ x\ /\ |\ /\ /\ |$$
White-headed and light-hearted, their true wits gone

with its seven stresses, its use of dipody, and the balanced, heavy spondees in first and fifth position, we can see something of Muir's expressive use of sound and his concern for craftsmanship. The deliberate emotional neutrality of the poem's ending is strengthened by the terseness of the syntax, with the short sentences twice ending in the middle of the line, creating a tension with the metrical line unit.

In "Telemachos Remembers," Muir returns to the theme of the wandering Odysseus and the waiting Penelope which he first treated in "The Return of Odysseus." Both poems focus on Penelope at her loom, weaving during the day and unpicking at night, to keep her suitors away, but "Telemachos Remembers" is a much more fully realized poem, better shaped and structured, and presenting human experience in more certain, more mature terms. The fully rhymed, tetrameter stanzas create the characteristic falling tone, heavy with

135

compassion yet full of won knowledge, which Muir achieved only after he had conquered the labyrinth and emerged beyond it:

> Twenty years, every day,
> The figures in the web she wove
> Came and stood and went away.
> Her fingers in their pitiless play
> Beat downward as the shuttle drove.

The sound and tone recreate the vast patience of the twenty years task which continues into the second stanza:

> Slowly, slowly did they come,
> With horse and chariot, spear and bow,
> Half-finished heroes sad and mum,
> Came slowly to the shuttle's hum.
> Time itself was not so slow.

The word "slowly" occurs three times and "slow" once in these few lines, making us feel almost physically the length of her task. This is strengthened by the repeated trochees of the first line, the slow list of "horse and chariot, spear and bow," and the end-stopping of every line.

The next stanza emphasizes the incompleteness — physical and psychological — of the whole process, by describing the partial results of her labours — "more odds and ends about to be" — for the twenty years is an experience of incompleteness, a denial of wholeness, where endless possibility never becomes real.

Stanza four introduces Odysseus in a brilliant image which parallels the image of the eternal circle of the loom:

> Far away Odysseus trod
> The treadmill of the turning road
> That did not bring him to his house.

The treadmill is a recurring pattern of experience which leads nowhere. Both Odysseus and Penelope are caught in parallel self-defeating processes which promise no release. With a ballad-like repetition, Muir stresses the futility of the experience in stanza five:

> The weary loom, the weary loom,
> The task grown sick from morn to night,
> From year to year. The treadle's boom
> Made a low thunder in the room
> The woven phantoms mazed her sight.

The sound-pattern is again important here. The rhyming words "loom," "loom," "boom," "room"; the web of assonance and consonance; the sudden dominance of iambic feet in three short sentences; all add a dimension to the feeling of the stanza and evoke an almost tangible sensation of depressed, unrelieved repetition. But this experience is valuable in human terms. If she had finished it, "She would have worked a matchless wrong." In the last stanza, for the first time, Telemachos enters the poem in his own voice, and Muir uses the strategy of his child's baffled response to complex experience to bring that experience into full focus:

> Instead, that jumble of heads and spears,
> Forlorn scraps of her treasure trove.
> I wet them with my childish tears
> Not knowing she wove into her fears
> Pride and fidelity and love.

Telemachos sees the pathos and the grief, which is only part of the experience. He misses the beauty of Penelope's task — the dignity, the symbolic weaving together of herself and Odysseus, the heroic single-mindedness with which she defeats time by creating an emblem of human potentiality.

Like "Orpheus' Dream" this is a deeply felt poem, not concerned with passion but with the triumphant experience of human love, which can transcend the world of time and sense and achieve eternal validity. Buried in this poem are the symbols of the journey, the labyrinth and the workings of time. Only in the last line do we find a positive answer. And yet, by the tone and quality of feeling, by the lyric pulse and the evocation of heroism and the possibility of love, Muir has inverted the obvious content, and created a poem where the total "meaning" is almost opposite to the conceptual "meaning" of the words.

On another level, we have to see Penelope as the creating artist, delicately balancing her life and her art. Muir himself made this clear in a broadcast when he said that, had Penelope finished her web, she "would have achieved the supreme work of art, but in doing so would have renounced her humanity." The poem, he continues, is

a fanciful statement of the claims of life and art, and describes the desolation which would follow if they were quite divorced from each other, as fortunately for us they cannot be.[23]

The web contains Penelope's expression of life and also links her to the symbol of life, Odysseus. If she finished it, the link would be gone; she would have put all her life into her art. The deepest possibilities of love and life exist in the constant tension between the symbolic web and the real man. As Odysseus voyages round in circles, she, at the centre of the web, is connected to him by real and symbolic threads.

This imaginative embodiment of the power and potential of human love clearly reveals Muir's new ability to transcend the antivision. The Fall is real, but even in the wake of its disruption, human beings can aspire to, and achieve, heroism and experience a redemption and a fulfilment undreamed of in the Prague poems. And yet, while the poems in *One Foot in Eden* were being written, Muir was again, in his personal life, experiencing crisis and despair. In 1953 he was unwell, and he became the victim of some very unpleasant political attacks by some who wanted Newbattle's function altered and who objected to Muir as Warden. He was deeply hurt by the hostility, and double-dealing and became worn down and depressed. He decided to leave. Beyond these local troubles, he was also depressed by the wider situation, writing to Kathleen Raine in 1954 that "I know how unpleasant the world is growing. I can feel it here as you feel it in London, though not so thickly. . . . "[24] Some of his anger and depression emerged, as we shall see, in "Effigies," where he attacks, in an uncharacteristic way, some of the people who were opposing him and the college. There is no simple relationship between the serenity of many of the poems in this volume and an easy, serene life. The overthrow of evil in his symbolism incorporates the darkness he still knew in his own story, but because his symbolic method incorporates far more than a "confessional" treatment of local experience, his poetry moves freely in an area which transcends his Newbattle difficulties.

"Abraham" is a rather cursory and incomplete treatment of a potentially viable symbol and the poem cannot be considered a success. Better is the next poem, "The Succession," which treats the Abraham story with more depth and confidence. It seems probable that Muir himself liked this poem, as he originally intended to call this collection *The Succession*, and only intervention by his wife and, according to Professor Butter, T. S. Eliot, persuaded him to choose the more striking title *One Foot in Eden*.

Here the symbols of Abraham and Isaac are used to express man's eternal pilgrimage. Abraham, in a superb image,

> First among these people came
> Cruising above them like a star
> That is in love with distances. . . .

The image continues with Isaac, "his twin star," who started by wheeling "around the father light," taking on Abraham's role as leader of the great pilgrimage. He can go "where the father could not go." We build on our ancestors who started us on the long road. The last section moves us through time to the present and the description, in the third person, of Abraham and Isaac becomes typically refined into "we" who still journey, continuing the eternal pattern:

> We through the generations came
> Here by a way we do not know
> From the fields of Abraham,
> And still the road is scarce begun.

The symbol of the eternal road, full of hazard and danger, is again evoked, and the new celebration of even fallen experience is continued here, though without the same intensity of other expressions of this hope. "The Succession," a rhymed tetrameter poem seems to falter after the fine image of the cruising star. Too many lines are end-stopped and the overall impression is of a rather tired, uninspired statement of a familiar theme. The poem lacks vitality, and exhibits little of the lyric felicity and symbolic richness we see in other poems of this period. This poem comes off badly when we compare it with the quality of feeling and dramatic construction of, say, "Adam's Dream," which deals essentially with the same theme of the succession.

"The Road" continues the symbolic journey. The participants are pilgrims; their journey is life. Like the anonymous dead in "The Heroes" these people are neither identified nor placed in time and space; the symbol is not called forth by a myth or hero of any sort.

The poem moves around the problem of choice and human movement through time, very much in the way of Robert Frost's "The Road Not Taken." The theme is embodied dramatically and with considerable vitality:

> The great road stretched before them, clear and still,
> Then from in front one cried: 'Turn back! Turn
>   back!'
> Yet they had never seen so fine a track,
> Honest and frank past any thought of ill.

From this beginning, looking to the future in spite of the ominous warning, the second half of the octave brings in time past; as past experience turns into chaos. Looking back, we see how we have been struggling in the labyrinth of patternless experience which we are powerless to alter. We cannot go back and renegotiate the labyrinth. Time cuts us off and leaves us stranded and isolated from our ancestors. We can only go forward, whatever our doubts and regrets:

> Yet as they travelled on, for many days
> These words rang in their ears as if they said,
> 'There was another road you did not see'.

The tragedy of man's fall into time is that he is never sure of his way and can do nothing about it. History closes its gates, like Eden, just behind us, and we must move on, however full of doubt.

From the world of the Greek myths and the Old Testament, Muir moves now into overtly Christian symbolism, where several strands of experience in previous poems — human love, the journey, man caught in time, the loss of Eden — are woven together symbolically. The first of the poems is "The Annunciation."

Lying behind the poem is an experience Muir had in Rome:

I remember stopping for a long time one day to look at a little plaque on the wall of a house in the Via degli Artisti, representing the Annunciation. An angel and a young girl, their bodies inclined towards each, other, their knees bent as if they were overcome by love, 'tutto tremante', gazed upon each like Dante's pair; and that representation of a human love so intense that it could not reach farther seemed the perfect earthly symbol of the love that passes understanding.[25]

The direct meeting of the girl and the angel, of this world and a higher world, in an act of love, is a perfect symbol for Muir, drawing together the Story and the Fable, the transfiguring power of love, and the restoration of the fragmented pattern. The symbols of earth and heaven mingle significantly and illuminate each other. The meaning of the experience derives from the resulting synthesis of the symbols; as they bridge the space between the two worlds, they give liberty from time.

The poem opens, as does "Orpheus' Dream," with a short wondering statement of achievement, which moves us directly to the heart of the experience:

> The angel and the girl are met.
> Earth was the only meeting place.
> For the embodied never yet
> Travelled beyond the shore of space.
> The eternal spirits in freedom go.

The four sentences in five lines and the positive rhyming give a definitive weight and an inevitability to the lines while the metre adds emphasis and points the meaning. The four heavy iambs of the first line, expressing their certainty, may be compared with the last line of the stanza, where the two anapests give a lightness and a break in pattern appropriate to the freedom of the eternal spirits:

> x   x / | x / | x x / | x / |
> The eternal spirits in freedom go

In lines of four feet (and fewer) the gain of two syllables can have a dramatic effect as it pulls away from and comments on the iambic norm.

The main section of the poem describes the miraculous union in language of remarkable energy as well as purity:

> See, they have come together, see,
> While the destroying minutes flow,
> Each reflects the other's face
> Till heaven in hers and earth in his
> Shine steady there.   He's come to her
> From far beyond the farthest star,
> Feathered through time. . . .

Far less physically evocative than the god/woman union in Yeats' "Leda and the Swan," this passage nevertheless has a great immediacy and is far from being abstract. The first line of this section — "See, they have come together, see" — has the wondering urgency of the speaking voice in the presence of a miracle. Although the line has only one substitution — the trochee in the first position — the two caesuras so alter the sound and tempo that the line sounds strikingly different. The reversed first foot is used brilliantly here in several lines to add intensity and a steady emphasis, and the sound is marvellously controlled:

He's come to her
From far beyond the farthest star,
Feathered through time.

These lines demonstrate Muir's control, not only by the emphatic trochee on "feathered," but by the alliteration and judicious repetition.

This section is dominated by wonder. The union is a highly spiritual consummation, in which each takes on the nature of the other; earth and heaven become one as the nature of each becomes overwhelmed by the experience "Of strangest strangeness."

The third section acts as a contrasting element which further points to the spiritual quality of the experience, by describing the world "Outside the window," where time, imperfect and unfulfilled "Rolls its numbered octaves out/And hoarsely grinds its battered tune." This is in direct contrast with the trembling ecstatic silence within the room to which the poem returns finally:

But through the endless afternoon
These neither speak nor movement make,
But stare into their deepening trance
As if their gaze would never break.

The resolution is confirmed by the metrical regularity and the unbroken syntax. The trance is "deepening" to the end; the union, outside time, seems eternal. The human love Muir celebrated in such poems as "Love's Remorse" and "Love in Time's Despite" which could transcend time, becomes here an integral part of timeless spiritual qualities. In Kathleen Raine's words:

the meeting of the Angel and the woman is essentially a poem about love, not a poem describing a unique historical event. It is none the less holy for that; for Muir, like Plato, understood that lovers are winged — that is to say uplifted into a spiritual order, whose mystery is reflected in the earthly event.[26]

This is fair criticism, for the Christian symbolism in this poem is not used in any doctrinally assertive sense, but as a framework on which Muir explores the same theme of transcendental love he had used in "Orpheus' Dream." "There is no more need to be a Christian in order to admire that, than there was to be a Greek to admire 'Telemachos Remembers'," writes John Holloway,[27] and yet one cannot deny the fact that this, as is most of Muir's poetry, is profoundly religious in a wide sense. Kathleen Raine puts this well:

His poem on the Annunciation is as profoundly Christian as Fra Angelico, but it is not because he was a Christian but because he rediscovered the symbols from within that this is so.[28]

In Muir's imagination and technique, the actual source of the symbols is less important than the way the symbols are energized and used. In "The Annunciation," although he uses two interwoven symbols, Muir does not focus on the results of their opposing and testing each other as in a combat; rather he concentrates on the synthesis which comes as a result of their peaceful interpenetration in a place beyond the conflict. This is emphasized by the use of the present tense throughout, to remove the symbolic situation from time and to insist on its permanent validity, and by the supreme evocation of intense silence which gives the poem its iconic quality. Muir's whole life can be seen as a search for "the love which passes understanding"; his whole symbolist technique is the imaginative means by which he achieved it. "The Annunciation" is one result of that search and that technique, where symbols have converged, beyond time, and beyond good and evil, to create a visionary synthesis of man's highest aspirations.

In "The Killing," Muir attempts to deal with the Crucifixion of Christ, showing the event as one significant point where man's journey meets God's journey, but the poem does not wholly succeed, lacking the emotional and technical vitality of his best work.

"Antichrist" attempts to show the truth of Christ by describing Christ's opposite. The poem is a portrait of a usurper who has totally perverted values. The Antichrist is "shaped by ingenious devils" to dupe credulous man. He is steeped in sin and sickness, delighting in pain and anguish. He is a false god: "Ingeniously he postures on the Tree/(His crowning jest), an actor miming death." He seems, on the surface, "goodness, sweetness, harmony," but the poem ends in utter condemnation and scorn: "He is the lie; one true thought, and he's gone." This figure has elements of the Intercepter in his ability to thwart and deceive man and keep him from the truth. But there is probably more affinity to Nietzsche and the Superman Muir had come to see as a mirage. During his psychoanalysis Muir had a dream about Nietzsche

which contained a curious criticism of him and my infatuation with him. I dreamt that I was in a crowd watching a crucifixion. I expected the crucified man to be bearded like Christ, but saw with surprise that he was clean-shaven except for a heavy moustache. It was undoubtedly

143

Nietzsche; he looked as if he had usurped the Cross, though like many a usurper he appeared simultaneously to be perfectly at home on it. He stared round him with an air of defiant possession . . . he was like a man who had violently seized a position which belonged to someone else.[29]

This dream seems to be echoed in the image of the Antichrist posturing on the Tree, usurping Christ's role. The danger of Antichrist is that he is plausible, just as Nietzsche was to Muir in his Glasgow days, and has the power to keep men from truth. The poem can be seen as a symbolic re-enactment of Muir's rejection of Nietzsche, though in the poem his implied knowledge of the truth and the finality of "He is the Lie" show far more certainty and strength that he himself had when he cast off his Nietzschean mask.

In "The Annunciation," Muir incorporated Christian symbolism into his wider mythology with great success, bringing to bear all his powers of technique to create a poem of deep feeling and an effortless, luminous tone. After this, he seemed unable to find the right vehicle for the symbols of Christianity he tried to use, and became prone to a technique of flat assertion, where the symbols are taken for granted and not permitted to develop and display their full meanings. With the poem "One Foot in Eden," Muir leaves Christian symbolism and returns to the symbols of Eden, time and man's destiny.[30]

"One Foot in Eden" is perfectly controlled. The tone and technique deepen the poem's meaning and give it a grave, beautiful music somewhat reminiscent of Auden's "Lay Your Sleeping Head." The feeling is powerful, the symbols are dense and relevant, and the poem is richly evocative. The theme of the poem — or rather the meanings emerging from the moving symbols — takes us from an acknowledgement of man's loss of Eden and his subsequent fallen journey, to a celebration, not of Eden and eternity, but of the fallen state itself. The Fall places man in the grip of time and history, with all its accompanying grief, but also makes possible "hope and faith and pity and love," which, as Muir has finally come to realize, is as worthy of acceptance as Eden itself. His symbolism has led him to a point where human life can be seen as a "strange blessing" to be entirely accepted in spite of its imperfections. The poem embodies this new certainty. No mythical or real love, nor visitor from eternity is here necessary as a touchstone for celebration; life itself is embraced and understood. "One Foot in Eden" represents Muir's symbolic acceptance of a full humanity, which survives in a kind of holiness in spite of the destruction caused by time.

The poem approaches its significance through a typical symbolist process. The positive first-person in the opening line seems a direct reference to the poet, but it is never repeated. In the third line, it changes imperceptibly to "we" and the second paragraph turns into an impersonally related, but deeply human, account of the Fall and human history. The tense is present and acts through this deliberate complexity of narrative stance to create a universal pattern which encompasses and transcends the individual Story. Time, space and narrator become irrelevant as the symbols develop and carry the meaning. The Story is one man's, the Fable is everyman's, and the poem shows them to be the same.

The opening image is a rich one: "One foot in Eden still, I stand/ And look across the other land." Reminiscent of "Adam's Dream," where Adam, fresh from Eden, looked over the fallen world, the image shows man in two states. He is part of the timeless innocent world, the intimations of which never leave him, and simultaneously is anchored in the human world of time. This fallen world, where good and evil are organically and inevitably entwined is embodied in the next lines:

> The world's great day is growing late,
> Yet strange these fields that we have planted
> So long with crops of love and hate.
> Time's handiworks by time are haunted,
> And nothing now can separate
> The corn and tares compactly grown.
> The armorial weed in stillness bound
> About the stalk;   these are our own.
> Evil and good stand thick around
> In the fields of charity and sin
> Where we shall lead our harvest in.

This long sustained image of crops, fields and growth has a great stillness and power. The landscape is fixed into time, with all its weeds and tares, and Muir manages to give it an impressive silence and inevitability, partly by the heraldic references, like "armorial weed," which create a static pattern, but also by removing the narrator, and thus man, from the landscape. We observe the growth, but are, in this poem, detached from it and not deeply involved in the evil. We shall reap what we have sown, but Muir does not break the observed silence of his landscape by involving man actively, as he has done so often in earlier poems. The scene remains neutral. A strong feeling of choking growth and confused good and evil is conveyed by the agricultural imagery.

The second section contrasts this fallen landscape with original innocence. Time destroys innocence, harms the "archetypal leaf" of Eden and introduces random terror and grief. And yet there is still the innocence of "the root" which cannot be altered or destroyed.

The poem concludes with its celebration of the life of "terror and of grief." Thus far the poem has used the symbolic values we are familiar with, contrasting the symbols of Eden and time, and showing the tragic imperfection of fallen man. But now Muir adds complexity by accepting joyfully what he has shown to be imperfect:

> But famished field and blackened tree
> Bear flowers in Eden never known.
> Blossoms of grief and charity
> Bloom in these darkened fields alone.
> What had Eden ever to say
> Of hope and faith and pity and love
> Until was buried all its day
> And memory found its treasure trove?
> Strange blessings never in Paradise
> Fall from these beclouded skies.

The "beclouded skies" of man's fallen state contain things unknown in Eden. Grief, charity, hope, faith, pity and memory are direct consequences of evil and man's attempt to overcome it. In Paradise, for all its innocence, there is no need for the deeply human impulse of pity, nor the modifying, comforting force of memory. The strength of this acceptance becomes clear by the rhetorical question, embodying an implied criticism of prelapsarian innocence: "What had Eden ever to say/Of hope and faith and pity and love?" And the acceptance here convinces more firmly by the acknowledgement of the "beclouded," "famished," "blackened," "darkened," "buried" and burned state of our existence. All this, Muir is saying, we cannot accept because of the deeply human forces it released in us and without which our life would be diminished.

The poem's solemn music, undisturbed by its incorporation of evil, affirms this acceptance. Together with the formal wholeness stated by the opening and concluding rhyming couplets, which join, imitatively and by sound, the symbolic circle of completeness, the metre, syntax and rhyme assert a full harmony and bear a wisdom and a humility which adds a significant level to the total "meaning" of the poem. The symbols, free again of time and space, move in and out of each other, opposing and supporting, vindicating their existence by generating powerful and evocative emotion, exactly justified and held by the formal pattern. In this poem their initial opposition becomes a full synthesis, where each incorporates the other to create the concluding harmony. This is strengthened by the local imagery of growth, decay and blossom which runs throughout the poem as a unifying force embodied within the wider symbolic landscapes, and culminating with the last two lines, where the "strange blessings" fall as healing rain from the "beclouded skies," promoting growth, and also assuming abstraction into the concrete image, which, in its turn, is absorbed by the overall symbolism. "One Foot in Eden" combines the perfected symbolist method with complete assurance of tone and technique, and displays Muir's deep human qualities of acceptance, compassion and thirst for wholeness.

The next two poems again bring the state of Scotland into Muir's symbolic pattern. The total acceptance of "One Foot in Eden" cannot be the last word, as Muir sees too much evidence about him of incompleteness, as well as forces which destroy the pattern he celebrates. Returning to the theme of the Incarnation, which had so inspired his thought in Rome, he contrasts the Italian and Scottish concepts of Christ in "The Incarnate One." Elsewhere, about the plaque representing the Annunciation in Rome, he writes:

A religion that dared to show forth such a mystery for everyone to see would have shocked the congregation of the north, would have seemed a sort of blasphemy, perhaps even an indecency. But here it was publicly shown, as Christ showed himself on the earth.[31]

The Presbyterian religion in Orkney and Scotland "did not tell me by any outward sign that the Word had been made flesh,"[32] and this poem is a firm criticism of the tradition which has cloaked the real meaning of Christianity in solemnity and abstraction, killing its wonder and murdering the "mystery." Presbyterianism, to Muir, is thin and bloodless, with a tradition fundamentally repressive and hostile to the essential vitality of Christianity. Scotland has betrayed the Incarnate Christ; Calvinism has impoverished religion, and Muir accuses it through the sterile, angry imagery of the first two stanzas:

> The windless northern surge, the sea-gull's scream,
> And Calvin's kirk crowning the barren brae. . . .

> The Word made flesh here is made word again,
> A word made word in flourish and arrogant crook,
> See there King Calvin with his iron pen,
> And God three angry letters in a book,
> And there the logical hook
> On which the Mystery is impaled and bent
> Into an ideological instrument.

The condemnation is powerful, reminiscent of the earlier "Scotland 1941" in *The Narrow Place* where Muir used the same imagery of iron to represent the anti-life destructive power of Knox, Melville and Peden. Here, "King Calvin" has an "iron pen," and the mystery, inaccessible to cold logic, is "impaled and bent" on a "logical hook."

"There's better gospel in man's natural tongue," Muir continues, among "The archaic peoples in their ancient awe" who were full of "Ignorant wonder." What will bring us down is the turning of God into abstraction by those who "Build their cold empire on the abstract man." The poem concludes with a resigned awareness that this sort of "bloodless" religion is so deeply embedded that

> the One has far to go
> Past the mirages and the murdering snow.

There is no possible synthesis of the images here. The one is cold, barren, inflexible; the other warm, simple, imaginative and full of wonder. Man is threatened by impersonal systems, industrial and political as well as religious. Muir's later writings, especially in *The Estate of Poetry*, show how concerned he was about the dehumanizing processes which work on modern man. His anger in this poem no doubt contains remnants of his feelings about the Nazis and the Russians, who subjected individuality to the pressures of massive impersonal systems. Like these systems, Calvinism suppresses individuality and joy:

> The fleshless word, growing, will bring us down,
> Pagan and Christian man alike will fall,
> The auguries say, the white and black and brown,
> The merry and sad, theorist, lover, all
> Invisibly will fall. . . .

"The Incarnate One" is part of Muir's symbolism of betrayal. In a world of pain and evil, it is, to him, intolerable that things of strength and completeness should be undermined and destroyed. Troy and Prague, as well as Christianity, have suffered this fate, and the great betrayal in Eden lies at the back of it all. "Scotland's Winter" continues the idea of a Scotland which has lost its strength and has suffered a fall.

A dead, consciously anti-lyrical free verse presents a picture of a once fine and noble country now drowned in the trivial. The dead heroes of Scotland's past — Percy, Douglas, Bruce — are replaced and walked over by

> . . . common heels that do not know
> Whence they come or where they go
> And are content
> With their poor frozen life and shallow banishment.

As in the previous poem, the moral and social characteristics of Scotland are embodied through imagery of coldness and thinness; again the main theme is that of a people cut off from the true sources of meaning, betrayed from their rightful heritage. In his little book *Scottish Journey*, Muir wrote of the "contrast between its (Scotland's) legendary past and its tawdry present"[33] and printed this poem there to illustrate his point. Now the poem, resurrected for this volume, reinforces "The Incarnate One," and, although by no means one of his best poems, helps to develop the theme of betrayal.

"The Great House" may be loosely grouped with these two poems on Scotland, as it deals with decay and ruin. The Fall is not purely a matter of the human spirit, but also of towns and houses and nature. And yet there is something which preserves itself and remains intact in the midst of chaos, and the poem ends with the words "Praise the few/Who built in chaos our bastion and our home."

The last poem in Part One of *One Foot in Eden*, another Italian sonnet called "The Emblem," is more successful. This poem, together with the essays on Hölderlin,[34] is the closest Muir came to describing his own poetic method. The poem is a justification for his symbolist technique and his refusal to use more normal subjective confessional methods of analysing experience. He indirectly defends himself from the charge of being old-fashioned by insisting on the timelessness and truth of symbol, which is always alive and relevant, and which can expand to include experience far wider than that presented by any other method. Muir invites us to step out of the "little tangled field" of the Story and enter the ordered, emblematic world of the Fable.

By creating his world of symbols and emblems, he has created "space and order magistral" which transcend the world of private experience and contain truth. The "scant-acre kingdom" is not dead; although containing heraldic stillness, it aspires to life through the quality of its timelessness, as do the figures on Keats' Urn.

Muir is here asserting the superiority of the symbolist method as a means of perception. In the symbolistic imagination all things are ordered and accessible. In his wife's words, "His kingdom kept no state at all, in accordance with his own simplicity. But its scant acre on earth reached far up and down into timelessness."[35] Through the symbol, Muir can take us into this timelessness where everything, as so often he has said in his poetry, is in its "due place and honour," and where the unbalanced fallen world of purely human experience is transformed into icons, emblems and symbols which give the pattern and form men are lacking. "The emblem on the shield" contains human experience, but becomes untouchable, free from time and space in the permanence of the symbolic world.

Part II of *One Foot in Eden* opens with a sonnet "To Franz Kafka," in which Muir pays tribute to the humanity and authenticity of a writer who had been of great importance to him. When Edwin and Willa Muir translated *The Castle* in 1930, Kafka's name was virtually unknown in the English-speaking world, and it is largely due to the eagerness and perception of the Muirs that Kafka has become a recognized major novelist.

An essay by Elgin Mellown on Muir's developing critical attitude towards Kafka[36] shows how the poet started in 1930 by defending Kafka as an allegorist who was concerned with religion, but by 1947[37] was rejecting the theory of allegory in favour of religious symbolism and "serious fantasy." Before he read Kafka, Muir was discovering his own symbolism of the road and the search for salvation, as we have seen, and was obviously excited to find a novelist working with similar symbols towards a similar end. In a 1930 essay called "A Note on Franz Kafka" Muir wrote that "For anyone who wants to have a serious imaginative treatment of religion, Kafka is infinitely more satisfying than Dostoevski,"[38] and in 1940 he was describing Kafka's theme and technique in a way which makes clear how much he identified with the Czech novelist. He might have been describing his own poetry when he claimed that Kafka

believed in the fundamental tenets of religion, divine justice, divine grace, damnation and salvation; they are the framework of his world.

The problem which posseses him is how man, stationed in one dimension, can direct his life in accordance with a law belonging to another, a law whose workings he can never interpret truly, though they are always before his eyes. . . .

Kafka's most ordinary scenes have a fullness which gives them simultaneously several meanings, one beneath the other, until in a trivial situation we find an image of some universal or mythical event such as the Fall. . . . He has been blamed for confusing two worlds, for introducing real people and then by a sudden twist making all their actions symbolical and bringing them into contact with mythical figures. But that was exactly what he set out to do.[39]

Like Kafka's, Muir's use of symbol enabled him to link "man, stationed in one dimension" and "a law belonging to another." In his essay "Franz Kafka" written in 1947, Muir looks at Kafka's work in terms of the endless road and the labyrinth, where "the right turn may easily chance to be the wrong, and the wrong the right,"[40] but also as the technician who re-created and made available to contemporary literature the timeless and archetypal story, in which is the source of all stories.

Muir saw in Kafka the justification of his own methods. Elgin Mellown writes:

Many of Muir's poems being based on 'universal situations', inevitably remind one of Kafka's stories; and certainly Kafka, even if he did not directly influence Muir, strengthened the poet's faith in his own ideas.[41]

Like Muir, Kafka "created a world" through symbol; like Muir, Kafka's massive pessimism and frustration became transformed into a more hopeful view of human life, though he did not live long enough for us to judge whether his final acceptance and celebration would have been as complete as Muir's.

This great affinity with Kafka lies behind "To Franz Kafka." Kafka is one of "the authentic ones" who shame us by their stature and certainty. Kafka not only accepts but embraces and celebrates the world of sin, poverty and shameful people:

> But you, dear Franz, sad champion of the drab
> And half, would watch the tell-tale shames drift in
> (As if they were troves of treasure) not aloof,
> But with a famishing passion quick to grab
> Meaning, and read on all the leaves of sin
> Eternity's secret script, the saving proof.

This assertion of Kafka's deep humanity is also an assertion of his religious, Christ-like power, which, by taking in the experience of sin and suffering, discovers meaning and Eternity at the very heart of inadequacy and failure. Kafka understands the necessity of sin and evil for attaining redemption. It is difficult not to see such poems as "To Franz Kafka," or "One Foot in Eden" and "The Annunciation" as more deeply "religious" than any of Muir's poems dealing directly with Christianity. Certainly the relationship of sin and redemption in the non-Christian "To Frank Kafka" shows how adaptable and all-inclusive Muir's mythology has become.

The fine "Effigies" form another part of Muir's symbolism of betrayal. Written during his unhappy time at Newbattle, these poems reflect some of the uncharacteristic bitterness caused by the machinations of the people who were trying to manipulate and undermine the college and Muir's position. After the first, third and fifth poems of "Effigies" were published in 1954, he wrote to Kathleen Raine, in a letter full of worry about his wife's health, the state of the world and his own inability to write:

The three poems in the New Statesman are affected by it (the unpleasantness of the world) — a little infusion of poison in them except for the third, which comes from an old memory.[42]

The first poem is a strong indictment of a man who lives through his manipulation of others. Behind this terrible portrait is the character of one of the powerful politician/educationalists who was hostile to Muir and what he was doing at Newbattle, though this picture of one man is absorbed into a wider context, somewhat reminiscent of the faceless, inhuman forms he wrote about in the Prague poems. (It is interesting in this context, that Muir reintroduces the symbol of the labyrinth in the first two poems of "Effigies.")

A strong feeling of hostility energizes this poem. The unnamed man controls others as if they are mere chess-pieces, and outside the immediate chess-board of his own power and influence — probably in Muir's mind an image of the executive committee in charge of Newbattle — the world is a labyrinth:

> Past that arena
> Stretched out a winding moonlight labyrinth,
> A shining limbo filled with vanishing faces,
> Propitious or dangerous, to be scanned
> In a passion of repulsion or desire.
> His glances knew two syllables: 'Come' and 'Go'.

The poem continues by introducing images of the manipulator's eyes and face. His eyes had "narrowed to the semi-circle before him"; and his face was like

> The shining front of a rich and loveless house,
> The doors all shut.   The windows cast such brightness
> Outwards that none could see what was within,
> Half-blinded by the strong repelling dazzle.
> Set in the doors two little judas windows. . . .

There is a controlled violence of feeling in these lines; words like "rich," "loveless," "shut," "repelling" and, above all, "judas" convey a condemnation never explicitly expressed. The poem concludes with a return to the chess image, picturing the manipulator dying and no longer able to control others, but not expressed with any compassion·

> When he was dying
> The pieces sauntered freely about the board
> Like lawless vagrants, and would not be controlled.
> He would whisper 'Stop',
> Starting awake, and weep to think they were free.

The last words complete the indictment, as even in death the manipulator cannot stand the thought that the ones he has controlled, through his power and position, might be free.

The portrait is of a non-human man, who reacts like a computer to others in his cold exploitation of power. Muir's personal antipathy is clear, but he controls it by means of the labyrinth/chessboard and the eyes/face imagery. This faceless committee-man, so hostile to what Muir believed about the individual and the free exercise of imagination, resembles the man in "The Helmet" and is of the same lineage as the Intercepter and the betrayers of "The Good Town." All betray freedom and restrict full humanity.

The second poem refers again to Judas and the labyrinth. If the subject of the first poem is guilty of betraying human potential, the subject of this poem stands indicted on a more specific charge, that of betraying a friend: the man has betrayed a friend to death through envy and is now imprisoned in the labyrinth of conscience. Totally sealed in the consequences of his act, he wants to be reunited with his victim but cannot escape. In a less harsh conclusion Muir calls for pity on his helplessness:

> Pity him, for he cannot think the thought
> Nor feel the pang that yet might set him free,
> and Judas ransomed dangle from the tree.

153

Miserable, the man cannot properly repent or understand. He too is short of humanity and imagination, but in a much less controlled and calculating way than the manipulator of the first poem.

The poem is remarkable for its treatment of the labyrinth image, here representing total self-involvement and imprisonment with the guilt of action, and the inability to empathise or grasp the humanity of others. He cannot feel or think the things which drove Judas to kill himself; his total absorption in self distorts perception.

The third effigy develops this theme of isolation and psychic imbalance. The man described has retreated into himself, and has had to kill and betray in order to do it:

> Revolving in his own
> Immovable danger zone,
> Having killed his enemy
> And betrayed his troublesome friend
> To be with himself alone. . . .

Completely alone he waits for eternity, seeing the world outside as wrong and sinful, as he remains "Cut off in blind desire." Sometimes he dreams of peace, but his life consists purely of watching time pass and waiting for a knock on the door of his retreat.

The poem deals obviously with a psychological state, and the confused, lonely paranoid, although guilty of betrayal, emerges as more sad and sick than evil. Again the denial of human life is strongly emphasized. The first three effigies are all portraits of men who cannot, or will not, relate, and whose suspicions, weaknesses and machinations deny humanity to other people. All are too deeply involved with the self, and the symbolic presentation of this, through images of labyrinth, prison and sealed rooms, reminds us of the previous use of the labyrinth, symbolizing all that is fallen and selfish and obstructive in man.

The fourth poem has a quality of dream or nightmare strongly reminiscent of "The Combat." The symbolic situation is again one of recurring battle, but this time by unspecified, unlocated armies. The poet's stance here is as one of the killers, using "We" throughout the poem, and if this is a portrait of a particular person the fact is completely obscured. The poem seems concerned with the inner realization of the destructive act, which occurs only after harm is done. The subdued Christian symbolism, reminding us of Christ's rising again after death, and also of Thomas' doubt and need of proof, is no more than a half-submerged hint, and we are left with

154

the image of conscience and terror as our guilts keep rising before us. No amount of killing can kill conscience, which lies in wait on the next ridge. Machine-oriented men who walk over humanity will find ultimately that "the dead/Were real."

The nightmare obscurity and lack of reference points here is repeated in the curious metrical treatment which uses two-, three-, four- and five-stress lines in a random pattern, not allowing the ear to settle and find formal harmony. Only with the terrible realization of the last two lines — "I do not think we knew the dead/Were real, or really dead, till then" — does Muir, through a regular tetrameter couplet, allow a pattern to emerge and conclude the poem.

The last of the "Effigies" is the one which "comes from an old memory." Its subject is a woman, betrayed by her lover and living subsequently on dream. By switching his focus from betrayer to betrayed, Muir is able to treat this theme with a strong compassion. The woman's hurt is strong and her life has been irretrievably altered, so that she seems not really to exist physically on earth:

> Her life was all an aria and an echo
> And when the aria ceased the echo led her
> Gently to alight somewhere that seemed the earth.

Her lover had stolen her angelic properties and "Her flying wings struck root upon his shoulders" and bore him away.

The pathos of this poem is considerable, as Muir evokes with pity a woman spiritually ravished, forced to end her days listening to the echo of what life was and might have been. Out of her finer element she waits for death:

> There gradually she withered towards her harvest,
> That grew as she grew less, until at last
> She stared in grief at mounds and mounds of grain.

This last image adds to the fertility/sterility movement of the poem, linking the conclusion to the opening where "She lived in comfort on her poor few pence/And sweetly starved to feed her swelling dream." At the end, her dreams are "mounds and mounds of grain" but she knows only grief as her body has withered away.

"Effigies" deals with betrayal, evil and suffering, and is a timely reminder that, although Muir has been able to find a synthesis and to celebrate human life in general terms, he is still aware of the imperfections and inhuman brutality of man's nature and is ready, if necessary, to pass moral judgment. Of the five poems, the first and fifth seem the most successful, mainly because of the intensity of feeling released by the images. Muir was by no means always in another world, creating figures in a symbolic landscape. "Effigies" is full of the flesh and blood, the mind and conscience we meet every day.

From this partial excursion into actuality the poet returns more fully to the symbolic world in his poem "The Difficult Land," which is a looser, more discursive meditation on the theme of "One Foot in Eden." The poem accepts the difficulty of life, and, after a struggle, finds a redeeming vision of hope emerging from the loss.

The symbolic base is a description by an unlocated primitive society of the problems of living, where nature and man conspire against fulfilment. "Things miscarry" and "You'd think there was malice in the very air." To the men, involved in the ceaseless round of planting and reaping, "the earth itself looks sad and senseless." Haunted by dreams, oppressed by war and invasion, sustained by a sense of "ancestral rite and custom," they survive and endure like the Jews, the Czechs or even the Scots. The poem creates a strong feeling of eternal loss and frustration, made real by the clear lyricism and the resigned, wistful tone. It is a compassionate symbolization of the Fall and by no means bitter or angry. Endurance becomes quietly heroic; the sense of "continuance of fold and hearth," of belonging to a pattern gives a sustaining strength. And yet

> . . . there are times
> When name, identity, and our very hands,
> Senselessly labouring, grow most hateful to us,
> And we would gladly rid us of these burdens,
> Enter our darkness through the doors of wheat
> And the light veil of grass (leaving behind
> Name, body, country, speech, vocation, faith)
> And gather into the secrecy of the earth
> Furrowed by broken ploughs lost deep in time.

This pressure for release, through a lyrically conceived death, follows the revulsion from self, strongly reminiscent of the same experience in "The Journey Back" in the previous volume. The realization of life's broken incompleteness leads to nausea with the self and forces the psychological craving for assumption into a wider pattern — in this case, appropriately for farmers, into "the secrecy of the earth" and the rhythm of the seasons. But, as in "Telemachos Remembers," from the enduring and deprivation comes something positive and deeply human which ultimately proves stronger and more permanent than the nausea, and "The Difficult Land" ends with a strong assertion of positive values which lie beneath the random pain of history and experience:

> We have such hours, but are drawn back again
> By faces of goodness, faithful masks of sorrow,
> Honesty, kindness, courage, fidelity,
> The love that lasts a life's time. . . .
> . . . And the dead
> Who lodge in us so strangely, unremembered,
> Yet in their place.

The vision of everything being in place is familiar to us, as it almost always heralds Muir's symbolic Eden, opposing the symbol of fractured, random evil in the historical process. We cannot reject, the poem concludes, the pattern we are ultimately part of, nor "refrain from love," for "This is a difficult country, and our home." This concluding line sums up concisely Muir's response to human experience in this volume, which presents the opposing visions of evil hopeless chaos and the possibility of a full redeeming acceptance of this in terms of the pattern which sustains and underpins our experience of the fallen state.

Whereas "Telemachos Remembers" uses a more dramatic, swaying symbolism to embody this vision, and "One Foot in Eden" relies on its tight compression of image and emblem, this poem uses a slow reflective lyricism to achieve its end. The symbolic landscape, devoid of individual man, is a free and timeless place on which the human race plays out its life experience. The positive vision is released only through a strenuous exploration of the negative and emerges organically and convincingly from it. There is no hint of a pattern imposed from outside; the poem remains a fluent process, enacted through symbol, embodying a wide knowledge of the fluctuations and extremes of experience, which is given conviction by the superb control of sound and syntax:

> . . .   our fields
> Mile after mile of soft and useless dust.
> On dull delusive days presaging rain
> We yoke the oxen, go out harrowing,
> Walk in the middle of an ochre cloud,
> Dust rising before us and falling again behind us,
> Slowly and gently settling where it lay.
> These days the earth itself looks sad and senseless.

The effect of these lines, the way in which they express and embody meaning, is partly due to the patterns of alliteration and consonance and partly to the subtle metrical variations in the iambic pentameter pattern:

/   / | x   x / | x   x / | x x /| x / |x
Dust rising before us and falling again behind us

where the spondee and the iamb, on each side of the three anapests, give a balance and pattern, and the final pyrrhic foot tails away with a dissolving helplessness, completely at one with the meaning of the line. At this stage, Muir is so much in control of his technique that lines as metrically complex as

/   x |x / | x   / | x   x /|x/|
Honesty, kindness, courage, fidelity

and

/   / |x / | x / | x x / | x / |
Name, body, country, speech, vocation, faith

can be incorporated with no sense of uneasiness.

In the using of a symbolist technique the handling of prosody is vital, for a poem's tone depends largely on sound-pattern, and this controlling tone is essential in the presentation of freely moving symbols. Without logic or local context, the rhythms and tones become controlling agencies of the first importance, without which the symbols would fly wildly and randomly and achieve little strength of ordered meaning and articulation. In all of Muir's greatest poems there is a creative tension binding symbol, tone, syntax and sound, each of which has a strong expressive function within the unified poetic utterance.

"Day and Night" is one of the most openly autobiographical of Muir's poems, justifying his faith in dreams and the shapes of the night and showing how, in poetry and in life, he tries to join the world of day/time to that of night/timelessness.

The first two sections contrast day and night as informing forces upon the innocent child. Daytime brings richness and immediacy but lack of pattern. The brash newness of waking experience is "too wild" and unformed, and this is strongly contrasted, in the second section of the poem, with the experience of night, which links us to archetypal repositories of meaning and simple, basic patterns of life. In this comparison, Muir is again pointing to the difference between the Story and the Fable, between the vivid, random sense-impressions of our daily experience and the deep archaic patterns of dreams and the unconscious which link us to all men in all times and all places.

The poem concludes with twelve lines which read as if they are taken directly from *An Autobiography*. Muir is giving a statement of the preoccupations which lie behind his symbolism, but also making the "I" refer to everyman, in spite of the obvious very personal details:

> A man now, gone with time so long —
> My youth to myself grown fabulous
> As an old land's memories, a song
> To trouble or to pleasure us —
> I try to fit that world to this,
> The hidden to the visible play,
> Would have them both, would nothing miss,
> Learn from the shepherd of the dark,
> Here in the light, the paths to know
> That thread the labyrinthine park,
> And the great Roman roads that go
> Striding across the untrodden way.

There is nothing to add to this summary of Muir's symbolism. It charts the loss of the fabulous, the attempt to fit the Story and the Fable together, the desire for timeless knowledge of how to defeat the labyrinth and to reach the straight road towards Eden/eternity. This is Muir's personal history; the unified pattern, its breakdown, the restored pattern lie deep in the human psyche and shape experience and life. The very simple and direct juxtaposition of the Story and the Fable, and the day and night symbols is resolved by fitting them together, without protest or tension, within the uncharacteristically personal framework. The symbolist technique allows the deeply personal articulation of experience a validity outside the time and place of Muir's own treatment of self.

"The Other Story" meditates on man's attitude to the Fall in a more metaphysical way. How can we attain innocence again now. The poem muses more abstractly than usual on the theme of innocence and knowledge, but behind the rather facile metaphysics and the arbitrary free verse runs Muir's terrible knowledge of man's central paradoxical predicament, as he moves inevitably in time and guilt, yet cannot forget his original state nor subdue the insistent desire to return to it.

"Song for a Hypothetical Age" returns, for the third time, to the symbol of Penelope's weaving as example of deep humanity, and places against this a hypothetical future time when such humanity has gone and men live impersonally, "exempt from grief and rage." Muir returns here to his symbolist method, introducing the Penelope symbol into the "impersonality" symbol with no logical or syntactical explanation or support, and letting meaning generate from the resulting clash.

The hypothetical age is presented in the present tense, and clearly the symbol defies a placing within time. This brave new world is Muir's vision of the Fall, and incorporates past, present and future. The only restriction on the time dislocation is that the old men tell of Penelope's story as happening "long, long ago," but even this, taken in the context of symbolist syntax, could be interpreted as a twentieth century interjection by the poet, within and yet removed from the poem. The whole Penelope section is in parenthesis.

This timeless world has gone beyond grief and joy into petrified emotional sterility:

> ... the round earth to rock is grown
> In the winter of our eyes;
> Heart and earth a single stone.
> Until the stony barrier break
> Grief and joy no more shall wake.

It is a vision of anti-humanity, where men are divorced from the things which make them human, and against this, introduced right into the heart of the present-tense description, the recalled story of Penelope takes on a strong meaning. In the past tense, with reported speech in the present, the myth takes on timeless qualities. More than in "Telemachos Remembers" Muir emphasizes Penelope's artistry in conflict with her individual experience of love and grief. The great web

> ... might have been a masterpiece —
> If she had let it have its way —
> To drive all artistry to despair
> And set the sober world at play
> Beyond the other side of care,
> And lead a fabulous era in.

This is brilliantly linked with the "fabulous era" of the hypothetical age, which is, having transcended emotion, "Beyond the other side of care." But the inhumanity and stony barriers of this age are dramatically challenged by the developing symbol of Penelope, who refuses to abandon the intensity of her grief and faith for the "hypo-thetical" world of the imagination, which would have ended her suffering, but also her humanity. She saves Odysseus who would be "shipwrecked on my art" had she finished the web, which, as she tears it again, is "No more divided from her heart."

Thus the poem opposes two symbolic worlds and sets of values. The concern of the Penelope section is to preserve humanity at all costs, even though this means accepting suffering and endurance, and rejecting all forms of escapism. The other symbolic world, by eliminating that painful humanity (finishing the web and abandon-ing the suffering individual) has managed to pass beyond pain, but only into a sterile waste-land, devoid of personality and feeling.

This great plea for the need to accept humanity and all its atten-dant suffering is made solely by releasing the two symbols. There is no argument or discussion, no logic or comment. The two symbols are left to mean what they can without the support of any conceptual apparatus. The only control comes from the subtle modulation of tone and sound, whereby the symbolic life of the hypothetical age is shown to be hard and inhuman by the use, especially in the first section, of completely enclosed tetrameter couplets, totally lacking buoyancy and vitality and, syntactically, unable to progress:

> Grief, they say, is personal,
> Else there'd be no grief at all.
> We, exempt from grief and rage,
> Rule here our new impersonal age.
> Now while dry is every eye
> The last grief is passing by.
> History takes its final turn
> Where all's to mourn for, none to mourn.
> Idle justice sits alone
> In a world to order grown.

The remarkable, rigid, computer-like movement of these lines is another example of Muir's ability to use sound and syntax as a vital instrument. Compare with this the sound, speed, energy and texture of the "positive" section:

> (Long, long ago, the old men say,
> A famous wife, Penelope,
> For twenty years the pride of Greece,
> Wove and unwove a web all day
> That might have been a masterpiece. . . .

But still she said, 'Where I begin
Must I return, else all is lost,
And great Odysseus tempest-tossed
Will perish, shipwrecked on my art.
But so, I guide him to the shore'.

This section has been released from the shackles of the closed couplets, the abstraction and the lack of energy of the first section. The
lines move buoyantly onwards and the reported speech gives a
concreteness and strength to the positive feelings being embodied.
After this, we return to the waste-land with six lines of sterility and
petrification of sound and sense. Not only do the symbols start a
chemical reaction as they mix, but they are supported and made
more meaningful by the sound and tone. The poem demonstrates
poetic craftsmanship of the highest order, as well as a deep understanding and celebration of the qualities in human-beings that make
life most precious and valuable.

That his symbolist technique has not yet been fully exploited may
be seen from "The Cloud" and "The Horses," each of which uses
rather surprising methods to achieve symbolic unity and pattern.

"The Cloud" is untypically close to a direct confessional mode of
describing experience. Instead of moving the reader directly into the
symbolic landscape, Muir leads him into the symbolism through the
reporting of a real experience, described in time and space:

One late spring evening in Bohemia,
Driving to the Writers' House, we lost our way
In a maze of little winding roads that led
To nothing but themselves. . . .

This casual autobiographical directness is only gradually merged into
the wider subject. The roads become "a rustic web for thoughtless
travellers" and removed from "sign and sound of life" the dusty
agricultural scene takes on qualities of a more universal landscape.
But this poem never escapes completely from actuality. Details of the
visit to the Writers' House serve to strengthen the concentration
upon the real focus of meditation — the solitary man in his cloud of
dust, who becomes a potent image of "fallen Adam filling the barren
fields with the sweat of his brow." However lowly and blind, however close to being merely "A pillar of dust moving in dust; no
more," man is part of Adam and Adam's spiritual destiny.

Muir's technique in "The Cloud" is to bring actual personal
experience much more closely to bear upon the symbols than usual

and to present a wide meaning growing naturally out of a concretely described private experience. This keeps the symbol of man as Adam much closer to time and space, becoming real only in terms of the local experience it grows from. Thus the poem is less symbolistic than most of Muir's work, where the technique, as we have seen, requires a comparison between emotions, perceptions and reasonings, and a freely moving, layered treatment of time and space. In "The Cloud" the symbolic world is not self-sufficient, but shown as the individual's imagination brooding over local experience. The Adam symbol comes alive in "our minds" and "our memory." In his most symbolistic vein, Muir would not have written that "cloud and message fused." Instead he would have presented the two perceptions, or experiences, as free symbols, rotating them, opposing them and finally mating them with no comment on what was happening or how, thus achieving a more self-sufficient dramatic effect.

At the other extreme, "The Horses" uses the full potential of the symbolist technique. Here Muir's symbolism is able to assimilate simultaneously the themes of nuclear war, politics, the Fall, rebirth, industrialization, man's relationship with the animals, all within a strong pseudo-narrative framework. This thematic relativism is made possible by the achievement of an impressive time/space dislocation whereby the poem is placed in the future, related in the past tense, and contains implications of the death of old time and the start of a new time. The place is remote — outside the nuclear conflict "that put the world to sleep," near the ocean, yet attached to the destroyed world. This brilliantly evoked confusion of space and time is further strengthened by the strategy, in the first lines, of creating a deliberate parallel between the "seven days war that put the world to sleep" and the original seven days of creation which brought it to life. This scheme of creation in reverse, where each day leads further towards nothingness and total silence, is even further heightened by the magic, ballad-like description of the ship: "On the third day a warship passed us, heading north,/Dead bodies piled on the deck." Here the symbolized death of the fishes of the sea is followed by the death of the fowls of the air as:

> On the sixth day
> A plane plunged over us into the sea.   Thereafter
> Nothing.

The seventh day leaves the radios dumb and the world gone. Thus time and space in this poem are not deliberately confused and dislocated by the usual symbolist methods, but are simultaneously described and embodied into the poem's content. The horses which come to the little community, arrive "Barely a twelvemonth" after the war, and "Late in the evening." The archaism of "twelvemonth," so striking in relation to the nuclear bombs and military hardware, is not only there for its vagueness, but adds to the theme of a new/old system of life and time being established. "Late in the evening," with its seemingly ridiculous precision under the circumstances of the poem, adds to the time cofusion, but also helps to make the "strange horses" more related to the unconscious world of night, and to emphasize their mysterious, emblematic, non-human qualities. Thus, simply by approaching the poem's treatment of time and space in terms of technique, we are taken to the very heart of its meaning. Here time, presented almost ritualistically in the poem's mythology, forms the structural skeleton which carries the other themes. In this, one of the most densely realized of all Muir's poems, the symbolistic structure embodies in itself much of the meaning and is directly responsible for the depth and range of perception and suggestion.

The surface narrative of the poem is simple. The seven day war is described in terms of increasing deadness and silence until the group of survivors is totally isolated from a dead world. They vow that they would never have that world back again, as it was a world of genocide. Now that world that "swallowed its children" lies destroyed, the nations like foetuses are "Curled blindly in impenetrable sorrow."[43] Around the survivors lie relics of the old world, symbolized here by tractors left to rust, which the survivors do not want to use. They revert instinctively to pre-industrial society:

> We make our oxen drag our rusty ploughs,
> Long laid aside.   We have gone back
> Far past our father's land.

The second half of the poem describes the arrival of the "strange horses" already mentioned in the first lines. They come like a threat, "Like a wild wave charging," introducing a vast noise in the silent landscape. The people do not dare to go near them at first, but the horses waited:

164

Stubborn and shy, as if they had been sent
By an old command to find our whereabouts
And that long-lost archaic companionship.

The horses are in control of the relationship, possessing a knowledge that men have forgotten. The colts, "Dropped in some wilderness of the broken world" form a kind of link with the realities outside the outpost of the survivors, who come to realize that the animals are willing to help them establish a fruitful relationship. The poem ends with the men moved by the "free servitude" of the animals, who have effected a rebirth and a beginning: "Our life is changed; their coming our beginning."

This narrative structure is obviously rich with potential meaning on many levels. The poem can be considered as a symbolic representation of the Fall of man and his subsequent acceptance of the fallen world as he works in harmony with innocence to bear his loads. Certainly it is concerned with industrial man's loss of innocence, for, by relying on the mechanical, we have lost that essential "archaic companionship" with the world of nature and the animals, without which our life is sterile and likely to lead to calamity. Only when, like the Ancient Mariner blessing the creatures of the sea, we regain our contact with innocence and nature can the disaster and punishment be mitigated and new hope introduced. Until then, man is seen busily and blindly undoing God's creation and misusing nature for destructive ends. Seen in this way, the poem is a "science-fiction" warning against the loss of humanity and the evils of a purely technological, soulless ethos. Even in a post-nuclear world, the young horses are "new as if they had come from their own Eden," and the poem can be seen in terms of Muir's accumulated use of the Eden-myth as a source of possibility at the very heart of this world. Life is possible through a rebirth of innocence.

Professor Cox, I think, is right to see submerged Christian references at the end of the poem.[44] The force which comes to bear our loads and serve us freely, as well as to put us in contact with Eden and give us the chance of a resurrection and new life, is certainly more than the horses. And yet Muir does not insist upon this. As with all his great symbols, the meaning is accumulative and impossible to interpret fully on any one level. It is certainly inadequate to suggest that:

Muir's primitivism, returning all post-atomic mankind to an Orkney farm, not without a certain austere satisfaction, seems ... to be far more insulting than comforting to man's restless spirit and aspiring brain.[45]

"The Horses" is not a poem dealing specifically with "post-atomic mankind," nor should the symbolism of innocence be taken literally. The poem deals with the basic problems in human existence; the great swaying battle between good and evil, man's losses and gains as he becomes more sophisticated, the conflicting destructive and creative impulses which can alienate or bring fulfilment, the possibilities of a renewal of life in an increasingly dehumanized situation, and the permanent struggle, in whatever form it takes, to relate the real world of experience to a wider reality in order to find pattern and wholeness, and to allow the self to escape from its inward-looking and self-obsession which can lead to paralysis and destruction.

Professor Butter claims that Muir "does not so much leave normal reality for the world of fable as perceive the fable beneath the surface of normal reality."[46] But the poem, ranging through time and space, quite deliberately confusing them, and bringing the two symbols of man/world/war and horses/Eden/peace into conjunction, is following symbolist technique where, as Edmund Wilson says, "links in association of ideas are dropped down into the unconscious mind so that we are obliged to divine them for ourselves."[47] The surface of the poem is by no means "normal reality," but a landscape for freely associating symbols which, by their conjunction, have accrued many layers of significance, certainly relating closely to mid-twentieth century experience, but which, even in the most precisely observed details, use realism only to promote the total structural symbolism of the poem.

Muir's choice of horses as the basis for the symbolism can easily be traced in his writings. From early childhood he had a curious fascination for and emotional ambivalence towards horses:

When my father and Sutherland brought in the horses from the fields I stood trembling among their legs ... looking up at the stationary hulks and the tossing heads, which in the winter dusk were lost in the sky. I felt beaten down by an enormous weight and a real terror: yet I did not hate the horses as I hated the insects; my fear turned into something else, for it was infused by a longing to go up to them and touch them and simultaneously checked by the knowledge that their hoofs were dangerous; a combination of emotions which added up to worship in the Old Testament sense. Everything about them ... filled me with a stationary terror and delight for which I could get no relief. One day two of our horses began to fight in the field below the house rearing at each other like steeds on a shield. . . . [48]

Behind the symbolism of "The Horses," too, is Muir's attitude towards the relationship of man, god and animal, seen so often in his visions of Eden. On this subject he writes of "an age when animal and man and god lived densely together in the same world: the timeless crowded age of organic heraldry."[49] He goes on to talk of man's guilt towards the animals because of taking their lives, but also of the curiously close relationship that existed between them:

The age which felt this connexion between men and animals was so much longer than the brief historical period known to us that we cannot conceive it: but our unconscious life goes back to it.[50]

And this last point is further emphasized:

My passion for animals comes partly from being brought up so close to them, in a place where people had lived as they had lived for two hundred years; partly from I do not know where. . . . But it is certain that people who have been brought up in close contact with animals, including the vast majority of the generations from whom we spring, have dreamed and dreamed of animals, and my own experience shows that these dreams are often tinged with a guilt of which consciously we are unaware.[51]

This belief in animals as part of man's unconscious and dream life, linked to the guilt we feel for breaking trust with them and losing contact, can be seen in "The Horses," where the reconciliation between man and animals symbolizes a return from the fallen, self-conscious state to the archetypal harmony known in our unconscious. The lines from "The Difficult Land":

> And the dead
> Who lodge in us so strongly, unremembered,
> Yet in their place

may be seen in the context of this poem, where the old relationship is restored, the conscious and the unconscious are reconciled, and, ultimately in this mythology, the broken circle, caused by the Fall, is joined.

Standing starkly in contrast to this symbol of restoration and redemption are the rusting tractors, products of the conscious, technological mind which is impervious to the workings of the imagination. This contrast between the animate and inanimate is clarified in Muir's essay called "The Natural Estate" where he claims that the vast dissemination of secondary objects isolates us from the natural world in a way which is new to mankind, and that this cannot help affecting our sensibilities and our imagination. It is possible to write a poem about horses, for, apart from the work they do for us, they have a life of their own; it is impossible to write a poem about motor cars, except in the false rhetorical vein, for they have no life except what we give them by pushing a starter. The finished article is finished in a final sense; sometimes we can admire its functional beauty, but it is impervious to the imagination.[52]

It is perhaps easy to disagree with this point. There have been many good poems written "about" secondary objects which are not "in the false rhetorical vein," but clearly this statement is a defence of the symbolist imagination and technique as we have seen it at work in Muir's poetry. The key difference between the horse and the car in this argument is that the horse has life and comes from the natural world whereas the car has no life, is "finished in a final sense" and is "impervious to the imagination." In terms of Muir's poetic, this is a valid distinction, for his symbols derive from the world of the unconscious, from myth, from religion and from nature, and are always deeply resonant with old, accumulated meaning. Horses can become "fabulous steeds set on an ancient shield," and symbols of terror and innocence and rebirth, but the car has no wealth of embodied meaning from which to draw symbol and pattern. Secondary objects are products of time, soon obsolete and not impinging upon man's inner life. Only those things which are natural, timeless, charged with meaning and pattern are fully accessible to the imagination. Objects purely from the Story are ultimately worthless if they do not penetrate into the world of the Fable.

This statement would not have been made by a non-symbolist poet, using concrete reality as his base for exploring experience. It deals with the necessary difficulty of the symbolistic approach which, at its most extreme, foregoes actuality in its attempt to create its own complete world of symbols. Muir, as I have said, is not this extreme — his symbolic world is always penetrated by the social and political realities he lived through — but he always tries to create, through symbol, a world out of time, the reality of which can reach beyond rusting tractors. "The Horses" shows this opposition very clearly. The horses are as concretely realized as the tractors, but they bear meanings and powers which postulate a transcendental reality.

Returning to our examination of the poem, we see that the sound and tone once again provide an effective and necessary controlling presence. The poem is "narrated," as if to a reporter, by one of the survivors, looking back at the events during and after the war, and mixing, naturally and effectively, narrative with personal comment. The language is unrhetorical and subdued, taking on, in the catalogue of the days of the war, a ritualistic, liturgical tone which deepens the reference to and contrast with the account of the Creation in Genesis. Following this, the tone changes to elegy as the strange, silent reality of the "new" world is realized and life is slowly picked up. With the coming of the horses and their semi-violent intrusion, the tension mounts, the sound becomes ominous and powerful and the metre speeds the poem up and breaks the quiet regularity until the horses and men find their relationship and the poem ends in a wondering tranquillity.

The metrical base is the five-foot blank line, but Muir handles this with considerable flexibility throughout the poem, making the prosody a highly expressive reinforcement for the symbolism. Four times he substitutes a short dimeter or trimeter line with dramatic effect. The brilliant opening lines, taking us straight into the strange timeless world, rely on their understatement and the metrical and syntactical pattern:

> Barely a twelve-month after
> The seven days war that put the world to sleep,
> Late in the evening the strange horses came . . .

The vague, seemingly unimportant evocation of time and the tentative human voice trying to pick up a story of such magnitude is reflected in the wavering metre, as both the iambic norm and the five-foot line struggle for establishment. The opening trimeter

> /   x|x / | x   / | x
> Barely a twelvemonth after

with its three and a half feet and opening trochee moves into the pentameter pattern as the narrator gathers confidence and memory returns:

> x / | x x / | x / | x / |x / |
> The seven days war that put the world to sleep.

The seventh line of two feet

> x   x / | x / |
> On the second day

effectively breaks the pattern of metrical expectancy and leads to the solemn liturgy of the description of the war, full of apocalypse and religious undertones, which is given life by the metre and syntax:

```
x    x / | x  /  |
On the second day

x   / | xx  /  |  x   / | x  /  |  / / | x
The radios failed;  we turned the knobs;  no answer.

x   x  /   / | x / | x  /  |  x  /  | x /  |
On the third day a warship passed us, heading north,

/     / | x / | x  x  / |  x  x /    / |
Dead bodies piled on the deck.   On the sixth day

x  /   | /    / | x x / | x x  / |   x / | x
A plane plunged over us into the sea.   Thereafter

/    x |    x / | xx    / |
Nothing.   The radios dumb . . .
```

The short ritualistic sentences, the terse compressed syntax and the irregular, highly expressive use of metre, create the strength of this passage. The opening two-foot line prepares us for the list; the closing trimeter, its two missing feet embodying and describing the total silence of the dumb radios, concludes the catalogue with finality. The phrases — "On the third day," and "On the sixth day," both at the start of a sentence, give a heavy biblical pattern; the unnatural six-foot line describing the warship heightens the feeling of the bizarre and supernatural; the two lines with final pyrrhic feet and the wide usage of anapests and trochees give a strange unnatural rhythm to the description of the unnatural events being recalled. Only after this, when the survivors start to reconstruct an ordered existence does the poem settle on an ordered pattern of pentameter lines.

The breaking of the peace with the sudden arrival of the horses is also expressed through sound and form; the disruption and sudden energy being mirrored in the tone, metre, syntax and language:

> . . . We have gone back
> Far past our father's land.
>   And then, that evening
> Late in the summer the strange horses came.
> We heard a distant tapping on the road,
> A deepening drumming; it stopped, went on again
> And at the corner changed to hollow thunder.

> We saw the heads
> Like a wild wave charging and were afraid.

Here the slow peace of the scene is violently disrupted by the dropping of "and then that evening" from its place in the line above and the sudden urgency of the language which builds to a crescendo of noise and action through progressive stages of "tapping," "drumming," "thunder," "charging," where the verbal concreteness and energy creates the sensation of physical presence. The dimeter line "We saw the heads" comes in a climactic position, and Muir uses the short line and its spaces as an agent of suspense and emotional climax as the men actually see what is approaching. The movement and strength of the animals is expressed by the piled up stresses and final tailing away of the line

$$ x \quad x \; / \quad / \; | \; / \quad x \; | \; x \quad / \; | \; x \; / \; | $$
Like a wild wave charging and were afraid

Again, following this action, the men can return to normality and the metre and syntax become regular again. The two climaxes of the war and the arrival of the horses each are reflected by the poem's sound and form.

"The Horses" is a poem of extreme richness, but always controlled by the poet in spite of the breadth of its symbolic possibilities. It embodies dramatically Muir's main themes, which emerge through symbol, sound and tone held in an active tension. The rebirth theme is movingly handled and the symbolist method is remarkable for the amount of actuality it incorporates while still achieving the release from time and the universality so important to Muir. The poem is filled with hope for the rediscovery of man's deepest forces and potentialities, which are seen as miraculously capable of surviving the ultimate of horror and the full unleashing of the world's destructive powers. The worst that the Intercepter, the usurpers and the face under the helmet can do is here faced and symbolically transcended by something simple yet timelessly valid within the pattern of life. "The Horses" gives dramatic and symbolic confirmation of Muir's acknowledgement, at the very end of his autobiography, that

we receive more than we can ever give; we receive it from the past, on which we draw with every breath, but also — and this is a point of faith — from the Source of the mystery itself, by the means which religious people call Grace.[53]

"Song" ("This will not pass so soon"), returns to Greek myth and much less dramatic symbolism. The poem is based on the myth of Persephone, the goddess who spent half her time in the underworld and half on earth, upon which Muir builds a plangent lyric about the division between the two worlds of "the quick and the dead." Because

> time is out of tune
> With all beneath the moon,
> Man and woman and flower and grass . . .

there is a barrier between the two worlds, which means grief when beauty leaves one to go to the other. The theme is loss. Because of time, the two worlds are separated and only the immortal Persephone can move between them, leaving behind grief in each as she leaves for the other. Emblematically described as "the lily," Persephone is linked with flowers in her myth and in this poem. Just as the pale lily comes and goes from the underworld, so does the rose on earth suffer its "death and resurrection."

Muir is here outlining the tragic division between the two realities, by emphasizing its potential for loss and grief through an understatement addressed to Persephone:

> Surely all this can only be
> A light exchange and amorous interplay
> In your strange twofold immortality;
> And a diversion for a summer day
> The death and resurrection of the rose.

Implied in these lines is that for us, who are mortal and caught in time, the loss and division is not "light" or "amorous" or "a diversion." The rose, emblem of love and beauty, dies and reappears like Persephone, but we, caught in the constant process of time and its rhythms, cannot transcend this loss of love and beauty, even though its return is certain. The poem symbolizes the schizophrenia implicit in man, who, since the Fall, has been banished from the timeless world without being able to forget its possibility and perfection. "Song" meditates on the symbolic themes of time and the Fall, by presenting emblematically through the Persephone myth an intense lyrical awareness of loss through the passing of time. The semiformal wistfulness of the poem is achieved by its close, regular rhymescheme and the odd semi-regular pattern of trimeter, tetrameter and pentameter lines.

"Into Thirty Centuries Born" returns to the relationship between Story and Fable, leading to an apocalyptic vision of man's escape from time. The poem opens with an assertion of our being part of a timeless pattern, and uses the symbol of Troy as an example of the eternal present:

> Ilium burns before our eyes
> For thirty centuries never put out,
> And we walk the streets of Troy
> And breathe in the air its fabulous name.
> The king, the courtier and the rout
> Shall never perish in that flame;
> Old Priam shall become a boy
> For ever changed, for ever the same.

This is more than anti-historicism. Muir claims that the ancestral pattern, the Fable, which supports life, remains accessible through symbol and emblem. Time is static; myth and symbol, the realities of the imagination, are permanent.

The final achievement, according to this poem, lies in attaining the knowledge of "grief and joy," and passing beyond the encumbrance of emotion into a new reality. It is a symbolic dying into life before suffering and process can be transcended. This poem bears out the general theme of this volume, that reality comes only through acceptance of suffering as well as joy and that time can be defeated by man's redemption through pain, endurance, faith and belief in a transcendent pattern, just as, in poetry, time can be defeated by the successful resolution of opposing symbols or symbolic states. Above all, this poem shows again the inadequacy of the Story, which must become fused with the Fable if we are to redeem our fallen state and achieve what "religious people call Grace."

The sonnet "My Own," using the symbol of the journey and the road, again treats the possibilities of attaining "the true knowledge and the real power." The poem studies the evasions and self-deceptions of fallen man who becomes "lost in the dreaming route" instead of staying, undeceived, in touch with the wider reality he seeks. The soul turns away from the self-deception as the cowardly self, pretending to be on the right road, allows itself to be "willingly duped." The sonnet ends with regret. Because of the temptations and the self-indulgent delights of avoiding reality, truth has been lost even though "I might have stayed, unshaken, with my own." The Story tempts man to evade the responsibility of the Fable, but the poem is not pessimistic. There is a clear choice postulated, and truth is presented as a real possibility.

Technically, the poem cleverly reflects its theme of self-preoccupation through its rhyming. Six of the fourteen lines end with the word "me," thus hammering home the labyrinth of self-obsession which Muir is warning against. Further, these are all double rhymes — beguile me/defile me; deceive me/believe me; behave me/save me — which gives them a tremendous force in the poem's sound pattern. This poem again shows the importance of sound in Muir's poetry and the result of his struggle to master the techniques of lyric poetry. In his late work, the seeming effortlessness and quietness of the surface-texture mask, for the casual reader, the craftsmanship and mastery of technique.

Perhaps the most surprising omission from *Collected Poems* is the little 14-line poem "The Choice,"[54] a sonnet in its syntactical and intellectual structure, but with four-foot lines and an irregular rhyme-scheme. It is possible that Muir decided to omit the poem because of its rather uncharacteristic Auden-like astringency and its somewhat inflexible treatment of necessity at a time when his ideas were moving towards a much greater inclusiveness and a more generous attitude to human existence.

The poem's tenseness is impressive, heightened by the sentence-structure which divides the thought and the construction into sentences of eight, three and three lines:

> The prisoner wasting in the pit,
> The player bending over the strings,
> The wise man tangled in his wit,
> The angel grafted to his wings
> Are governed by necessity
> Condemned to be whatever they are
> Not once from that to move away,
> Each his appointed prisoner.

This conception of necessity is expressed in harsh, almost Calvinistic terms of total imprisonment and inability to escape from time and destiny.

The conclusion opposes this with the argued position that only through imprisoning necessity can man find liberty and escape from chaos. The abstract image of imprisonment is worked into an organically developed concrete metaphor:

> But the riddling sages say,
> It is your prison that sets you free,
> Else chaos would appropriate all.
> Out of chaos you built this wall,
> Raised this hovel of bone and clay
> To be a refuge for liberty.

The "hovel of bone and clay," inside the prison walls, is now the means of finding freedom and keeping chaos out. The sustained image is brilliant; the prison walls becoming a defence instead of a restriction, and carrying subdued reminders of the walls of Eden.

"The Choice" is a starkly presented view of man, sustained not by any originality of idea but by the running and expanding image, which perfectly contains the argument. Symbolism is here replaced by the tight local metaphorical construction which, in its own fairly narrow terms, must be considered a success.

One Foot in Eden ends with three short lyrics, which give a dissolving effect through their lyric beauty and emotional purity. "The Horses," with its drama and complexity, forms the natural climax to the volume. After that intensity, Muir concentrates on a mild, lyrical reinforcement of the implications of peace and rebirth contained in the volume as a whole.

Professor Butter is right to say that "The Late Wasp" and "The Late Swallow" "should be read together."[55] The poems, in effect, form two similar, but significantly different symbols, which, when allowed to act together draw meaning and feeling from each other, while at the same time each poem exists clearly and satisfactorily in its own right.

"The Late Wasp," another irregular sonnet, rhymed but metrically inconsistent, presents a movement downward into cold emptiness. The time is "the dying summer" and the wasp which previously, in its full strength, had fed from the year's fullness has grown old with the season. The movement of the poem is from heat, fullness and strength to coldness, thinness and oblivion; a process of ageing and diminishing power leading to emptiness and despair:

> ... the good air will not hold,
> All cracked and perished with the cold;
> And down you dive through nothing and through
>   despair.

The theme is spare and unassuring, but the understanding and empathy of the attitude and tone work against the pessimism implied in the stated treatment of death.

"The Late Swallow" presents a similar symbolic situation. One bird is left after the others have migrated south and the poet urges it to depart as the world is cold, "ageing" and "narrowing." But this poem concludes very differently from "The Late Wasp":

> Prepare;
> Shake out your pinions long untried
> That now must bear you there where you would be
> Through all the heavens of ice;
> Till falling down the homing air
> You light and perch upon the radiant tree.

Again the final image is of falling, but the swallow is achieving a symbolic "southern paradise" and is coming home, whereas the wasp simply passes into oblivion. The first poem works in terms of the journey (through the "avenues of the air") which ends in cold death, whereas the second presents the journey "Across the great earth's downward sloping side" followed by the arrival at a place outside the cold necessity of the winter world. The swallow has achieved an escape from the world to a higher reality. The wasp remains and is destroyed.

If we take the two poems as symbols for the process of ageing and dying, we can see that Muir is raising the question about the reality of death. Will it be a slow perishing followed by nothingness, or will it be a transformation into a longed-for, radiant world and a higher reality? The two conflicting symbols are allowed to live side by side and they provide no conceptual answer, but the energy of the Platonism in "The Late Swallow," where the soul as much as the bird is obviously being asked to use its "pinions long untried," and the sense of achieved finality in the migrant's arrival, add a strong dimension to the deliberately worldly, everyday surroundings of the first poem, with its "breakfast table" and "marmalade." The two poems are mirrors of the same process, but one stops, tragically incomplete, while the other achieves itself. Nearing seventy when he wrote these poems, Muir must have considered this process in terms of his own life, and the two poems seem to echo the spiritual progress he had made — from a thin, cold, inadequate state of uncertainty and breakdown to a belief in transcendence and the resolving power of symbol and faith, which convinced him of the existence of a higher reality into which the individual "Story" can become absorbed and fulfilled.

One Foot in Eden ends, appropriately, with a quietly spoken "Amen," a simple love poem entitled "Song," where Muir shows that the giving and taking of the love relationship leads to something wider:

> With it all must be well,
> There where the invisible
> Loom sweetly plies its trade.
> All made there is well-made
> So be it between us two;
> A giving be our taking,
> A making our unmaking,
> A doing what we undo.

The loose strands of the "Story" become woven together in the "Fable" where "all must be well" and in its pattern and appointed place.

This volume is remarkable not only for the high quality of the poetry but for its confirmation of the healing process. The symbols of Eden and harmony have defined themselves completely, and through them Muir has come to a state of reconciliation and acceptance, where the pressures of time, the Fall and the labyrinth no longer have the power to break down the intimations of grace. With these poems a spiritual, psychological and symbolic journey seems over and Muir has arrived at a place where he is fulfilled.

The movement from the tragic vision of *The Labyrinth* to the acceptance of *One Foot in Eden* may be loosely compared with the movement from Shakespeare's tragedies to his last plays, where the deceptions, evil motives, breakdown and disintegration become absorbed into a wider vision of redemption. In the tragedies, as in the poems of *The Labyrinth*, the symbols of disease, corruption and bestiality cruelly dominate the symbols of innocence and hope, but in *The Tempest*, *The Winter's Tale* and *Cymbeline*, this tragic vision, although still present as possibility, is ultimately defeated by the music of grace and regeneration. To achieve this symbolic healing, Shakespeare had to remove his last plays from actuality into a setting both of this world and beyond it, where magic is easily accepted, time and place are irrelevant, and the images of water, sleep, flowers and music saturate the texture and limit the tragic possibilities. Prospero, finally, has "pardoned the deceiver" and his ending will be despair unless "relieved by prayer."

In much the same way, Muir's symbolism can now include evil and suffering without being swamped by it. The potential tragedy inherent in man's tortured, fallen existence is transcended, and the symbols of harmony and forgiveness dominate the volume, even in the face of nuclear destruction. Like Shakespeare, Muir copes with actual evil by creating a symbolic world beyond actuality, and in that setting shows clearly and dramatically that the long symbolic battle is ultimately won by the powers of life and harmony.

Thus Muir has come to a state of psychological balance and integration. He has descended into the labyrinth and by doing so has been able to emerge beyond evil with a terrible knowledge but with a tested strength. The journey to this point of acceptance took him nearly seventy years of living and thirty-five years of writing, but only with this volume has his imagination and his use of symbolism been able to come to terms with the extremes of experience and attain the full personal possession of the pattern he had long known from his time in Orkney and from the symbols of his unconscious. *One Foot in Eden* is a personal victory as well as a poetic one. Muir has learned to celebrate all experience and to look beyond the prison of the self into "the clear eternal weather," which releases man from the tragedy of the Fall. This is not "religious" poetry in the narrow sense; rather it celebrates the depths and possibilities of man's spiritual identity, and, by its symbolist method, not only describes but creates the realities of that identity which are shown dramatically to be stronger than any forces of destruction which threaten it.

CHAPTER SIX

Last Poems

One Foot in Eden was the last volume of poetry that Muir published, and, in a very real sense, it marked the end of a journey. Muir had found a mature poetic technique which wonderfully expressed the spiritual synthesis he had arrived at. In the last years of his life, he had reached, through the conflict and resolution of symbol, a visionary, even mystical, position of acceptance, and the poetry of *One Foot in Eden* is Muir's expression of a final compatibility between the primary elements in his experience. He forgot none of the pain and tragedy which had undermined his life and his art in the late 1940's, but was able to absorb this into an inclusive vision of pattern and flux, always modified and sustained by the knowledge of a higher reality. A personal healing process has been completed with the acceptance by Muir of the fact that suffering is inevitable when one is human and that it is, ultimately, a means by which man can see more clearly and come to a meaningful knowledge of good and evil and the forces which shape life. His final acceptance is never escapist, as he can never omit from his vision the knowledge of tragedy, evil and the Fall, but the serenity and radiance of the achieved vision is fuller and richer for including this knowledge and transcending it.

So, in his last poems, we still find strong intimations of fear and evil, but often more universally imagined, in terms of war and political realities. With the inner conflicts resolved, Muir was able to bring to bear the experience of his own journey through the labyrinth of time and suffering to the suffering of a tragic world which, with its oppressions, sterilities, and the constant threat of annihilation, was still struggling in the labyrinth of evil.

There is, understandably, less unity in these last poems. The first twenty-two were published in various places or sent, in final form, to his publishers. The next six were found in typescript among his papers, and the last few poems had to be constructed from manuscript after his death. The poems were written in America and in Swaffham Prior, near Cambridge, where the poet spent his last years, which seem to have been happy and quiet, and mercifully free from the stresses of politics which had so exhausted him at Newbattle. He spent the summer of 1956 in Orkney, which gave him enormous pleasure, and put him in touch again with the landscape and people of his childhood, and the most important generating source of his symbols. The darkness and premonition of disaster which appear in many of his last poems certainly do not derive from his experience of these peaceful few years, but from his passionate awareness of the plight of others who had not attained the peace and fulfilment he had strugged all his life to reach. These poems have the unmistakable authority of an observer who has personally lived through the experiences he is describing and in whom the terrible, yet joyful, knowledge is still fresh and present.

"The Song" is one of Muir's most interesting poems. It is, I believe, the most completely symbolist poem he wrote, in which he pushed his technique to the limit with dramatic effect. Not only does the poem use dream material — like "The Combat" it seems to derive mainly from the unconscious — but it departs from Muir's own developed system of symbols. As with all his great symbolist poems, "The Song" dislocates the tense sequence and moves disturbingly through various levels of dream-experience and actuality, transcending normal time and space. But this poem goes further. It remains unlocated within myth, biography or any known symbology — a fact which allows the symbolism to move freely and to attain an almost musical state of non-conceptuality. The poem comments on itself as it proceeds, creating its own meanings as it develops, disintegrating, resolving and confirming itself purely in its own terms, and in its own time and space. In this way, "The Song" becomes a self-enclosed, non-referential act, feeding on itself, using the ambiguities of tense to drive the reader from line to line through the time of the poem. The poem has the elusive yet strongly dramatic quality of the dream it describes, its strange tone being largely the result of its rejection of rational, propositional thought. What seems to be a logical development is, on closer examination, merely pseudo-logic, as the vision is far too wide and intense to be contained or shaped by logic. In fact the only controlling elements in "The Song" are the tense-shifts and the metrical pattern. Muir simply allows the dream symbols to present and then exhaust themselves, whereas in most of his other deeply symbolistic poems, he has had the framework of a myth to help him shape the symbolic progression with a given set of at least partially referential points.

The core of this poem is a dream of a fabulous creature, a symbol from somewhere else invading reality and bearing witness to a huge anguish, a "wound in the world's side," before it leaves. But this vision of the creature is complicated by the observing "I" of the poem, whose witness is recorded. The opening lines of the poem distort time and reality, as a necessary pre-requisite for the introduction of the beast-symbol:

> I was haunted *all that day by memories* knocking
> At a disused, deaf, dead door of my mind
> Sealed up *for forty years* by myself and time.
> They could not get to me nor I to them.
> And yet they knocked.   And since I could not answer,
> *Since time was past* for that sole assignation,
> I was oppressed by the unspoken thought
> *That they and I were not contemporary,*
> *For I had gone away.   Yet still in dreams*
> *Where all is changed,* time, place, identity,
> Where fables turn to beasts and beasts to fables,
> And anything can be in a natural wonder,
> These meetings are renewed, dead dialogues
> Utter their antique speech.
>   *That night I dreamed*
> That towards the end of *such another day*
> Spent in such thoughts, but *in some other place,*
> I was returning from a long day's work —
> *What work I have forgotten* — and had to cross
> A park *lost somewhere in the world,* yet now
> Present and whole to me as I to it:

(my italics)

This shows the deliberate attempt by Muir to confuse the time and space of the experience and remove it from the exigencies of logic. The experience seems relevant to the poet's own years in Glasgow and London, when the harmony and order of his childhood were so fiercely undermined and he was cut off from the "memories knocking" until his psycho-analysis released the visions of his unconscious.

Also in these lines, we see a celebration of dream and archetype, which is ultimately a description of Muir's own art. When the unconscious is admitted " ... fables turn to beasts and beasts to fables,/And anything can be in a natural wonder. . . . " These lines adumbrate the dream of the beast and lie at the heart of the poem's symbolism, where every day reality is penetrated by forces from outside our time and place. These forces can be fabulous and harmonious, like the archteypal intimations of order in dreams, or, like the beast, bearers of a sickening knowledge of pain and helplessness.

The poem continues with the dream of the great creature, come into suburbia like some monster in a science-fiction film:

> . . . from the park poured out the resonant moaning
> Of some great beast in anguish.   Could it be
> For us, *I wondered dreaming*, the strange beast
>   mourned,
> Or for some deed *once done and done for ever*
> And done in vain?

> (my italics)

Again the words "I wondered dreaming" allow the poem to move simultaneously on two levels, commenting on the dream as it is being recorded. For the dreamer, the experience removes him from reality:

> . . . or had I strayed
> Into some place forgotten in old time?
> The dream worked on. . . .

The symbolic beast is enormous, like a cliff, and strange beyond description:

> As heavy as earth it stood and mourned alone,
> Horse, or centaur, or wide-winged Pegasus,
> But far too strange for any fabulous name.

The creature's presence and its enormous private grief impinge upon the dreamer who runs " . . . lest the thing should move/And come to me. . . . " but remains listening to the "long breath drawn by pain, intolerable."

The poem arrives at an emotional climax as the creature moves in a strange combination of gentleness, holiness and brute strength:

> I thought, now it will move.   And then it moved.
> The moaning ceased, the hoofs rose up and fell
> Gently, as treading out a meditation,
> Then broke in thunder; the wild thing charged the
>   gate,
> Yet could not pass — oh pity! — that simple barrier
> (subservient to any common touch),

> Turned back again in absolute overthrow,
> And beat on the ground as if for entrance there.
> The dream worked on. The clamour died; the hoofs
> Beat on no common ground; silence; a drumming
> As of wild swans taking their highway south
> From the murdering ice; hoofs, wings far overhead
> Climbing the sky; pain raised that wonder there;
> Nothing but pain. The drumming died away.

These remarkable lines combine dream narrative with comment on the narrative. The unreality of the scene is magnified and echoed by the distorted syntax of the penultimate sentence as the bulk of the great beast dissolves into nothing more than a distant sound, like birds' wings, and then into silence. The only remaining certainty for the observer is that " . . . pain raised that wonder there;/Nothing but pain."

The poem concludes with twelve lines which question the significance of the beast and the vision of pain. Muir returns us to the opening of the poem, where the dreamer is haunted by "memories knocking" which cannot enter the "dead door of my mind." Now questions are posed:

> Was it these hoofs, I thought, that knocked all day
> With no articulate message, but this vision
> That had no tongue to speak its mystery?
> What wound in the world's side and we unknowing
> Lay open and bleeding now? What present anguish
> Drew that long dirge from the earth-haunting marvel?
> And why that earthly visit, unearthly pain?
> I was not dreaming now, but thinking the dream.

These lines make clear the pain and suffering embodied in the vision, while remaining through their questioning, completely non-didactic. There are no words to explain this experience; the words of "The Song" are events in themselves, not descriptive of events, and the vision creates and destroys its own existence without outside reference.

The last few lines, though still a report of the dream, bring us one step closer to reality:

> Then all was quiet, the park was its own again,
> And I on my road to my familiar lodgings
> A world away; and all its poor own again.
> Yet I woke up saying, 'The song — the song'.

The final note is of celebration. The dream, so full of pain and fear, has been reduced, finally, to the only spoken words in the poem — " 'The song — the song'." The cry of anguish, the thunder of the hoofs, the drumming wings are all included here as the dream-experience is translated into language. The vision is accepted with joy by the conscious mind which had previously been "disused, deaf, dead" and "sealed up," and a process of liberation and transformation is complete.

The symbolism of "The Song" does not allow of any definitive interpretation. Quite clearly, however, the poem presents a process which leaves the narrating human-being altered in some significant way through the working on his mind of the great creature. The blocked mind, rejecting memory and any healing contact with a wider reality, can finally admit and transcend both the knowledge of pain and suffering and the existence of a reality beyond the time and place of the park, the lodging-houses and the city. On one level, the poem merely recounts a bizarre dream, but the symbolism insists on wider meanings, however unlocated. Firstly, the poem is a discussion of the making of poetry, which celebrates unconscious realities, which it can penetrate to give meaning and to enlarge experience. When open to these forces of dream and symbol, the poetic imagination can "turn . . . beasts to fables." And the organic structural device of the poem, where the dream is both enacted and discussed, itself symbolizes the act of poetic creation, with the "I" of the poem fusing the problems of "thinking the dream" and turning a one-dimensioned drab, blocked actuality into an all-embracing cry of "The song — the song." To achieve this, suffering and pain, so strong as to terrify the creator, must be seen, felt, understood and accepted; only then will the subsequent perception of reality be free and mature enough to create "the song."

It is difficult not to see references to Muir's own psychological journey here. This symbolic movement — from blockage and neurosis, through vision and intense suffering to a final acceptance, balance and serenity — is the process Muir lived through. The stages correspond closely to his deep neurosis in Glasgow, the release of memory, vision and symbol through psycho-analysis, the slow but urgent coming to terms with evil and suffering in Prague and the final transcending vision, attaining a reality both higher than and yet including the reality of his life, which we have seen demonstrated in the poems of *One Foot in Eden*. This poem is the symbolic record of the breakthrough of a human mind, released from sterility and neurosis by dream, vision and knowledge into a state of balance and celebration.

It is possible, too, to feel a subdued Christian element in "The Song." The living thing from a higher world come to this earth to bring understanding of a wider purpose and pattern is seen suffering intensely, as if bearing the whole world's pain. As in the Christ story, the great powers are not allowed to prevail in order to release it from suffering. Here a simple park gate "defeats" the huge animal, just as a wooden cross "defeats" Christ, as it kicks perhaps at the gate of Eden. Here, too, following the agony, there is a mysterious rising from the world as the creature returns to its place of origin, and what is left is pain transformed into song.

The symbolism cannot be made to bear, exclusively, any one of these interpretations without mortally restricting it. It reverberates and moves too deeply and freely to be fixed in any way. But we can see from this poem how, through the symbolist method, Muir came to see his own experience as archetypal and deeply meaningful. The processes of liberation through poetry and the imagination, through psychological balance and through mystical and religious sources all merge into one great utterance about the possibilities of man's defying the Fall, with its implicit weight of pain and frustration, and achieving a transcendental vision which liberates him and brings him closer to his true nature. This journey dominates Muir's imagination, and in no other poem does he treat it so inclusively and with such a perfectly resolved tension between the experience he himself lived through and the universal experience he knew was common to all men.

"The Song" is one of Muir's best poems and one central to an understanding of his mind and his technique. Here he approaches the full symbolist method more closely than in any other poem, which gives him a freedom he seldom allows himself. It can be argued that true symbolist poetry requires the elocutionary disappearance of the poet, which only partially occurs here, but in every other sense — the illusion of logic, the dislocated tense-sequence, the time/space, dream/reality confusion, the description of itself as it progresses, the discussion of the writing of poetry, the approach to the condition of music, the active use of syntax — "The Song" fully embodies symbolist technique. And it is only through the full use of this technique that Muir is able to enact, in such all-inclusive richness, the vital human process of the preservation and integration of the self, and the intimations of a redemptive pattern of coherence.

It is remarkable that, nearing seventy and in failing health, Muir was able to extend his poetic achievement through this new, dynamic use of symbolist technique. The last poems are amazingly eclectic and full of new technical experiment, showing a genuine progression from the earlier poems, without any loss of intensity. The poet feared that he was repeating himself, but this was not so. In a letter he wrote:

I've been rather daunted in the last year or two by the fear that I am keeping on writing the same poem, and I fancy that it has inhibited (horrid word) the flow. I have written very few poems lately, but many parts of poems which ceased when they seemed to be taking the same old course.[1]

In one sense, of course, Muir was right. As a visionary poet, his creative life was obsessed with expressing his vision, and his individual poems may be seen as pieces which together make up one great, revelatory pattern. But his diffidence is not justified, as the technical innovation and the wide range of these last poems ensure that they are not repetitive in any easy sense.

"Images," as well as "The Song," illustrates this perfectly. "Images," first published in 1955, is really three separate poems with no apparent logical connection. Again Muir extends his method so far that we are forced to abandon any attempt to interpret the poem logically or to refer it to external points of reference. The poem describes images of permanence, the symbols which transcend time, the act of creation by which the artist captures these symbols and the tension between art and reality. Like "The Song," the poem may be seen, on one level, as autobiographical; a record of how Muir himself has managed to transcend time and suffering through an active and creative use of symbol, but the poem is clearly more than this.

The first section is deeply symbolist in method, in that it uses symbol and syntax to describe symbol and syntax and their place in the creative act. The heart of the poem is a symbolic face, which is not identified, which is "the face of life" confronting man and which man must try and describe and recreate. The face is the source of knowledge, like Keats' Moneta, and also the mystery of timelessness in art. The first lines again remind us of Keats:

186

Take one look at that face and go your way.
Regard these lines of motionless desire
Perpetually assuaged yet unappeased,
Still yearning for what still is about to be.
What you see there is something else than beauty.

Like the figures on the urn, the face contains the timeless stillness of
art, which, in order to defeat time, has to forego movement and
remain, in one sense, "unappeased." Through a brilliant, instinctive
transition, Muir turns the lines of the face into his lines of poetry, as
he goes on to warn of the inability of mere syntax and language to
recreate the felt knowledge of the face. Simultaneously, he uses his
own syntax to embody what he is saying about it:

Look once.   But do not hope to find a sentence
To tell what you have seen.   Stop at the colon:
And set a silence after to speak the word
That you will always seek and never find,
Perhaps, if found, the good and beautiful end.
You will not reach that place.   So leave the hiatus
There in the broken sentence.   What is missing
You will always think of.

This poetry is purely symbolist, describing itself and commenting on
itself, using syntax as expressive agent, confusing present and future
tenses, allowing the meaning to create itself as it progresses, being
concerned with the creation of art. We can also see here, barely
submerged, Muir's obsessive symbolism of the road and the journey,
of the impossibility of achieving perfection in this life. The poet
continues with a warning about the attainment of symbolic truth.
The face — the poetic symbol — must be seen quickly and then
released, but it must not be contaminated by the individual observer.
Although one glance at truth is never enough for man to know it,
any further contact will interfere with its self-sufficiency:

And do not turn again
To scan the face lest you should leave upon it
Your personal load of trouble and desire.

This image of the broken sentence is continued to the end by the use
of "postscript" and "limping sentence," and the mystery and value
of the face is emphasized by the last line. This first section is about
the symbolist poet's use of symbol to attain vision and knowledge. It
is about Muir's own poetic method, and it reasserts the existence of
two places of reality which must be joined — by art and symbol —

before "the good and beautiful" vision can be experienced. But, more than this, the poem *embodies*, in its syntax and symbolism, the very activity it discusses, the time-locked human-being trying, through symbol and language, to incarnate, in a permanent form, the intimation of truth he has gleaned from his occasional glimpses of a higher world of meaning.

The second section again uses syntax for vital expressive effect. Its eighteen lines are contained in one sentence, slowly unravelling itself through fear and inadequacy to an ordered conclusion. Again we have the reference to Muir's familiar symbolism of the journey and the labyrinth, the more autobiographical indications in the symbolic movement from psychological disturbance to an achieved stillness and balance beyond time and space. The poem describes the artist and how he must forge serenity and song out of the chaos of often desperate experience. The opening lines show the psychological labyrinth, but the poem is deliberately freed from referential possibility by the insistence that the labyrinth, or wood, "has no place but in your mind," and the mind-breaking terrors are never specified.

The process of the artist, from this point, is towards blindness from which comes vision and prophecy as he joins "blind Tiresias." From this point experience is seen and felt clearly and becomes capable of transmutation:

> You look in wonder at the bird,
> Round ball of appetite and fear,
> That sings at ease upon the branch,
> Time a long silence in its ear
> That never heard of time or space;
> You who hear the avalanche
> Must fabricate a temporal tale
> To bring the timeless nightingale
> And swallow to your trysting place.

The poetic symbol of the bird is free of time and space. The artist must create in order to bring that timelessness and permanence into this life. Once more, we can see that Muir is describing his own poetic method. The poem celebrates Romantic and symbolist theories of poetry by its implied movement into the world of imagination, whence derive inspiration, image and symbol.

The third section again deals with the poetic symbol, itself symbolized here as a little god, weaving, teasingly, through time and space, perfectly free in his magic powers. There is no human presence in this poem; no poet addressing or being addressed; no hint of autobiography. The god, or symbol, is allowed to dominate, as Muir presents its possibilities and healing powers. The tone is lighter. Like the god it is "little, sly, absconding," full of childish wryness as if, in fact the poet were reading a fairy-story to a child:

> He is the little, sly, absconding god,
> Hides in the moment.   Look and he is gone,
> But turn away, and there he is back again.
> He is more quick than movement,
> Present and gone, absent and safe in hiding,
> No spell can bind him.

Just as, in the first poem, the face could not be contained in language, so this god cannot be found in time, as he "Hides in the moment." He is not available to those who are over-seriously involved in time and time's things, or who have lost innocence of imagination:

> But idle fools and children
> Take him for granted, are at their ease with him,
> And he's the true friend of the absentminded.

These lines are followed by a great symbolist statement:

> He is too agile for time's dull iambics,
> Lightly dives in and out of stale duration,
> Poised on the endless present.   There he is free,
> Having no past or future.

This is a justification of the symbolist technique as a valid means of defeating time and space. The "endless present" — the condition of music — is achieved only by the free symbol. The line "He is too agile for time's dull iambics" refers us back to the first section of "Images" and its discussion of the inadequacy of syntax and language to capture the whole truth. The poem ends with an assertion of value, modified by the sly tone:

> All things know him.
> And then are eased as by a heavenly chance.
> The greater gods sometimes in grave amusement
> Smile at his tricks, yet nod in approbation.

The symbol unites all things and brings healing and restoration to the fallen world of time and place. The "greater gods" — the symbols of universal order and meaning higher even than art and the

189

human act of creation — approve, amusedly, of the elusive thing which men can never wholly grasp.

Thus the three poems are really one. In each section Muir is directly concerned with the possibilities and limitations of art as a means of apprehending reality. The poetic symbol, seen in turn as the face full of knowledge, the eternal singing bird and the little god, can and does bridge the distance between this world and a higher one, but, because of our limitations in time and space, the gap remains. Visions of true reality are temporary and fleeting because we have only "time's dull iambics" in which to embody our glimpses of eternity, and yet these "images" which transcend time and space are vital to us, bestowing visionary and healing qualities. This poem is a beautifully constructed celebration of the transcendental powers of the creative act. Only through symbol and syntax can Muir describe the limitations and possibilities of symbol and syntax with such density, conviction and tonal variety. "Images" is a justification and explanation of Muir's use of freely-moving, non-anchored symbols (like the great creature in "The Song") as instruments which link time to eternity and which, in so doing, bring balance and integration to the confused, disoriented psyche of fallen man.

The technical control of the sustained images in each section and the remarkable integral expressiveness of the syntax are enhanced by the metrical virtuosity. The first and third sections use a blank pentameter line, with subtle, non-iambic variations, whereas the one long sentence of the second section is controlled and modulated by rhymed, four-foot lines. Two examples of Muir's expressive and organic use of metre can be seen in the third section. Of the fifteen lines, only one is not of five-feet: "He is more quick than movement," where the missing two stresses and three syllables embody the sense of the line. The god is too quick even for the movement of the line and its established space and time. This truncating of the pattern of expectancy makes the reader stop, ironically after the word "movement," thus allowing the poem to actually embody the "Present and gone" quality of the god's flitting in and out of time and place.

A further example is of Muir's almost humourous use of the discrepancy between content and metre in the line "He is too agile for time's dull iambics." We would probably scan the line

x x / / | x x / / | x / | x

which is about as far as a poet can get from "dull iambics" in a pentameter line. The metrics fracture the iambic line just as strongly as the agile god escapes from the pattern of normal time.

After such complex symbolist poems as "The Song" and "Images," the little song "Complaint of the Dying Peasantry" reverts to a non-symbolist simplicity. Its theme is closely related to that of the first Harvard lecture which Muir gave and in which he analyses the traditional and natural possession of song and ballad by whole communities and contrasts this with the contemporary situation. Muir recalls that in Orkney:

We had a great number of ballads and songs which had been handed down from generation to generation. These, sometimes with the airs traditionally belonging to them, were known in all the farms; there must have been hundreds of them. They were part of our life, all the more because we knew them by heart, and had not acquired but inherited them. They were not contemporary in any sense, but entered our present from the past.[2]

"Complaint of the Dying Peasantry" is a rather bitter elegy for the world of the peasant community and its spontaneous poetry, but, unlike the Harvard lectures, it does not develop Muir's arguments about the mass-media and technology, and, as a result, stands too boldly and sentimentally for a romanticized past.

We can understand this elegy for a lost, archaic way of life, which Muir knew as a boy, and we can agree, partially, that the collecting and printing of the creative, collective art-form of the ballad, by such as Scott and Hogg, killed its vitality. We can accede, in part, to the vision of deadness and lost values in our world of instant communication and urbanization. But, as the poem stands, we must feel that such simplified and selective anti-historicism is naive to a fault. This vision of a lost Eden, presented in such purely nostalgic, sociological terms, does little justice to Muir's thought, and clearly demonstrates the inadequacy of a non-symbolist approach in interpreting experience which itself is symbolic and which derives from symbol.

The same inadequacy may be seen in the two poems directly about America: "The Church" and "Salem, Massachusetts." Both poems are over-descriptive, and suffer from a thinness of texture and a flatness of tone, as if the poet were standing too far away from his creation. One feels that this is not his style, nor his material, and a comparison of "The Church" with Philip Larkin's "Church Going," or "Salem, Massachusetts" with Robert Lowell's "A Quaker Graveyard in Nantucket" — poems which relate fairly closely in theme — will show the unmistakable inferiority of Muir's poems.

The sense of some vital missing ingredient in the poems can possibly be explained by Muir's feeling of rootlessness while he was in the United States. In a letter from America to Kathleen Raine, he wrote:

I know I have been writing some very queer poetry since I came, with a good deal of new horror in it; why, Heaven alone knows, for everyone here has been extraordinarily kind, and considerate at the same time. But I am not at home here. . . . I was far more at home in Italy. . . . I want the landscape, the soil . . . things shaped by generations with affection and made into a human scene. I shall try to get up to Orkney this summer if it can be managed at all. I suppose what is wrong with me here is I am hungry. Horrible thought: I don't know whether Eden was ever here.[3]

This sense of the deprivation of Eden, of the loss of contact with the landscape, is apparent in the two poems. America left his imagination unmoved and threw up no symbols by which Muir could penetrate into the deeper and more rewarding areas of his apprehension of life.

Professor Butter claims that the next poem "After a Hypothetical War" "was probably written in America,"[4] and, if this is the case, it would explain Muir's remark about his poetry having "a good deal of new horror in it." The poem is deeply pessimistic. In "The Horses," we have seen how the survivors of nuclear war tenatively establish new relationships with the horses as the first stage in the development of a new order, but in "After A Hypothetical War" there are neither horses nor any symbolic messengers of hope. Post-atomic existence here is a terrible mixture of selfishness, greed, sterility of nature, overthrow of law, unnatural mutations, infection — in short it is a complete collapse or order and of those patterns and values which make human life bearable. Never has Muir evoked so terrible a picture of distorted life and hell on earth without a balancing, conflicting symbol to impose or at least intimate some sort of order. Here is chaos and distortion with "no rule nor ruler" in a world of "water and clay," of drought, famine, murder and encroaching mud. There is a desperate sense of inevitability in the poem, combined with intensely realized depictions of twisted humanity and addled nature:

Chaotic breed of misbegotten things,
Embryos of what could never wish to be.
Soil and air breed crookedly here, and men
Are dumb and twisted as the envious scrub
That spreads in silent malice on the fields.
Lost lands infected by an enmity
Deeper than lust or greed, that works by stealth
Yet in the sun is helpless as the blindworm,
Making bad worse.   The mud has sucked half in
People and cattle until they eat and breathe
Nothing but mud.

This is the essence of chaos, with infection having undermined the
very springs of life and the process of breeding. There is no chance
of release:

> ... Poor tribe so meanly cheated,
> Their very cradle an image of the grave.
> What rule or governance can save them now?

This terrible vision of a ruined world is softened only by its being
projected into the future as a hypothesis, though Muir writes in the
present tense to give dramatic immediacy. The poem is a warning of
the possibilities of universal breakdown, but still outside the pattern
of Muir's own symbolic journey. It is written by a man whose own
psychological integration has been achieved by his ability to encompass the worst of evil. The self remains more detached from this
poem than in "The Horses," where the symbol-conflict reflects the
psychological struggle towards assimilation. For this reason, "The
Horses" is a greater poem, as it includes within its symbolic structure
much more of human experience. "After A Hypothetical War"
presents just one symbol — the shattered landscape and its broken
humanity — and this precludes further development through interpenetration of symbol.

"The Conqueror," a gentle rhyming lyric, returns to the kind of
emblematic imagery of Muir's middle-period poetry. The proud,
armoured conqueror rides out from a cloud and proudly surveys the
world he is going to capture. But something makes him hesitate —
perhaps "the little roads" — and defeated, he sinks back into his
cloud.

This little symbolic situation is unpretentious, and relates to man's
journey on "the little roads." Like conquerors, until we see the journey we must make, we plan to turn the world to our own uses and

advantages. But the world and the journey through it imply fear for fallen man and to conquer the world demands courage beyond the mere panoply of heraldic eternal glory and inner pride.

The poem is beautifully constructed. Its two stanzas reflect the proud advance of the conqueror and then his quiet retreat. In the first line he emerges from the cloud and in the last he returns to it, changed, in the poem's language, as well as psychologically, from the hard, proud, metallic warrior knight to something ethereal and insubstantial as "the soft cloud drank him in again."

The same metrical pattern and stanza form is used in "An Island Tale," but with more effect. One of Muir's most beautiful lyrics, the poem is filled with a quiet elegiac acceptance of mortality and a poignant awareness of the workings of time.

An old lady dies on an island — perhaps in Orkney — and becomes the subject of a local ballad which celebrates the love and grief which "became her well." The poem, written from the viewpoint of the watchers at her death, rejects this simplicity by its insistence on the human reality of the event and the tragedy of time and death which work on beauty and life.

The first two stanzas of "An Island Tale" achieve, through sound and tone, a great tenderness. The gravity and utter simplicity of language and feeling, the overwhelming sense of dissolution, ensure a powerful basic identification with the dying woman, which is essential for the ultimate success of the poem:

> She had endured so long a grief
> That from her breast we saw it grow,
> Branch, leaf and flower with such a grace
> We wondered at the summer place
> Which set that harvest there. But oh
> The softly, softly yellowing leaf.

These lines have a simplicity and an immense compassion for humanity caught in time. They are, seemingly, effortless, but this is an earned ability, perhaps possible only when the personality of the poet himself has emerged from suffering and a sense of tragedy, and when this knowledge is allied to an unerring formal and technical instinct. "An Island Tale" is one of Muir's most universal, timeless poems. What it lacks in size, range and ambition, it gains in purity and intensity of feeling, in its knowledge of the potencies of growth and decay, and in its quiet humble reduction of complexity into basic felt knowledge. The last question of the poem, which could so

easily have been trite, attains, through the intense lyric build-up, a
complex weight of significance:

> They sing her ballad yet,
> But all the simple verses tell
> Is, Love and grief became her well.
> Too well;   for how can we forget
> Her happy face when she was young?

The six-line tetrameter stanzas, rhymed *a b c c b a,* combine the
rich close harmony of the central couplet with the moving, separated,
more tentative rhymes of the first and last lines, giving each stanza
a slow growth to a point followed by a diminuendo effect, as sound
and sense fall away and, faintly echoing, dissolve.

"After 1984" and "The Strange Return" return to Muir's more
usual symbolic territory, dealing with man's potential and actual
release from hell into new forms of creative life. The confidence and
serenity of his late work were not achieved by closing off his darkest
vision, but by remaining open to it and transcending it by showing
movement through and beyond it; the process he himself had had to
undergo. In this way, the late poems are both deeply personal and
strangely objective. The poet's "I" remains outside their structure
and yet the symbolic movement is certainly derived from his own
journey. In these poems, the Story and the Fable, reality and symbol,
time and eternity, the labyrinth and Eden, are triumphantly and
creatively shown to be inseparable, thus affirming that individual
man is part of something meaningful and universal beyond his own
limited space and time. Always lying behind this vision is the related
symbolism of time and the Fall; the movement or journey from one
state to another with man dragged back by evil while striving to
attain the transfiguration which, as Muir's poetry and experience
develop, becomes more possible. The obvious danger is that the
poetry will become obsessively allegorical, even programmatic, but
such is Edwin Muir's imaginative power and the creative possibility
of his symbolism that the poems remain concrete, the symbols continue to develop and each poem achieves its own fully realized
individuality.

"After 1984," for example, attacks once more a theme which is
familiar, but the poem is in no way repetitive. Set far in the future,
it looks back through the eyes of a group of old men who are survivors of some unspecified vast event which dramaticaly altered

their lives. The title is well chosen. Orwell's *1984*, with its vision of men controlled and dehumanized, is the world in which the old men were brought up before the revolutionary day "That drove the murdering lies away." The old totalitarian society is deftly sketched. It was a world of total repression, where the things which make life human had been destroyed, and where there was no hope. In this version of the labyrinth, men were

> Shut from ourselves even in our mind;
> Only a twisting chaos within
> Turned on itself, not knowing where
> The exit was, salvation gate.

It is a picture of emptiness and spiritual nihilism, where people have been reduced as far as possible. It is not difficult to relate it to the political terrors of 1939-45 and 1948 in Prague, and the state of almost catatonic trance, of hopeless withdrawal, is very similar to Muir's state in Cambridge after his return from Prague.

Against this version of 1984, Edwin Muir places the picture of the society beyond 1984, after the revolutionary day which changed everything. This event is left vague. The old men still cannot understand it and regard it as a miracle or perhaps an accident. The new life represents salvation and a settled community life, but most remarkable is that the liberation is a familiar thing; a reversion to life before 1984, in fact to normal social reality:

> Then we fought
> On to this life that was before,
> Only that, no less, no more,
> Strangely familiar.   In the Nought
> Did we beget it in our thought?

The basis of their wonder is probably more religious than political; it is allied to their sense of the spiritual qualities involved in this miraculous rebirth of a dead past, and the new sense of connection and creative vitality (the children in stanza one) that accompanies it. Thus the poem celebrates ordinary social and spiritual life, which is apprehended as an order in which men can discover and fulfil themselves. In the face of total loss of liberty and the worst kind of dehumanizing oppression, Muir is suggesting, there is something in man which will conquer and survive.

"After 1984" can be read as a political poem; a symbolic re-enactment of Muir's own spiritual renaissance; a poetic patterning of the Fall, the labyrinth and man's ability to escape; a meditation on chance and purpose in history; a science-fiction prophecy. The poem's expressiveness and resonance derive from the two opposing visions of human life, which create a tone of positive, wondering acceptance, deepened by questioning and an only half-submerged recollection of the great possibilities for destruction and anarchy with which man must always contend. Here, the positive defeat of evil is tempered, too, by the question mark at the end of the poem and by the feeling of being poised throughout on the edge of an experience which is near the limits of human understanding.

Technically, the rhymed and loosely accentual tetrameters, forming irregular paragraphs, provide a relaxed vehicle for the mutterings and subdued meditations of the old men. The poem is appropriately low-toned and casual, although the metrical regularity and the rhyming keep a firm control over the rather abstract language. The poet's technical confidence may be gauged by his almost playful use of the two archaisms "manumitted" (released) and "widdershins" (wrong way), which, placed against the magnitude of theme and the striving for clarity and explanation, add a relieving tonal dimension.

"The Strange Return" seems to spring from the same imaginative root as "After 1984," being concerned with the same miraculous, unspecified release from bondage and the wondering discovery and awareness of a new free existence. Whereas "After 1984" deals with this shift of state largely in terms of time, seized through memory, "The Strange Return" approaches the theme through images of space. Here the time, although written in the past tense, is the dramatic moment immediately after release, as the man moves away from Hell and its prison towers, out into a symbolic land. We are again made to apprehend experience by a journey through a universal landscape, removed from the exigencies of particular detail or recognizable referential points of focus:

> Behind him Hell sank in the plain.
> Of burning somewhere.   That was all
> He saw far off the liquid glaze
> A burning there or in his brain?
> He could not tell . . .

It is not accidental that the opening lines present a sense of spatial disorientation. Hell sinks into the landscape; the burning is "liquid," imprecisely "somewhere," perhaps even inside his brain and not in the landscape at all. His very existence there "put all Hell in doubt" and puts in doubt the physical reality of the scene. He is somewhere "half-way from Heaven to Hell," but even this might be "a dream of stone." This brilliantly imagined state of semi-solid, semi-concrete place and experience is much more symbolist than the treatment of the theme in "After 1984." Is it real or a dream? "No matter," Muir says. He is establishing a structure of symbol and a state of mind, helped by the syntax. The first twelve lines contain nine sentences, three of which are direct questions, which embody the ambiguity of the experience by their own uncertainty and lack of sustained vitality and express a disordered experience in terms of a dislocated functioning. The rhyme, too, reinforces this lack of confidence by its irregularity and lack of pattern.

The poem continues more fluently as the escapee's mind starts to question more seriously his strange predicament. Still conditioned, Hell following him like his footprints on the sand, he cannot grasp freedom and remains disorientated and suspicious.

The second section of the poem deals expressly with his coming to terms with the full range of human experience, and especially with the perplexing problems of evil which he begins to remember:

> ... how could he counter these,
> Make friends with the evils, take his part,
> Salute the outer and inner strife,
> The bickering between doubt and faith,
> Inherit the tangle he had left,
> Outface the trembling at his heart?

These questions form the core of the poem. As in "After 1984," the strange and new reality is the ordinary world he had known before his imprisonment in Hell, but now it has to be seen and dealt with again, with all its complexities and evil, before full humanity can come. The details of this passage are somewhat reminiscent of Muir's reaction to the complexities of Glasgow. They have the tone, too, of the bewildered wonder seemingly felt by newly released long-term prisoners or patients, and perhaps felt by those in a society after a revolution, forced to interpret social and spiritual life in a new context.

The poem concludes with an affirmation as the fear and trembling is overcome by the sight of a flowering tree and the man is suddenly possessed with his humanity once again, the "desire" which had been destroyed in him in Hell. He accepts the world, finally, with all its contradictions, and by doing so, accepts his own identity and his place in it. The deliberate echo of Genesis in the last line emphasizes the symbolic new creation, the rebirth into the world, the finding of form and shape after chaos. The vague liquid dream-like landscape of the opening lines has now moved into a sharp precise singular thing; "a little tree" putting out "in pain a single bud." Vision, reality, hardness have been restored to the poem's language and landscape as well as to the man's understanding. The emergence from Hell is complete as perception and emotional response sharpen and focus, and the long list of questions falls away leaving the strongly assertive statements of the last six lines. Caught in time, "half-way from Heaven to Hell," full of doubts and questioning, lost in a vast landscape, man not only survives but, stimulated by new forms of perception after long years of alienation, can discover in all the ambiguities of life a positive creative hope; a symbol of unity and fulfilment.

In "Three Tales," Muir returns to a direct treatment of time, some twenty-five years after writing *Variations on a Time Theme*, and although "Three Tales" is not fully successful — its great abstractions are not adequately energized — the poem shows that time remained a subject of central concern to the poet.

Apart from love poems to Willa, Edwin Muir was able only once to write directly, in verse, about members of his family. We have seen how his life in Orkney, with its security and unity, played a vital role in creating his system of symbols, and how the terrible shock of moving to Glasgow and seeing his parents and brothers die almost simultaneously contributed both to his great psychological breakdown and to his awareness of evil and suffering. But the "raging desolations" of Glasgow (and later Prague) and the sense of unity and timelessness in Orkney seemed impervious to any non-symbolic treatment. "The Brothers" is in some ways an exception to this, but even so the poem — one of his purest, and most tender and lyrical — derives from a dream. In a letter to Kathleen Raine, Muir wrote:

I'm trying to write one now about a dream I had recently about my two brothers, Willy and Johnnie, dead fifty years ago. I watched them playing in a field, racing about in some game, and it was not a game either of them was trying to win (there was no winning in it), and because of that they were infinitely happy in making each other happy, and all that was left in their hearts and their bodies was grace. It was very difficult to convey this in a poem. I had not thought of them for a long time. And when I did know them (I was little more than a boy then) there was affection, but also little grouses and jealousies, assertions of the will, a cloud of petty disagreements and passions which hid their true shape from me and from themselves. In the dream it seemed to me the cloud was dispelled and I saw them as they were. I'm sure Blake could have told me everything about it.[5]

This sums up the poem's content as well as prose could ever do, but it conveys little of the deeply moving quality of this elegy, written fifty years after those tragic deaths. The poem turns on the well-known human characteristic, inevitable after the death of a loved person, of guilt; of a sense of not having valued, or shown that appreciation of value, until it is too late. "The Brothers" is an elegy, but it is also a plea for expiation, as the poet explains that he has only reached an understanding of their relationship with the long passing of time. This realization that only slow years have been able to bring vision serves to emphasize the poignant quality achieved here, which perhaps is only possible when an artist is dealing with time at its cruellest, when it cuts down youth and innocence and thereby chokes the growth and potentialities of love. It is this awareness of loss, terrible because of its calm presentation, which informs the emotional centre of the poem:

> For then we played for victory
> And not to make each other glad.
> A darkness covered every head,
> Frowns twisted the original face,
> And through that mask we could not see
> The beauty and the buried grace.

In these lines the quiet regularity of the tetrameter is given a controlled emotional charge in the imitative metrical distortion of

/   / | x / |x /|x x / |
Frowns twisted the original face

and especially by the moving ambiguity of the word "buried" in "The beauty and the buried grace." A quiet progression of tonal and emotional logic develops in the poem's three sections. The first section describes in almost purely visual terms the dream-vision of the two brothers transfigured and mystically beautiful:

> Last night I watched my brothers play,
> The gentle and the reckless one,

In a field two yards away. . . .
For still they raced about the green
And were like two revolving suns;
A brightness poured from head to head,
So strong I could not see their eyes
Or look into their paradise.

The hyperbole of "two yards away" and the pouring brightness
remain acceptable in the low-toned dream context and the un-
wavering certainty of the poet's statement. It is a vision of ecstasy,
modified throughout by the felt dimension of death and loss. The
second section is concerned with the poet-observer's own self-
examination and guilt brought on by the vision, and the final section
resolves the poem by moving outwards into a more public area in
order to examine, and implicitly condemn, the application of justice
in a world of public and private inhumanity and tragedy. The lines
have tremendous authority:

I have observed in foolish awe
The dateless mid-days of the law
And seen indifferent justice done
By everyone on everyone.
And in a vision I have seen
My brothers playing on the green.

The seemingly inconsequential last couplet, following the general
statement on human conduct, provides the perfect conclusion.
Totally simple, apparently unprotesting, it somehow welds together
Muir's vision of his own private grief and guilt, the lack of humanity
in the world at large, and a powerful, resigned acknowledgement of,
and response to, the inexorable workings of time among the ruins of
human hopes. This resolution is strongly reinforced by the sound and
the language. For example, the last six lines consist of three rhyming
couplets, whereas the rest of the poem, though fully rhymed, is
rhymed at random, each verse paragraph being taken as a long
rhyming unit, and rhyme words being separated by as much as seven
lines. Thus the sudden insistent regularity of the couplet forms a
drawing together, a resolution of sound and feeling, an inevitable,
shaped closing together.

The poem's choice of language, too, is an integral part of the total
expressiveness. We have seen that the poem turns on the idea of
injustice, loss of love and the blind inhumane activities of necessity,
without ever raising its voice explicitly. That Muir's feelings strike

so powerfully is largely due to his use of words suggesting youth, innocence and growth, against which the death of the brothers is tellingly placed. The description of the brothers as "gentle" and "reckless"; the emphasis "So wildly spent"; the use of the Scots word "green," instead of field or garden, with all its symbolic associations with growth and health; the repeated insistence on beauty and happiness — all these words implicitly build up a powerful emotional resistance to the fact of the deaths, which culminates in the last couplet. Here the repeating of the word "green," the activity of children's innocence and happiness, the poignant realization that this is obtainable and accessible now only in vision and not reality, become deeply significant juxtaposed as they are with the flat statement about "indifferent justice."

"The Brothers," according to Professor Butter,[6] was one of Muir's favourite poems. This is understandable, as he succeeded here in writing a well-nigh faultless lyric, technically and tonally perfect, and containing deep, complex and universal feelings about the nature of death, bereavement, time and justice. Much less formally ambitious than his great symbolist poems, "The Brothers" is nevertheless a triumph of Muir's technique of simplicity and of the fruitful mingling through sound, tone, image and vision, of the deeply personal and the universal. It remains one of his most unflawed and deeply felt poems.

In the first of three poems entitled "Dialogue," Muir returns to a meditative treatment of the Fable and man's journey in time, in terms of a dialogue between two unspecified people. The poem has a strange quality of remoteness, of experience distilled into formal ceremonial utterance. The poem's pulse is slow and almost ethereal, with long stately sentences in loose blank five-foot lines sometimes gaining an extra foot and all the weight of the hexameter. This feeling of formality and stateliness is further expressed by Muir's extended use of the long list of details, piled up, mainly in strongly patterned end-stopped lines, upon repetitive syntactical bases. The long sentence in section two, for instance, reporting what the traveller sees, reads like a solemn liturgy, every line but two of the nineteen-line sentence being end-stopped, every detail dependent on the words "I see that all is in its place." The tone is that of a psalm, gaining expressiveness from repetitive, ritualistic constructs of syntax and sound.

The dialogue form enables Muir to present two voices, but as each meditates, as well as entering into a question and answer dialogue, the device seems almost unnecessary. Each voice has two statements; the first questions the second, who is "adventurer seeking your home," about his experiences "at the back of the world" and "the antipodes of time," formally asking the traveller to confirm his own imagined vision of the journey:

> What were you doing in the dragon's kingdom?
> Did you see yourself when you were not looking,
> Or take the desert lion by surprise,
> Entering his gaze following the antelope
> To the watering place, watching the watcher, still
> So far away from the unreachable beginning,
> A soul seeking its soul in fell and claw?

In the fabulous kingdom of archetype and purely heraldic presence, is it possible to lose identity, to be assumed into an emblematic existence?

The second voice, more solemn, replies like an Old Testament prophet newly returned from the desert, eyes filled with strangeness and long-vision, man's destiny still clear in his mind. The vision he has on returning "from the other side of time" is one of acceptance. The world, he now sees, is made of things which are in their place — Muir's old recurring expression — and which co-exist to form a pattern as measured and heraldic as the vision of the first speaker:

> Now, passing, I see that all is in its place,
> The good and the evil, equal and strange order:
> Hunter and quarry, each in a separate day,
> The hecatombs of slaughter upon the hills,
> The shepherds watching from the eastern slopes,
> New gods and kings sitting upon their chairs. . . .

This great all-inclusive vision of human life and history, absorbing evil and death without strain, is ultimately a celebration of the patterns of existence. It is a statement of complete acceptance, which does not avoid the manifestations of inhumanity and death, but sees them as part of an ordained richness, at the centre of which is "Jack and Jill/And Kate and Harry, black and brown and white." This is emphasized by the repeated metrical and syntactical figures, "men and women and children," "child and youth and man," "black and brown and white." The passage embraces Muir's mature vision of life's pattern probably more fully than any other poem;

including man, the gods, the animals, the family, war, atrocity, mutability, good and evil, and the home, all resting together and yielding to a powerful unifying destiny. But the section ends with three lines making clear that this reality cannot be all:

> But now, looking again, I see wall, roof and door
> Are changed, and my house looks out on foreign
> ground.
> This is not the end of the world's road.

For all the pattern and unity, this world is subject to change and the processes of time, and the final two sections of the poem discuss time in this context, taking up the abstract intellectual propositions of "Three Tales" in the new context of the two voices.

The first voice now has stopped questioning and meditates, telling the traveller that he has seen him in this world responding to beauty as if time had stopped "In an endless stasis." His argument is that

> What was given before
> You opened your eyes upon the changing earth
> Is there, and for a moment you are at home.

Time can stop here, he argues, and at least temporarily man can recover the state of timelessness which existed before he opened his eyes. But the traveller rejects this argument, and he goes on to argue the case for the Fall of man, which has left uncertainty, loss of direction and the terrible ambiguity of living with "the ghost of an ethereal sorrow" and "in half-memory." The temporary and instinctive glimpses of the real home make the pattern of worldly life, however unified, no more than a plangent echo:

> For my kinsmen say: 'Long since we lost a road,
> Then reached this place, on earth the first and last,
> Neither good nor bad, the right place nor the wrong;
> A house, and there we nourish a heavenly hope.
> For this a great god died and all heaven mourned
> That earth might, in extremity, have such fortune.

The vision here is Christian. Christ's atonement is recognized as an antidote to the Fall, but this cannot be the whole answer. The poem ends ambiguously:

> Does that road still run somewhere in the world?
> Question on question.
> Hope and sorrow ethereal roof our house.

Here the celebration of human life and history must be modified by the uncertainty and the questioning. The evolved patterns we live by, though rich and comforting, are, in the context of the Fall and the journey, "Neither good nor bad, the right place nor the wrong." Our home is ambiguously roofed with both hope and sorrow.

The theme of necessary suffering is continued in "Sick Caliban," a poem which carries the weight of the suffering of the creatures and the dilemmas posed by our relationship with that suffering. I do not think the poem should be too closely associated with *The Tempest*. Caliban here represents misfortune, ugliness, sickness and deprivation in the widest sense, and the "he" who sees him is more Everyman (or the poet) than Prospero or any of the temporary inhabitants of the island.

The poem describes the reactions of the man to the suffering creature and the effect this meeting has on him as he takes on its suffering and carries it, not understanding, to his death. Again there are strong ambiguities and constant questioning about the nature of suffering man; the poem ending in uncertainty and a plea for meaning and alteration. Something is far wrong and the last lines have a quiet desperation:

> If he could keep his eyes
> On that far distant mourner, would it save
> Something?   Would he find a breath to call
> To the others, and all be changed, that thing, and all?

The strange, untypical syntax of the last line is indicative of a state of fragmentation, of duty left undone and of necessary pain, but the poem seems more concerned with the inevitability of world-wide suffering and loss of meaning than with the local moral question of whether the man could have helped by stopping. The process is seen as an inevitable, ordained one, as if the creature exists as a necessary confrontation to make the nature of the world's suffering clear to men as they pass.

Loosely constructed, in a mixture of five, four and two-foot lines, and irregularly rhymed, "Sick Caliban" shows a surprising energy and vitality. The typical Muirean tone of elegy, though present, is vivified by the speed and compression of language, rhythm and syntax. The sentences are mainly short, the pseudo-narrative structure allows the symbolic action to be merged easily with meditation on that action, and the tautness of the final questions gives an urgency to the structure. Again Muir shows his ability to move

easily and convincingly from the local to the universal; in this case
bringing compassion and understanding to the suffering endemic in
the human condition:

> No remedy here or anywhere
> For that poor bag of bone
> And hank of hair....

Muir attains here, as in many of these late poems, a deeply compassionate, almost priestly quality, as if his perception, however
benevolent, has absorbed experience which is astonishingly compre-
hensive and wise.

Pursuing further the theme of suffering, though in nothing like
such an intense way, Muir returns for the last time to the Greek
myth which fascinated him the most. "Penelope in Doubt" is another
exploration of the moment of reunion between Odysseus and Penelope, concentrating on the human sufferings and deprivation of
Penelope turned into an old uncertain woman by the ravages of
time. The poem, apart from the implication of its final line, sets out
to be anti-heroic, adding a further dimension to the character of
Penelope in "Telemachos Remembers." Age and passed time dominate the poem; the earlier "pride and fidelity and love," the very
core and justification of her waiting existence, is replaced by the
shock of non-recognition as she confronts a "stranger." The treatment of time is enhanced by the comparison of the frozen emblematic figures of hound and doe on a brooch Odysseus reminds her
of, which serves as an ironic comment on the dreadful effects of
time's work in the twenty year separation:

> The brooch came closer as he told —
> Grown suddenly young — how he had lost
> The wild doe and the raging hound
> That battled in the golden round.
> She listened, but what shook her most
> Was that these creatures made her old.

The unchanging nature of the brooch, untouched by time, bears no
relation to the real battles of Odysseus and their effect on both of
them.

Muir describes the genesis of this poem in a 1957 notebook:

While wandering along, I remembered the meeting between Penelope
and Odysseus, and thought the only thing which identified him for her
(after twenty years) was a brooch he described from memory, a brooch

of beaten gold showing a dog and a fawn, the dog fastened to the fawn's throat, the fawn striking at him with its slender hoofs, the brooch lost now and the combat still going on, unchanged. She remembered it when he spoke of it. Then he spoke of the time when he was hunting in Parnassus and a wild boar gashed him in the thigh, far up. The scar was still there. The brooch and the scar, these were all that brought him back to her. For his hair was grey, his shoulders had shrunken, though his back was still straight, and his eyes were cold and pale, as if they had looked at things she would never know, or had been bleached in the snows of time.[7]

The poem picks up nearly every one of these details, but adds little of substance to them. The poem is essentially there in the notebook.

Based on the biblical legend of the tower of Babel, "The Tower" seems to be concerned with tyranny and oppression. The great tower, hewn from a nearby quarry, contains the faceless rulers, who use methods of terror and military strength to rule the people. The tower absorbs the young men and the lords, growing ever bigger as a symbol of power and domination over the weak and the old who remain outside to help construct it. Pervading the description of the tower, by the old men outside, is a desperate, Kafka-like feeling of disoriented helplessness in the face of an inaccessible, brutal and undefinable structure of power. The old men have been reduced to impotent, child-like imprecations:

> What are our masters?   Who are you there?
> We scarcely see you.   May there come
> A great wind from a stormier star,
> Blow tower and shadow to kingdom come.

Once voices and songs, both noble and simple, were there, but these "suddenly ended," and the state of silent, censored terror is communicated by a startling dramatic image:

> No message drops from the middle air
> Except when a dead lord flutters down
> Light as a frozen and mummied fly
> From the perpendicular town.
> (They have no license there to die).

The relevance of this poem's imagery to the Nazi and Russian occupations in Europe, with all the apparatus of silence, murder, menace and terror, is clear. The innocent population, faced with an utterly distorted and terrifying reality, is left with nothing but a pathological sense of divorce from reality and known identity. The poem concludes:

> We too die. *So* look the dead
> Whose breath stopped on a different star.
> Who are they? We are what we are.

The broken thought-processes, the sense of utter alienation, the lack of any hope, all characteristics of a totally subjugated people are crystallized here. Once more Muir is exploring the possibilities of suffering, this time without a compensating symbolism of fulfilment, and we are reminded very clearly by "The Tower" that he is a poet steeped in the dreadful realities of mid-twentieth century Europe, the experience of which forms an essential part of his view of man.

"The Voices" is another late poem which demonstrates great imaginative vigour, immediately evident in the language and movement of the verse:

> The lid flew off, and all the desolations
> As through a roaring poet's shameless throat,
> Poured out their lamentations.

There is a buoyancy and springiness here, in spite of the desperately heavy feminine rhymes and yet "The Voices," with its erratic rhyming and its jumbled mixture of three-, four-, five- and six-foot lines, also suggests a certain technical carelessness or, at least, some lack of polish.

The predicament of man is here symbolized through a dream-like set of images of noise. The poem assails the ear and the hubbub described becomes a symbol of the desolations, of meaningless chaos threatening tranquillity and stability. The voices shout despair, and man, noisily trying to reject this, so deafens himself that he cannot hear the quiet antithetical voice of hope, "That calmly said, 'Rejoice'." The poem's pessimism, the presentation of chaos which accompanies man as constant companion, is modified by man's inability to hear it. The poem deals, in its own way, with time and the Fall. At the end of the first section man is described as:

> . . . a tribe who having lost their tongue
> Could find no articulate word to say,
> Having forgotten what was fresh and young:
> All so debased by time it was almost mad.

The Fall has led to loss of quietness, sanity and articulation. The battle against undermining confusion has led us into confusion and blinded us to what is real.

"The Voices," with its energy, its impressively concentrated images of noise as a holding, shaping device, its powerful, George Herbert-like, tonally contrasting conclusion and its odd, unlocated dream-like setting, does not say anything that Muir has not said before, but illustrates the obsessive concentration of his imagination on the results of the Fall into time and his astonishing ability to keep finding new images and approaches with which to explore this theme.

Continuing this group of poems about suffering, "Impersonal Calamity" deals again with the forces of brutalizing dehumanization which have been set loose in our time, with devastating results to the balance and health of the psyche. The poem turns on a comparison between "traditional grief," such as the death of a loved one, and the "impersonal calamities" of "gutted towns and the millions dead." Not only are these different in scale, but different in kind. Man is equipped to deal with the former, for all its pain:

> A son or daughter dead
> Can bend the back or whiten the head,
> Break and remould the heart,
> Stiffen the face into a mask of grief.
> It is an ancient art.

This kind of calamity is natural, part of an old, cyclical process, and deeply part of being fully human. It rises, says Muir, "from old and worn and simple springs." The other calamities of mass destruction can not be responded to in a normal human way:

> The impersonal calamities estrange us
> From our own selves, send us abroad
> In desolate thoughtlessness,
> While far behind our hearts know what they know,
> Yet cannot feel, nor ever express.

This radically altered situation, the one we are so used to on our television screens, presents us with so much vicarious suffering that we become unable to respond, however deeply changed we may be. This is yet another expression of Muir's strong sense of the disparity between man's present experience and an older, more finely shaped order of existence from which he has become tragically alienated. Our hearts have been left "far behind," as Muir's had in Glasgow and in Prague, and we have become removed from the natural patterns and rhythms of our responses to experience. Again, the only modification of this terrible indictment of the twentieth century is the subdued awareness of a real humanity, but this is at a depth which, faced with Hitler, Stalin, Auschwitz, Hiroshima and Dresden, we can no longer attain and can only just remember. Contemporary experience has driven an impersonal wedge between man and his true self.

Unlike "The Voices," this poem uses form in a highly expressive and coherent way. Again the structure is a loose collection of two-, three-, four- and five-foot lines and random rhyming, but the metrical properties are very much part of the poem's expressiveness. The first eight lines, describing the apparent ordinariness of men and evoking the "worn and simple springs" of human response, are all regular penameters, giving the poem a grave, sober start. But when Muir continues to describe the chaos he sees today, deliberately moving us away from the "simple springs," the metre breaks with the subject, physically embodying the breakdown being described:

<pre>
      x   / | x / | x   / |
How can an eye or brow
      x   / | x   / | x   / | x x   / |xx   / |
Disclose the gutted towns and the millions dead?
    x   / | /   / | x / |x / |
They have too slight an artistry.
    x   / | / x | x   / | x   / | x
Between us and the things that change us
    x / |x x   / | x / |x   / |
A covenant long ago was set
    x   / | x   / | x   / |
And is prescriptive yet.
    x / |x / | x   / | x / |
A single grief from man or God
  /   x | x / |
Freely will let
   /   / | x   / | x / |x / |
Change in and bring a stern relief.
</pre>

These lines create, in their irregularity and swaying instability, the sense of disintegrated order which Muir wants to emphasize. Coming after the strong pentameter bases of the first eight lines, and continuing to the end of the poem, this irregular pattern draws strong attention to the poem's pessimism by refusing to give metrical consolation and by deliberately avoiding a return to coherence. The effect is to leave the ear and eye as dissatisfied as the mind and feelings; all the senses finally full of a broken order, which, at least at the present time, is not amenable to any form of shaping or joining together.

In "The Two Sisters" Muir reverts to a simple, song-like, perfectly regular form as a means of commenting on mortality and human nature. This deceptively simple lyric achieves a remarkable universality and emotional richness:

> Her beauty was so rare,
> It wore her body down
> With leading through the air
> That marvel not her own.
> At last to set it free
> From enmity of change
> And time's incontinence
> To drink from beauty's bone,
> Snatching her last defence,
> She locked it in the sea.
>
> The other, not content
> That fault of hers should bring
> Grief and mismanagement
> To make an end of grace
> And snap the slender ring,
> Pulled death down on her head,
> Completed destiny.
> So each from her own place,
> These ladies put to sea
> To join the intrepid dead.

The subtle emotion of this poem certainly does not derive from any surface complexity. The words are astonishingly simple, largely monosyllabic; the rhyme, though not identical in each stanza, is full and straightforward, and, apart from the last line, with its seven syllables, the poem is completely accentual-syllabic throughout, having three feet and six syllables in each line. Yet working elusively through this surface simplicity is a tonal and emotional complexity which makes "The Two Sisters" one of Muir's finest achievements.

Firstly, in order to come at this complexity, we must realize that this is not — or not merely — a narrative. The images of the deaths of the two sisters — one full of beauty; one full of grace and manners — lie side by side in time and in space, completely unspecific, ultimately, in spite of their detailed particularities. The two sisters may or may not have existed. They may be from life, from art, from dream or from the poet's imagination. The only locality that matters is "the sea" of "the intrepid dead," which exists as a free-moving symbol. The poem deals with human death and the effect of "time's incontinence" on the most delicate and rare human things. The two representative figures are, like all humans, engaged upon a battle or contest with time before they consent to its demands, and it is this final consenting, or acceptance, which makes the poem so moving. Death comes finally without any protest. The human-beings are absorbed into a great natural process which means the end of struggle and some sort of fulfilment.

In coming to a sense of this poem's emotional richness, we may be helped by an observation, based on a study of another poet, by Archibald MacLeish:

How will you "describe" in words the poignancy of the recognition of the *obstacle* of time — its recognition not on the clock face or among the stars but on the nerves of the body and in the blood itself? But if you cannot 'describe' it in words how then can words contain it? . . . By speaking of two things which, like parentheses can include between them what neither of them says. By leaving a space between one sensed image and another where what cannot be said can *be*. . . . [8]

This seems peculiarly relevant in "The Two Sisters." It is a poem deeply concerned with time and human experience, articulating to the senses something which could never be directly described, and using juxtaposed images, or attitudes, to make possible this articulation. There is no comment whatsoever from the poet here. The pictures of the two deaths are left side by side and somehow generate a meaning from their mutual proximity. Similarly, and vitally, two attitudes, or tones, are placed together, again without comment, to generate meaning. As well as the overwhelming tone of dissolution into death, of mortality celebrated and elegized, there appears an attitude of chiding, of gentle mockery towards these two highly motivated ladies, who to preserve decently their attributes of good looks and good manners consciously choose death rather than a loss of appearance. This is done so affectionately and gently by Muir that it remains merely an impression. Certainly there is no question of condemnation or judgment, but rather a whimsical recognition, only slightly mocking, of people's concern with behaviour, which lies next to the serious emotional knowledge of death.

What then is the emotion of the poem? It is not simply affectionate amusement at human vanity, nor is it simply grief in the face of mortality. As MacLeish suggests, the meaning lies between the two, where the two things penetrate each other and reveal each other on a totally non-logical level. It becomes a completely "felt" meaning, elusive but humanly recognizable and important, in which the fact of death, far from being reduced in potency by the mockery is actually heightened. Human fallibility and individual eccentricity become valuable beyond measure in this context, and can be expressed only through image and tone. When this is successfully achieved in the lyric poem, it can make us aware of the deepest patterns and possibilities in life and can give us an awareness of our human place in a great living process, constantly creating and dissolving. "The Two Sisters" celebrates life by celebrating death. It celebrates human strength and dignity by recognizing human weakness. In this poem Muir achieves a perfect harmony of form and meaning and the result is a clear, steady, luminous poetry, full of the elusive wisdom and converged feeling that only a lifetime of experience could bring. To use MacLeish's words once more:

To face the truth of the passing away of the world and make song of it, make beauty of it, is not to solve the riddle of our mortal lives but perhaps to accomplish something more.[9]

In the long poem "The Last War" Muir reverts partially to a symbolist approach, using certain ambiguities and shifts of time and tense, of reality and dream, to develop a meditation on war and suffering. The poem's tenses shift throughout from rhetorical present to future speculation, to past recollection, to the contemporary present and finally into the visionary present of an actual recalled dream. Hence the war and suffering presented encompass the refugees of twentieth-century Europe, blight and decay in nature and imagination, a possible future annihilation of mankind, and a symbolic extra-temporal pattern of fear and hope.

In the context of these late poems, "The Last War" is a continuation of the poet's exploration of suffering in terms of both contemporary Europe and the wider pattern of the Fall and time. Hence each local detail is merely part of a complex structure of interconnected references. The future atomic war and the refugees from the past cannot be imaginatively separated:

> Perhaps nothing at all will be but pain,
> A choking and floundering, or gigantic stupor
> Of a world-wide deserted hospital ward.
> There will be strange goodbyes, more strange than
>   those
> That once were spoken by terrified refugees,
> Our harbingers: some of them lost in shipwreck,
> Spilling salt angry tears in the salt waves,
> Their lives waste-water sucked through a gaping hole,
> Yet all the world around them;   hope and fear.

These lines, from section three, are certainly not just about a future war, but include past, present and future suffering in one act of imagination, which can have no tense. In the first three sections, Muir explores the destruction of both concrete and abstract things by war and evil, a vision which culminates in section two with an uncharacteristically daring image which points to the fracturing of natural life in a terrifying way:

> Or shall we picture bird and tree
> Silently falling, and think of all the words
> By which we forged earth, night and day
> And ruled with such strange ease our work and play?
> Now only the lexicon of a dream.
> And we see our bodies buried in falling birds.

This works on several levels, again combining past, present and future, to embody the fallen state of man and nature, the loss of our birthright, the possibilities of unnatural destruction and unbalancing which man has developed in his lost and fallen state. The almost surrealistic vision of "our bodies buried in falling birds," with its charge of silent terror and its admitting of the utter breakdown of nature and man, serves to emphasize the intensity of these meditations. The world is losing its possibilities for bravery, for saving the young, for hoping, for believing in a recurring revitalizing force which will always create new, hopeful patterns of life in spite of tragedy. All that our past and present, and our clearest looks into the future can offer is a meditation on the power of suffering; a questioning not so much of whether, but of *how* we will come to destroy ourselves and the world.

   This vision of "the vacant earth" and "the turncoat sun" contains little hope. All that Muir offers are the poignant lines:

> Will great visions come,
> And life lie clear at last as it says, Good-bye,
> Good-bye, I have born with you a little while?

But sections four and five do something to restore a balance in the face of suffering, giving strong intimations of a supporting reality underneath the things gone wrong.

Leaving the ostensibly future-tense posture of the first sections, part four moves into a past/present sequence. The "we" and "us" of the first sections now become "I," as the poet as individual moves closer to the surface of the poem, instead of functioning as one of the generalized human race. Section four recounts a search for permanence in nature and art, in terms of the disruptive realities of suffering already presented in the poem. In this context, "ordinary sights appal," Muir says, having seen a blighted tree· Nature can be infected — as with the dead birds in section two — and when natural things or made things are neglected or distorted, like man after the Fall, it "wounds the heart." Perception becomes inaccurate and partial, unnaturalness is seen in terms of procreation itself:

> Face mirrors face,
> Mixing to generate an image sown
> By casual desire or disaffection. . . .

But in the third stanza of this section — itself a sonnet of sorts — Muir adds a new dimension to balance the vision of war and destruction and mutation:

> I thought, our help is in all that is full-grown
> In nature, and all that is with hands well-made,
> Carved in verse or stone
> Or a harvest yield.   There is the harmony
> By which we know our own and the world's health,
> The simply good, great counterpoise
> To blind nonentity,
> Ever renewed and squandered wealth.

But this assertion of a creative pattern is not enough in face of the image of an empty dead world previously presented with such authority. Because of the Fall and man's distorted nature, these things have been neglected:

> Yet not enough.   Because we could not wait
> To untwist the twisted smile and make it straight
> Or render restitution to the tree.

> We who were wrapped so warm in foolish joys
> Did not have time to call on pity
> For all that is sick, and heal and remake our city.

For this reason we are vulnerable to the worst effects of suffering and war. This is Muir's explanation for past, present and future chaos — a tragic break in the fabric which lets in all the terror of the forces of disintegration.

Section five attempts to resolve the poem by moving even further away from time and place into the world of dream where the pattern is visible and all-meaning. The wavering three-, four- and five-foot lines of the preceding sections image this new reality and pattern by settling firmly into a five-foot norm and expressing, in the sound of the lines, an achieved harmony. The section — a vision of the "well of life" in contrast to the previous images of distorted procreation — is saturated with shining light, flowers, and water, symbolically embodying qualities of redemptive strength, regeneration and the reconciliation of warring opposites. Man is here firmly united with eternity, earth with heaven, good with evil, body with spirit, in a state of "pure commingled being."

The dream on which these lines are based was recorded by Muir in a notebook, marked "Dreams and Diary Items." In November 1957 he wrote:

Dreams in the last few weeks. Dream of the watchers in a dark place (coming on the words somewhere, 'The Well of Life', I have associated them with that, though the words come later, in some poem or other in a book). Except for the watchers, all was deep darkness, and I could see only their faces, which were lighted by a brilliant beam of light. . . . It seemed to be an underworld and how the beam of light came, and from what source I did not know. The faces strongly radiant, serene . . . Radiance above all.[10]

Muir captures this radiance in the poem. It is a radiance not merely visual, but one which illuminates man in terms of his potential, as part of the widest, most all-inclusive pattern:

> About the well of life where we are made
> Spirits of earth and heaven together lie.
> They do no turn their bright heads at our coming,
> So deep their dream of pure commingled being,
> So still the air and the level beam that flows
> Along the ground, shed by the flowers and waters:
> All above and beneath them a deep darkness.

Their bodies lie in shadow or buried in earth,
Their heads shine in the light of the underworld.
Loaded with fear and crowned with every hope
The born stream past them to the longed for place.

At this level, at the mystical source of life, man is "loaded with fear," as in the early sections of the poem, but has gained the hope which has previously seemed denied. Instead of heading towards total destruction, he is seen as moving inevitably towards "the longed for place."

This resolution of the poem remains, perhaps, open to criticism. In order to solve the basic problems of suffering, war and human nature, Muir has had to move into dream, into a world where paradox is unknown, and which, in the context of this poem, has only very tenuous contacts with the preceding realities. "The Last War," for all its power and authority, is flawed by a lack of unity and a sense of structural uneasiness and awkwardness. Nevertheless, it remains a strong expression of actual and potential suffering, and the bitter paradoxes of human experience, doomed to alienation from its "longed for place."

The remaining poems, all found in typescript or manuscript form, must be regarded as not necessarily incomplete, but certainly subject to revision had the poet lived to collect them. But "The Poet" is most likely a finished product, formally well-rounded and a complete act in itself. The poem is a classic statement of the belief of the visionary poet; a justification for symbolism and a rejection of reason. The poet is described as a prophet, or perhaps a medium, through whom the non-rational symbols arise "And make a song":

What I shall never know
I must make known.
Where traveller never went
Is my domain.
Dear disembodiment
Through which is shown
The shapes that come and go
And turn again.

This serves as a perfect description of Muir's own poetic method, working intuitively in areas which can never be "known," creating journeys and places where no real traveller can go, disappearing himself as elocutionary functionary in order to become a medium for the active symbols, "The shapes that come and go," which play

217

against each other "And turn again." In the last stanza, thought is specifically rejected as a means of artistic "knowing":

> Heaven-sent perplexity —
> If thought should thieve
> One word of the mystery
> All would be wrong.

In the "bewilderment" of the creative process,

> Love's parable
> Into the world was sent
> To stammer its word.

The sudden use of the past tense here, in a poem of the dramatic present, suggests a reference to the Incarnation of Christ, coming to the world strangely and with love in the way the poem comes to the world. The beliefs shown in this poem — of the unconscious, of the overwhelming importance of symbol, of the rejection of intellect, reason and logic — are beliefs which Blake, Yeats, Rilke, Mallarmé, Rimbaud and other visionary poets would immediately have recognized. In this poem, Muir himself places his work firmly in their tradition, openly confessing the aesthetic to which his life and work had inevitably led him.

Muir's objections to the poem — based largely, one suspects, on the creative artist's highly personal awareness that the creation is not equal to, or the same as, the original conception — may perhaps be justified to a degree. "The Poet" lacks the singing quality and the concrete embodiment of feeling in image which we find in his best work, but there is a compensating quietness and simplicity. And the poem is by no means devoid of technical interest. The structure of three eight-line stanzas, written in alternate trimeter and dimeter, is one he had never used before and the result is fresh, light and interesting to the ear. The syntactical pattern is neatly based on four-line sentences, exactly bisecting each stanza, with the one exception of stanza two, which has an extra sentence after two lines, and this precision and structural harmony is further enhanced by the rhyme-scheme. The first stanza, rhyming *a b a c a b a c*, is beautifully pointed and the last stanza repeats this scheme. The second stanza, rhyming *a b c d c b a d*, picks up with the *c*-rhymes the four-times repeated *a*-rhymes of stanza one, which gives an interesting variation of rhyme-sound and enables the last stanza's reversion to the original scheme to be more dramatic and final. The result of these devices is a very tightly woven pattern of sound which controls the tone and, with the short lines, gives a melodic, song-like quality to the vast utterances of the theme. This counterpoint of sound and theme provides a distinctive quality which considerably enhances the poem's interest.

"Dialogue" ("I never saw the world until that day") is one of Edwin Muir's most puzzling poems simply because the reader receives so little information. It appears to be a conversation, probably between two women, offering conflicting attitudes and recollections about a man they both knew. The man was an artist and a visionary, striving to join the rarified world of the imagination with the real world of human life. The first speaker responds to what the man showed her:

> The real fabulous world newly reborn,
> And celebrated and crowned on every side
> With sun and sky and lands of fruit and corn,
> The dull ox and the high horse glorified,
> Red images on the red clay,
> And such a race of women and men,
> I thought the famous ones had never died.

In short, he had shown her the archetypal vision of Eden, presented here in familiar language and syntax, with its long lists and its picture of man, animals and nature living in harmony. This speaker is full of wonder, changed completely by the strange and permanent world of the imagination the man has shown her.

The second speaker is more knowing, less innocent and less amenable to the lure of the imagination. Her picture of the man is quite different, and she has resisted in the name of worldly values and self-presentation. To the charge that the man was trying to use people for his own purposes, the first speaker replies that he was a man who "Endured, accepted all," yet was never so much of a visionary that he did not demand use and function from things. But the ultimate defence brought by this speaker is that his vision is permanent for her: "Yet that first world was beautiful/And true, stands still where first it stood." But the poem concludes with three sharp, epigrammatic lines from the second speaker, showing that she still rejects this view and that she can never lose control of herself enough to be carried away by such a vision:

I have known men and horses many a day.
Men come and go, the wise and the fanciful.
I ride my horse and make it go my way.

The dialogue may be seen as between innocence and experience, where experience has self-sufficiency, pride, control, but where innocence, for all its breathless lack of sophistication, is malleable and open enough to receive and value intimations of a higher level of reality. One can read it, too, like "The Poet," as a justification of the symbolist method and the reality it proposes, in contrast to the knowing and literal world of logic and worldly preoccupations. It is also possible, though not likely, that it is a poem about religious attitudes, and that the man is Christ. In this case, the two speakers would represent the fertile and the barren soil on which the seeds were cast. And we must not overlook the possibility that Muir might be presenting, through the form of dialogue, an account of his own shifting, alternating attitude towards reality, as he is pulled between imagination and reality, eternity and time, sharing both the first speaker's obsessive vision of "the real fabulous world" and simultaneously having this checked by a part of him which insisted upon a literal self-sufficiency. The poem is amenable to any or all of these interpretations and it probably does not matter which the individual reader prefers. I suspect the poem might have been revised, had the poet lived, in order to give more precision of focus. As it stands, however, "Dialogue" is of very mixed quality. A certain prosiness and flatness characterize the tone, and the lack of sharpness in the content is reflected by a lack of sharpness in the language, imagery and sound, and one feels that a potentially interesting expression of conflicting modes of perception has been partially lost through a lack of sustained imaginative vitality. I suspect that what the poet was trying to say in this poem is that

... our passion for 'reality' has rendered absurd our desire for meaning. That our insistence on 'fact' has given the lie to truth. That our love of 'truth' has begotten an unlovable world.[11]

This is something that Muir says over and over again in his work as he celebrates, in practice and in theory, the unique power of symbol to transcend local reality and to express the permanent value of the heart's reasoning. True order, the pattern lying behind our lives, can only be grasped symbolically, whether in a poem or through myth, nature or religion. Fallen man, represented by the second speaker in

"Dialogue" has mislaid his symbols, become caught in a labyrinth of false logic, reason and ambiguity, until he is incapable of seeing the vision of permanence when it is put in front of him. These things are implied in "Dialogue," but never apprehended as fiercely and dramatically as in many of the earlier poems.

"Petrol Shortage" is a meditation on contrasts of life style; the poet juxtaposing modern technology with deeper permanent rhythms of existence:

> The planes are hunted from the sky,
> All around me is the natural day.
> I watch this empty country road
> Roll half a century away.
>
> And looking round me I recall
> That here the patient ploughmen came
> Long years ago, and so remember
> What they were and what I am.
>
> I think, the aeroplanes will pass,
> Power's stupendous equipage,
> And leave with simpler dynasties
> The mute detritus of an age.

In the "vacant silence" of the countryside, Muir is able to salvage this belief that "simpler dynasties" will take over the wrecked world, and one is reminded of the new simple post-war order imaged in "The Horses," the people living among useless "mute detritus" of a dead civilization. However, the last stanza adds ambiguity and a warning:

> A week refutes a prophecy
> That only ages can make true.
> The deafening distractions wait,
> Industrious fiends, for me and you.

In the face of loss of meaning, we can only believe in a long-term solution as some vast process takes its course. We must be aware of "The deafening distractions" which keep us from being part of this process and lead us, as well as the distractions, to become "Industrious fiends."

"Ballad of Everyman" and "Nightmare of Peace" must be taken together as they are different versions of the same poem, telling the same symbolic story and using the same images. "Ballad of Everyman," written in a strict tetrameter quatrain rhyming *a b c b*, seems to be the superior version; its formal precision adding a control, a tightness and an effective sound-pattern. "Nightmare of Peace," using long verse paragraphs, haphazard rhyming and a much looser metric, is more prose-like and more coarsely shaped, lacking the economy of "Ballad of Everyman."

The pseudo-narrative presents itself as a dream, outside reality and yet unmistakably partaking of cold-war actuality. Everyman, on a mission

> to meet
> His brothers gathered from every land,
> And make a peace for all the earth
> And link the nations hand to hand. . . .

finds himself in what appears to be the United Nations building,

> And there he saw a motionless dove
> Swung from the roof, but for the rest
> Found little sign of peace or love.

This assembly is seen by Everyman as merely an extension of the terrors of secret police and political terror and dishonesty so prevalent everywhere else. In the first version he openly rejects the assembly; the second version, more menacingly, makes Everyman less in control:

> But why was our old friend Everyman
> Among this false-faced company
> When we knew that he was sought
> Across the border a mile away
> By men the living spit of these?

In both versions he leaves and is not seen again. Challenging the assembly means death.

The second part of the poem refers to the death of Everyman; the poet, dreaming he is flying "In some contraption old and lame," witnesses below him a terrible, distorted, shifting image of mankind murdering Everyman. The poet sees at first a game between two sides, which changes into a monster "With iron hoofs and scourging tail," trampling down a harvest. Suddenly the beast is covered with eyes, representing "the lies" which "Spring open," and the temporary memory of "Something that long ago was said." The beast then changes into a ring of murderers surrounding the dead Everyman. The first version of the poem ends with the poet cursing "The traitorous men" who "murder peace to bring their peace"; the second version returns us to the conference room "With Peace the Tyrant's pitiless law," having attempted a more ambitious analysis of the death-scene in the field:

> ... we knew,
> These were God's creatures after all
> Ashamed and broken by the fall
> Into the dark.
> > Then one stepped out
> Who had been but now a hoof or horn
> Or drop of sweat on the animal,
> And waved and shouted: we must come down.
> And the animal was reborn.

The reference to the "fall/Into the dark" is perhaps a superfluous addition to what is implicit throughout, but it signifies the more symbolic, less allegorical, nature of the second vision. The lines about the animal's being "reborn" suggest a necessary connection between the beast and the dreaming observers; a pattern of recurring evil, with the poet now as possible victim. The first section presents its action as straightforward allegory, the second as a mixed mode of allegory, dream-material and symbolism. Perhaps neither version is fully satisfactory by the standards of Muir's best work, but the theme of innocence murdered by the treacherous all-powerful forces of political terror and human blindness remains a powerful image of the poet's vision not only of the cold-war, but of men who change into beasts, so inhuman have they become with lying, double-dealing and murder. It is another image of the Fall. The beast is both outside us, in the political world, and inside us, in our loss of grace.

The last ten poems in *Collected Poems* were the least finished of those found among Edwin Muir's papers. "There's Nothing Here" is apparently incomplete, ending in the middle of a sentence. The poem seems unworked metrically, being based on a loose pentameter line but wandering further off this norm as it progresses into lines of three, four, six and even seven feet. There is no rhyme.

The poem presents a negative reaction to heaven from someone, probably Muir's cousin, Sutherland, newly arrived from a simple farming existence. The speaker rejects the lack of "substance and shadow" in heaven and wants to be sent back to where he can hold things and be part of the physical properties of the earth. He goes on to celebrate the delights of earthly existence — taking his friends to meet girls; the summer; chatting with "Jock at the Bothy";

climbing in farm windows to visit the lasses — all part of the unsophisticated rhythm and identity which Muir valued so much in
Orkney life.

The next poem, yet another "Dialogue" ("I have heard you cry")
is again unfinished and thus any remarks must of necessity be tentative. The poem again shows Muir's increasing use, in these late
poems, of direct speech and the dialogue form to present opposing
or differing views, which is a more direct and unsophisticated technique than he uses in the more complex symbolist constructions.
The dangers of this method may be seen in this poem, where the
inverted commas become irritating and the poet, switching from
short speech to short speech, is forced into a stylized and repetitive
manner in the link passages. The result is a clumsy poem, awkward
to eye and ear, and, ironically, nothing like as dramatic, for all its
direct reporting of speech, as most of the more technically subtle
poems of conflict.

The poem concerns itself with two views of man's situation. The
"I" of the poem, reporting the dialogue, calls himself Adam and
stands for acceptance of man's existence. His attitude is religious,
praising the processes of which man is a part, and refusing to doubt
or despair because of man's limitations. He recognizes the tragic
obstacle of man's having fallen into time, but in spite of this remains
content to accept this world:

> Here you are not at ease, but must prefer
> What you were born for, this your place,
> Where all moves towards infinity
> At a snail's or a herd's pace.
> Plods, hurries, dawdles: finding, choosing its
>   rhyme. . . .

The other speaker cannot easily accept this. He is preoccupied with
time and mortality and cynical about man's fate when he is so
fettered and unable to achieve his destiny. He is just as concerned
with reaching the state of Eden, but psychologically less balanced in
his fear of losing it:

> As if you feared that unawares
> The indestructable flowers of Paradise
> Might suddenly droop and wither
> In a brief, thoughtless intermission of your eyes
> And all your journey thither
> End in consummate vacancy.

224

The first speaker claims that man chose this life, deliberately leaving Paradise and accepting this world where "all my kindred go"; the second fears that death will take everything away and leave man with nothing: " 'I am a footstep from eternity/And cannot lift my foot'." We are, for him, "the dupes of time," pawns of a malicious fate which shows us what we might gain and prevents our gaining it.

How Muir could have ended this poem is impossible to guess. Probably it would have finished on a note of positive optimism from the first speaker, but as the difference between the two is merely one of interpretation of the situation and not of fundamentally opposed values, it is hard to see this poem as an important receptacle of ideas. The attitudes of both these speakers have previously been treated and accepted by Muir several times, so it is not easy to simply reject one of them. The poem exists as a loose, rather intellectual, musing on time and the Fall, but its failure to find dynamic forms in which to embody its argument leaves it unconvincing, as well as unfinished. It does, however, show once again Muir's obsession with examining the real world in these last poems, and his increasing ability to come to terms with its imperfections, especially the problem of time.

A preoccupation with time also sustains the next poem, "The Heart Could Never Speak," which is a simple, three stanza lyric in the form of a prayer from man to time. Time has the "art" of humanizing, giving meaning, making whole, when it works on the human heart, breaking it and healing it. When time gives "the word," we are linked with the dead and animated in a new way. Time teaches the tongue to speak the meaningful word instead of mere "Syllables, joy and pain," and is finally addressed by the poet as "Time, merciful lord," as the implied source of life and salvation. This deification of time, in the light of Muir's frequently repeated hypothesis about time's being the enemy to eternity, fails to convince. Man's wisdom, the poet has told us so often, derives from the under-pinning of the Fable, which is timeless; the instinctive memory of, and search for, Eden; and grace, however received, which comes from beyond time. Whatever the definition of time is meant to be in this poem, it is not described in sufficient depth for us to find it anything but confusing. I suspect that Muir meant "time," in this context, to be some sort of amalgam of time and eternity, but the poem does not say this. All we can say with certainty is that it is a non-Christian poem which is urging man to look to outside powers for the strength to become newly human and revitalized.

The next two poems are more interesting. "I See the Image," a nine-line verse paragraph in blank pentameter, treats man's relationship with time much more in the manner of Muir's earlier symbolistic poems:

> I see the image of a naked man,
> He stoops and picks a smooth stone from the ground,
> Turns round and in a wide arc flings it backward
> Towards the beginning.   What will catch it,
> Hand, or paw, or gullet of sea-monster?
> He stoops again, turns round and flings a stone
> Straight on before him.   I listen for its fall,
> And hear a ringing on some hidden place
> As if against the wall of an iron tower.

The subject is fabulous, dream-like, confused in the first line by the disembodied observer's seeing "the image" of the man, as if in a vision or dream, and the whole poem has the tone and feel of dream. The man is a human archetype, and his actions, when he throws the stones, become symbolic equivalents of man's exploration of time past and future. The symbol of the thrown stones represents a testing of the past and future, of man's origins and destiny, implying with the utmost economy a huge journey through time and space in search of meaning. In this vision, man is seen isolated somewhere between evolutionary history ("Hand, or paw, or gullet of sea-monster") and an unknown but vaguely menacing future. Both past, present and future are suggested imprecisely, as befits the dream-like tone, and the poem benefits from this imprecision. The future holds an indefinite obstacle, in the symbol of the stone hitting an iron wall. There can be no easy progression for man. The road ahead has its blockages and labyrinths, just as the road behind has its monsters and terrors, and man cannot escape either. The journey leads always through a "vale of soul-making."

The nature of the "iron tower," however, while being suggestive of future blockage and obstruction, may be interpreted more positively as the gateway to Eden, or perhaps a symbolic repository of some new life beyond the desert. The stone, after all, is heard "ringing," and the iron tower is merely part of a simile. But this poem interests us less in its more intellectual prophetic stance than in its uncanny awareness, presented through symbol and tone, of man's predicament when surrounded by unknown stretches of time and space. We are taken backwards and forwards in time, never being allowed to leave the mood of almost disembodied dream, drawn completely into this world of archetypes which comes to seem utterly natural. This can be achieved in just nine lines only because of Muir's direct symbolist attack on the subject and the resonance and appropriateness of the embodying symbols. The journey through time and space is created here not by tense-shift, but by the simple device of the moving stone, which becomes, in terms of this set of images, a kind of time-machine.

In "Our Apprehensions Give," however, Muir reintroduces the tense-shift in order to distort reality for the purposes of this theme:

> Our apprehensions give
> Us to another time, and cast
> Our hapless horoscope;   we did not live
> Either in the present or the past.
>
> And thus afloat upon our fears
> We scarcely lived, and dread to be.
> Straight on the reckless pilot sheers;
> Our sons are born upon the sea,
>
> And in the waves will live and die,
> Not drift to the murderous strand
> But reading for portents in the sky,
> Knowing too well, too well, the land.

This simple poem, close in mood to the previous one, again suggests man caught and confused in time and "afloat upon our fears." The first stanza explicitly comments on the disorientation caused by a confused sense of time, but it is through syntactical techniques that this confusion is most vitally expressed. If we look at the verbs in the poem, we can see a deliberate shifting in and out of the past, present and future — "give," "cast," "did not live," "lived," "dread," "sheers," "are born," "will live and die," "drift," as well as the present participles "reading" and "knowing." The last three, ostensibly present, are, in fact, an implied future tense, though by this stage they incorporate past and present too. Present reality is strangely distorted by these tense-shifts, as it is by the lack of location, and the universal, archetypal quality. This symbolist technique, even in a poem so short, is highly effective. Even the blank space between stanzas two and three becomes meaningful, filling in an implied passing of time.

"The Refugees Born For A Land Unknown" demonstrates Muir's continuing preoccupation with war and suffering, and their effects on people:

> The refugees born for a land unknown
> We have dismissed their wrongs, now dull and old,
> And little judgment-days lost in the dark.

This little introduction, somewhat clumsily phrased, leads into the rest of the poem, which, again in inverted commas, is spoken by a displaced person now living in England:

> "I have fled through land and sea, blank land and sea,
> Because my house is besieged by murderers
> And I was wrecked in the ocean, crushed and swept,
> Spilling salt angry tears on the salt waves,
> My life waste water drawn down through a hole,
> Yet lived".[12]

Now the refugee sees flowers and trees "with alien eyes" in an English garden, feeling outside it all. The poem ends with his looking back:

> Footsteps on the stair, two heavy, two light,
> The door opens.   Since then I remember nothing,
> But this room in a place where no doors open.
> I think the world died many years ago.

This is a harrowing account of displacement and alienation, calling into question the very validity of the refugee's existence in a foreign land.

It is tempting to read parts of this poem as autobiographical, though I doubt whether the poet consciously intended this. As a story of violence, death and breakdown of personality it echoes Muir's own life, and the details of the "English garden" with "the bees among the lavender" are not hard to equate with Swaffham Prior. In a way, the poet and the refugee become mingled and confused here, as each dreams of other places and other times, and each recalls intense personal and universal suffering which changed his life.

"And Once I Knew" is much lighter in tone than most of Muir's late poems:

> And once I knew
> A hasty man,
> So small, so kind, and so perfunctory,
> Of such an eager kindness
> It flushed his little face with standing shame.

Wherever he came
He poured his alms into a single hand
That was full then empty.   He could not understand.
A foolish or a blessed blindness,
Saint or fool, a better man than you.

This represents, basically, a plea for humanity. The hasty man, willing to give everything away to help others, lives among people who take advantage, who behave completely differently, who live by different rules. The pathos of "He could not understand" shows the gulf between the giver and the receiver and between an older, more human world and the hard inhuman world of today. Whether he is "Saint or fool," the little man, so bewildered by the new and alien modes of behaviour, is "a better man than you." This unpretentious poem, a subdued elegy for a previous, Orkney-like, generosity of living, contains an indictment of the present time, full of people who abuse largeness of spirit and a genuine belief in the brotherhood of man.

It is rare to find direct natural description in Muir's poetry, but "Sunset," as we know from his notebook, derives from an evening walk. He describes it thus:

The evening extraordinarily still, bright clouds in the west, soft and suffused with all the colours of light flowing through them horizontally, yet lingering, reluctant to go. The trees along the road seemed conscious of this image of peace, and three horses in a field were subdued by it. Nothing which appeared to be unaware of it. Strange perfection of a common mood, sky and light and cloud and tree and the horses: I felt it too.[13]

This prose is remarkable for its detail and the way the observed experience becomes transformed into an experential unity, felt rather than perceived. In fact the first stanza of "Sunset" asks this very question. How can perception turn into felt experience?

How can a cloud give peace,
Peace speak through bodiless fire
And still the angry world?

The last stanza attempts to come at the visionary experience, picking up the light and fire references of these opening lines as key elements:

Yet now each bush and tree
Stands still within the fire,
And the bird sits on the tree.

Three horses in a field
That yesterday ran wild
Are bridled and reined by light
As in a heavenly field.
Man, beast and tree in fire,
The bright cloud showering peace.

The sunset has led into the vision of Eden, where man and nature and eternity are joined in harmony. Through light and fire, the transcendental has penetrated earthly reality and the result is a mystic experience which expels disparates, calms nature and brings an understood stillness to everything. The "fire" of the sunset is transformed into an elemental purifying flame which welds nature, man and the animals together with a total lack of turbulence or strain.

This poem presents us with the possibility of an earthly Eden, but it is only a temporary state of vision. The force which stills "the angry world" somehow comes from outside "As in a heavenly field," and peace drops onto the earth from "The bright cloud" as opposed to its being generated here. But "Sunset" shows Muir's preoccupation, which we have seen often in these late poems, with assessing the value of the experience of *this* world, as opposed to the world of the gods. The distillation of worldly things into fire and light may be a mystical act, but the poem unmistakably roots itself in the phenomena of every-day human experience and perception, which not only may be, but often are, transformed into something more meaningful and patterned, partaking of Eden.

This is a fresh visionary poem full of a sense of wonder and delight. The vitality and flexibility of Muir's vision and techniques in these last poems are startling when we remember he was an old man when they were written and not in the best of health. Somehow he had managed to preserve a visionary innocence, which he combined with the immense authenticity and authority of a long life full of the most tragic suffering and the most vital joy. It is a strangely luminous poetry, seemingly simple, but supported by as much knowledge of hell and heaven as any man is ever likely to acquire without its killing him or breaking him.

It is appropriate that the last two poems Edwin Muir wrote — "The Day Before the Last Day" and "I Have Been Taught" — should appear together at the end of the *Collected Poems*. These poems represent the two extremes of experience and vision and serve as a supremely fitting summary of his view of human life. "The Day Before the Last Day" embodies Muir's deepest fears for man in a great warning prophecy. Total destruction, hysteria, loss of identity, nightmare, all combine in a great expression of fallen man's propensities for evil. "I Have Been Taught," on the contrary, sums up the poet's deepest beliefs, and proposes, with the utmost certainty, a sustaining reality and the existence of creative forces which defeat evil. In earlier poems, like "The Labyrinth," for example, the opposing views coexist within one poetic structure and the resolution of their conflict is the resolution of the imaginative deed which is the poem, but in these late poems, Muir is more prone to either the cruder confrontation of dialogue form or to giving individual poems almost completely to a proposition of "evil" or "good." As we have seen throughout this analysis of his poetry, his vision implies a process, a pattern, intrinsic to which are both good and evil. It is impossible to dissociate the Fall from time and the labyrinth, but conversely, it is impossible to dissociate the Fall from Eden or the labyrinth from the escape towards Eden again. The Story, with all its terrors, obstacles, breakdown, war and suffering cannot be separated from the supporting Fable, which is not subject to the time-space limitations of human experience. Muir's vision is totally unified in a series of symbols which owe their existence to their mutual interpenetration. The descent into hell is a necessary prerequisite for the ascent to heaven. Neither means anything without the other. Archibald MacLeish puts it like this:

To taste the human tragedy one must taste at the same time the possibility of human happiness, for it is only when the two are known together in a single knowledge that either can be known.[14]

In the greatest art, good and evil, potentiality and blockage, suffering and intense joy become fused into a structure which contains them both and is, simultaneously, greater than they. And so it is with Edwin Muir. The often tragic facts of life in time, on this earth, are accepted without evasion in the same breath with which he asserts the truer realities of those eternities which only symbol and imagination can preserve from time and circumstance. These two last poems, one a terrifying prophecy of utter annihilation and the other a quiet assertion of wholeness, form a completed pattern, drawing together, from the furthest rim of human experience, one man's intuitions about chaos and order. There is nothing tidily rational about this equation; nor can we ever accuse Muir of writing a programmed set of poems, intended, in advance, to propound a theory. This is a symbolic order, full of paradox and shifting perspectives, as full of naked horror or overwhelming joy at the end of his life as at the beginning. Each poem has to be worked for and each symbol explored *for itself* as it emerges under the subconscious pressure of the creative act. The development and consistency of Muir's vision is a tribute to the authenticity of this vision rather than to any false, planned desire to "create a philosophy."

Let us consider "The Day Before the Last Day," Muir's last expression of the vision of evil and breakdown. The poem works partly by being a complete reversal of the Eden-vision, even to the point of using the same syntactical forms.

> If it could come to pass, and all kill all
> And in a day or a week we could destroy
> Ourselves, that is the beginning only
> Of the destruction, for so we murder all
> That ever has been, all species and forms,
> Man and woman and child, beast and bird,
> Tree, flower and herb, and that by which they were
>   known,
> Sight and hearing and touch, feeling and thought,
> And memory of our friends among the dead.

The long list of related forms of creation here, a device Muir often uses in celebrating unity, is twisted and reversed in a poem which postulates their destruction. The nuclear end of the world would mean obliteration of the chain of existence, shown as a monstrously *unnatural* event by this list of natural things which form a balanced harmony. It would be a "Mechanical parody of the Judgment Day/ That does not judge but only deals damnation."

The main body of the poem consists of a long visionary "hypothetical picture" of what might happen, written in the dramatic present, and evoking a weird archetypal situation of mankind facing extinction, standing at the end of the land looking over a dead, stagnant and indifferent sea. At first the people expect the traditional day of judgment, with the dead arising in triumph, but this is only a dream:

> They dream that the grave and the sea give up their
>   dead
> In wonder at the news of the death of death,
> Hearing that death itself is balked by death.

And those who were drowned a year or a thousand
     years
Come out with staring eyes, foam on their faces,
And quaint sea-creatures fixed like jewelled worms
Upon their salt-white crowns, sea-tangled breasts,
That they, the once dead, might know the second
     death.
And then a stir and rumour break their dream. . . .

From this point the horror of the vision takes over in a great picture
of human despair, alienation and denial of humanity. Natural
human instincts are reversed, and, as in *King Lear*, nature cracks
open and men are reduced to senseless things, selfish and cruel as
animals:

And women faint with child-birth lay their babes
Beside them on the earth and turn away
And lovers two by two estranged for ever
Lie each in place without a parting look.
And the dying awakened know
That the generous do not try to help their neighbours,
Nor the feeble and greedy ask for succour,
Nor the fastidious complain of their company
Nor the ambitious dream of a great chance lost
Nor the preacher try to save one soul.   For all
Think only of themselves and curse the faithless earth.

All concept of human value has gone as people wait for the end.
And the poem leaves the people dazed, afraid, suddenly aware of
the terrifying thing they have allowed to happen. There is no consolation or redemption here; not even an epitaph. Instead of a joyful
revolutionary day of judgment, bringing the glory of heaven to the
earth, man has made, through his evil and his blind use of technology, a situation of total annihilation, which is in every way
negative. All life, after becoming twisted and unnatural, will simply
cease to exist. Nature, history, time will vanish. All creation will be
negated because of man's choice which, only when it is far too late,
does he realize has been wrong.

This poem works on several levels. It is, of course, a "bomb"
poem; a massive political reminder of the realities of our age. It is,
too, a strong moral statement. But primarily, its impulse is religious;
a visionary view of man in terms of his purpose and destiny. It may
be seen as perhaps the extreme statement of Muir's symbolic Fall,
where the distortion and denial of all that is properly human,

creative and valuable lead inevitably to the total destruction of Eden, nature, and man himself. The broken pattern, caused by the Fall, is turned here into an annihilation of all patterns and possibilities, and, although ostensibly "set" in the future, the poem is, by extension, an exploration of the present state of the human psyche.

Coming after so many earlier attempts to explore and define the anti-vision, this poem is startling by the very intensity of its response to evil and destructive potentialities. Compared with the evil of the labyrinth symbol, this vision is altogether shorter and more extreme. It is not balanced by compensatory implications of salvation and comes more directly at its subject. There is an energy in the poem, too; an urgency to communicate and to warn which adds to the substance of the content and attacks the reader head-on, in a more openly challenging manner than is usual in Muir's work. The pentameters are roughly shaped and are driven quickly forward by an urgent syntax. The lack of rhyme denies comfort to the ear. Reading about the destruction of pattern, we are never allowed to find a formed pattern to give solace. Again, form is expressive and organic.

Other poets have written about the end of the world, about actual or latent evil, but few can command the authority which Edwin Muir brings to the subject. This is partly an authority gained by more than thirty years of exploring human experience through poetry, but, more, it lies in the inescapably authentic tone which could only come from a man who himself has seen hell and has travelled through the lowest reaches of experience.

The text of "I Have Been Taught," the last poem Muir wrote, is not complete. There are difficulties about punctuation (the poem, syntactically, is one long sentence, although not printed that way), about stanza breaks, about the penultimate stanza, which, as Butter admits, is "conjectural." But there is certainly enough for us to see this poem as a great statement of belief and an effective and dramatic contrast to "The Day Before the Last Day." As a summing-up of his life and art this poem is remarkable. For once Muir seems to be talking directly through a first-person "I," without a mask, and endeavouring to answer the question, "What do you finally *know* about being a human-being?" And never has he summarized his beliefs this clearly and movingly. His knowledge comes from the unconscious, with its symbols both "friendly" and "darker"; from those who have preceded him into death, having played their part in the Fable; from his parents, especially; from the "founts" of ritual, art, traditional patterns which sustain him; from a knowledge of the dark places of the psyche, "the sultry labyrinth," the powers of which are destructive and anti-creative; from time, which as well as being an enemy enables us to see the wholeness of eternity and harmony. And now, finally, as death approaches, he sees most clearly of all that "Plato's is the truest poetry," that the Platonic belief in perfect forms and order, of which our world is an imperfect reflection, does in fact sustain life. There is, he is saying, a true order, unaffected by time and change, which ultimately defeats doubt and negates the Fall. This distinction between an ideal world and our world of time and experience lies at the heart of Muir's thought. He uses symbolic concepts to explore and embody this concept of the tragic gulf between possibility and reality, intention and result. But finally he can celebrate life in spite of this gulf. Even the vision of nihilism in "The Day Before the Last Day" can be assimilated and included in this great *credo*, which asserts pattern, truth and permanence:

> Have drawn at last from time which takes away
> And taking leaves all things in their right place
> An image of forever
> One and whole.

> And now that time grows shorter, I perceive
> That Plato's is the truest poetry,
> And that these shadows
> Are cast by the true.

The labyrinth, and its power, can never be forgotten, but it can be seen as part of something larger, more generous and life-enhancing, which supports and illuminates existence. It is a religious conception, certainly, but one which absorbs Christian, Greek, Hebrew and modern mythology without strain or preference.

In these last two poems, we can see both extremes of Muir's vision. He is reporting from hell and then from heaven, balancing the equation. It would not be true to say that Muir was a pessimist who tried to preserve his sanity by creating an abstract system of hope. In his work evil and good are part of the same unified vision, deeply organic, and an authentic response to the complexities of experience. The journey downward into hell is intrinsically part of the journey upwards towards grace. As we have seen in his own life, as well as in his poetry, the vision of Eden, of renewed possibility, emerges from the very heart of evil and breakdown, in a patterned, rhythmical and recurrent way. By the deployment of the symbols rising from the unconscious, as well as the paradoxical events of actual living, Muir ultimately finds a balance. The symbols which embody breakdown are countered by those which affirm man as part of a great creative pattern. The graph of Muir's experience would be a Platonic circle, moving into, through and beyond good and evil as the Fable of existence continues.

Few men have found so much of heaven and hell in this life and been able to report it. Few poets have been given such creative and powerful symbols and the techniques to embody them with such compassion and understanding, such authenticity and integrity and ultimately with such concern for the nature and quality of life itself. In these last poems, by bringing the dual symbols of life and death closer to political and social realities, the poet is perhaps restricting their ability to float freely, but, at the same time, he is re-energizing them and guarding against their becoming too abstract and too tired. The late poems are vitalized by the actuality they embody, but the secondary world, the sense of Plato's "poetry," remains as firm as ever. The symbols show their flexibility by containing this new injection of actuality, and the result is a poetry which is both familiar and yet differently flavoured. The balance and achieved serenity is not at the expense of imaginative energy. Indeed, in his notebooks, Muir had sketched out plans for several ambitious new poems:

Odin hanging from the tree, seven days and nights?
Odysseus' meeting in Hades with his mother.
David: That he should have seemed a man after God's heart.
The dream: the traveller looking for a bed in Jerusalem at the Passover. Opens a door in a great inn; scene from a brothel. In haste tries another door; 13 men sitting at a table; something strange about them: they all look at him: he retreats. As he goes downstairs a man — one of the 13 — stumbles past him and runs away.[15]

Norse, Greek, Hebrew and Christian — we see in these ideas the symbols which obsessed him; patterns of death, reconciliation, harmony and betrayal, drawn from myth, which could embody imaginatively his vision of experience. His poetry bestows the kind of wisdom and knowledge that can only be fully felt at an elusive, pre-rational level. Poetic symbolism is an imaginative process which originates in sequences of images and is projected by the dynamics of those sequences. Through his deployment of symbol, Muir creates a world both remote and yet instantly recognizable. In his poetry, man's everyday experience of mortality and transitoriness is absorbed into a rich, all-inclusive pattern which harmoniously assumes time into eternity, and good and evil into wide rhythms of potentiality. The long journey of Edwin Muir's life and art is complete, come to a place of integration and perfected forms.

NOTES

CHAPTER ONE

[1] Helen Gardner, *Edwin Muir*. The W. D. Thomas Memorial Lecture (Cardiff, 1961), p. 9.

[2] Charles Tomlinson, "Poetry Today," *The Pelican Guide to English Literature*, Vol. 7 (London, 1961), p. 469.

[3] Kenneth Allott, ed., *The Penguin Book of Contemporary Verse* (London, 1963), p. 92.

[4] Graham Hough, Review of *Collected Poems, The Listener* (May 26, 1960), 941.

[5] J. A. M. Rillie, Review of *Collected Poems, The Glasgow Herald* (April 21, 1960).

[6] Edwin Morgan, "Edwin Muir," *The Review*, No. 5 (February 1963), 3.

[7] T. S. Eliot, "Edwin Muir: 1887-1959," *The Listener*, LXXI (May 28, 1964), 872.

[8] Gardner, p. 7.

[9] A. Alvarez, Review of *Collected Poems, The Observer* (May 8, 1960).

[10] Frederick Grubb, "The Poetry of Kathleen Raine," *The Poetry Review*, Vol. LIV, No. 3 (Autumn 1963), 237.

[11] Philip Larkin, Review of *Collected Poems, The Guardian* (April 29, 1960).

[12] "Not Afraid to Differ," B.B.C. television, (October 11, 1967).

[13] Kathleen Raine, *Defending Ancient Springs* (Oxford, 1967), p. 13.

[14] J. M. Cohen, *Poetry of this Age 1908-1965* (London, 1966), p. 80.

[15] Edwin Muir, *An Autobiography* (London, 1954), pp. 48-49.

[16] Willa Muir, *Belonging* (London, 1968), p. 70.

[17] *Ibid.*, p. 316.

[18] *An Autobiography*, p. 14.

[19] *Ibid.*, pp. 14-16.

[20] *Ibid.*, pp. 24-25.

[21] *Ibid.*, p. 25.

[22] *Ibid.*, p. 33.

[23] *Ibid.*, p. 48.

[24] *Ibid.*, p. 51.

[25] *Ibid.*, p. 77.

[26] Letter to Alec Aitken, July 1938. See Butter, P., *Selected Letters of Edwin Muir*, London, 1974, p. 103.

[27] Edwin Muir, *The Story and the Fable* (London, 1940), p. 263.

[28] *An Autobiography*, p. 96.

[29] *Ibid.*, p. 104.

[30] *Ibid.*, p. 104.

[31] *Ibid.*, p. 145.

[32] *Ibid.*, p. 34.

[33] *Ibid.*, p. 127.

[34] Muir contributed to *The New Age* from 1916 to 1924. His early aphorisms, written under the pseudonym of "Edward Moore," were collected in *We Moderns* (London 1918).

[35] *Belonging*, p. 13.

[36] *The New Age*, Vol. 20 (March 15, 1917), 470-471.

[37] *Ibid.*, Vol. 27 (September 9, 1920), 281.

[38] *Belonging*, p. 13.

[39] *Belonging*, p. 36.

[40] Willa Muir, "In Search of Edwin Muir," B.B.C. radio (May 13, 1964).

[41] *An Autobiography*, p. 170.

[42] *Belonging*, pp. 45-46.

[43] *An Autobiography*, p. 205.

CHAPTER TWO

[1] Suzanne Langer, *Philosophy in a New Key* (Harvard, 1951), p. 42.

[2] Thomas Carlyle, *Sartor Resartus*, ed. C. F. Harrold (New York, 1937), pp. 218-19.

[3] Alex Preminger, ed., *The Princeton Encyclopedia of Poetry and Poetics* (Princeton, 1968), p. 833.

[4] C. G. Jung, *Psychological Reflections* (New York, 1953), p. 39.

[5] Charles Chadwick, *Symbolism* (London, 1971), p. 3.

6 William York Tindall, *Forces in Modern British Literature, 1885-1956* (New York, 1956), p. 253.

7 *Ibid.,* p. 254.

8 *Princeton Encyclopedia,* p. 836.

9 Donald Davie, "Mr. Eliot," *The New Statesman* (October 11, 1963), 496.

10 Quoted in Arthur Symons, *The Symbolist Movement in Literature* (London, 1919), p. 7.

11 C. M. Bowra, *The Heritage of Symbolism* (London, 1943), p. 6.

12 Edward Engelberg, ed., *The Symbolist Poem* (New York, 1967), pp. 32-33.

13 William Blake, "A Vision of the Last Judgment," *The Complete Poetry and Prose,* ed. Keynes (London, 1967), p. 637.

CHAPTER THREE

1 Edwin Muir, *Collected Poems,* second ed. London (Faber) 1963. Except where otherwise stated, the extracts of poems printed in this book are taken from this text.

2 In the National Library of Scotland.

3 Peter Butter, *Edwin Muir: Man and Poet* (Edinburgh, 1966), p. 98. I shall henceforth refer to this book as Butter (2) and to Peter Butter's earlier book, *Edwin Muir* (Edinburgh, 1962) as Butter (1).

4 *An Autobiography,* p. 43.

5 *Belonging,* p. 103.

6 *An Autobiography,* p. 223.

7 *Ibid.,* p. 224.

8 *To Sydney Schiff,* May 7, 1924. See *Selected Letters,* p. 37.

9 Butter (2), p. 136.

10 S. Kierkegaard, *Words for Love,* trans. D. F. and L. F. Swenson (Princeton, 1946), p. 243.

11 Mircea Eliade, *Cosmos and History: The Myth of the Eternal Return* (New York, 1954).

12 Elizabeth Huberman, *The Poetry of Edwin Muir: The Field of Good and Ill* (New York, 1971), pp. 59-80.

13 Edwin Muir, *Journeys and Places* (London, 1937).

14 John Holloway, "The Poetry of Edwin Muir," *The Hudson Review,* Vol. XIII, No. 4 (1960-1961), 562-563.

15 Daniel Hoffman, *Barbarous Knowledge: Myth in the Poetry of Yeats, Graves and Muir* (New York, 1967), pp. 234-35.

[16] *Belonging*, p. 198.

[17] Quoted in Butter (2), pp. 182-83.

[18] *Ibid.*, p. 183.

[19] *Scots Magazine* (September 1940), 408.

[20] *Belonging*, p. 210.

[21] Huberman, p. 122.

[22] Huberman, p. 105.

[23] *Belonging*, p 210.

[24] "Chapbook," B.B.C. radio (September 3, 1952).

[25] In *Belonging*, p. 211, Willa Muir claims that the veteran Greeks in the poem are "an image of the homeless soldiers who turned up in Edinburgh with their terrible stories."

CHAPTER FOUR

[1] *An Autobiography*, p. 274.

[2] *Belonging*, p. 234.

[3] M. L. Rosenthal, *The Modern Poets* (New York, 1965), p. 138.

[4] *An Autobiography*, p. 271.

[5] "Chapbook," B.B.C. Radio, 3 September 1952.

[6] Charles Feidelson, *Symbolism and American Literature* (Chicago, 1953), p. 22.

[7] J. C. Hall, ed., *Collected Poems of Edwin Muir* (New York, 1957), p. 13.

[8] Edwin Muir, "Franz Kafka," *Essays on Literature and Society*, revised ed. (London, 1965), p. 121.

[9] *Ibid.*, p. 122.

[10] *An Autobiography*, p. 240.

[11] Elgin W. Mellown, "The Development of A Criticism: Edwin Muir and Franz Kafka," *Comparative Literature*, Vol. XVI, No. 4 (Fall 1964), 321.

[12] *Belonging*, pp. 244-50.

[13] Edwin Muir, *The Estate of Poetry* (London, 1962), p. 88.

[14] Kathleen Raine, "Edwin Muir. An Appreciation." *Texas Quarterly*, Vol. IV, No. 3 (Autumn 1961), 242.

[15] Elizabeth Jennings, "Edwin Muir as Poet and Allegorist," *The London Magazine*, Vol. 7, No. 3 (March 1960), 54.

[16] Huberman, p. 170.

[17] J. C. Hall, *Edwin Muir*, p. 24.

[18] "Little Gidding," *Four Quartets* (London, 1944), p. 43.

[19] Raine, *Texas Quarterly*, 242.

[20] Jennings, p. 54.

[21] Quoted in Butter (2), p. 214.

[22] Gardner, p. 22.

[23] Hugh Marwick, *Orkney* (London, 1951), p. 225.

[24] Rosenthal, *The Modern Poets*, p. 138.

[25] Quoted in Butter (1), p. 84.

[26] *Belonging*, pp. 238-39.

[27] *Ibid.*, p. 248.

[28] *Ibid.*, p. 248.

[29] *Ibid.*, p. 249.

[30] *Ibid.*, p. 250.

[31] B.B.C. "Chapbook," September 3, 1952.

[32] Letter to Chiari, quoted in Butter (2), pp. 214-15.

[33] Frederick Grubb, *A Vision of Reality: A Study of Liberalism in Twentieth-Century Verse* (London, 1965), p. 104.

[34] Morgan, p. 5.

[35] *Ibid.*, p. 5.

[36] *Ibid.*, p. 5.

[37] Rosenthal, *The Modern Poets*, p. 136.

[38] *Ibid.*, p. 139.

[39] Edwin Muir, "Oswald Spengler," *Essays on Literature and Society* (London, 1965), pp. 125-33.

[40] *An Autobiography*, pp. 261-62.

[41] Gardner, p. 25.

[42] Gardner, p. 24.

[43] "Chapbook," B.B.C. radio (September 3, 1952).

[44] Quoted in Butter (2), p. 221.

[45] *Belonging*, p. 248.

[46] Jennings, p. 55.

[47] *An Autobiography*, p. 114.

[48] *Ibid.*, p. 115.

[49] *Ibid.*, p. 170.

[50] *Belonging*, p. 244.

[51] *Ibid.*, p. 244.

[52] *Ibid.*, p. 245.

[53] *An Autobiography*, p. 274.

CHAPTER FIVE

[1] *An Autobiography*, p. 280.

[2] *Ibid.*, p. 275.

[3] *Ibid.*, p. 276.

[4] *Belonging*, p. 247.

[5] *Ibid.*, p. 255.

[6] *An Autobiography*, p. 278.

[7] *Ibid.*, p. 277.

[8] Quoted in Butter (2), p. 233.

[9] Raine, *Texas Quarterly*, 242-43.

[10] J. R. Watson, "Edwin Muir and the Problem of Evil," *Critical Quarterly*, Vol. 6, No. 3 (Autumn 1964), 247.

[11] Holloway, pp. 553-54.

[12] *Ibid.*, p. 554.

[13] *Ibid.*, p. 554.

[14] Rosenthal, *The Modern Poets*, p. 139.

[15] *Ibid.*, p. 139.

[16] Gross, p. 71.

[17] John Keats to Bailey (November 22, 1817). *Letters of John Keats*, ed. F. Page (Oxford, 1954), p. 49.

[18] Quoted in Butter (2), p. 252.

[19] Butter (2), p. 252.

[20] Holloway, p. 557.

[21] In Manuscript notes for this poem, Muir originally conceived of Plato sitting with Eurydice, "wordless and motionless in their arm chair," suggesting an even wider divergence from the myth.

[22] Holloway, p. 557.

[23] "Scottish Life and Letters," B.B.C. radio (May 23, 1954).

[24] Quoted in Butter (2), p. 255.

[25] *An Autobiography*, p. 278.

[26] Raine, *Texas Quarterly*, 243.

[27] Holloway, p. 567.

[28] Raine, *Texas Quarterly*, 243.

[29] *An Autobiography*, p. 128.

[30] The poem "returns" only chronologically within the volume. It was written earlier, in Rome.

[31] *An Autobiography*, p. 278.

[32] *Ibid.*, p. 237.

[33] Edwin Muir, *Scottish Journey* (London, 1935), p. 38.

[34] "Friedrich Hölderlin" and "Hölderlin's *Patmos*," both in *Essays on Literature and Society*, pp. 86-91, 92-103.

[35] *Belonging*, p. 276.

[36] Mellown, pp. 310-22.

[37] "Franz Kafka," *Essays on Literature and Society*, pp. 120-25.

[38] In *The Bookman*, LXXII (New York, 1930), p. 238.

[39] Edwin Muir, "Franz Kafka," *A Franz Kafka Miscellany* (New York, 1940), pp. 55-66.

[40] *Essays on Literature and Society*, p. 121.

[41] Mellown, p. 321.

[42] Quoted in Butter (2), p. 255.

[43] T. S. Eliot talks of "That great, that terrifying poem of the atomic age, 'The Horses'," ("In Search of Edwin Muir," B.B.C. radio, May 7, 1964) and there is certainly much terror in this vision of a destroyed world. Muir himself, in a review, claimed that "The thought of the bomb has made the world strangely quieter and everything uncertain," ("Recent American Poetry," in *The Observer*, No. 8601, May 6, 1956, 17). But the poem does not rely on this knowledge for its development. The specific references to war merge into wider and perhaps less harsh realities as the poem establishes its terms of reference.

[44] C. B. Cox, "Edwin Muir's 'The Horses'," *Critical Survey*, Vol. 1, No. 1 (1962), 19-21.

[45] Morgan, pp. 9-10.

[46] Butter (2), p. 260.

[47] Wilson, p. 165.

[48] *An Autobiography*, p. 22.

[49] *Ibid.*, p. 46.

[50] *Ibid.*, p. 47.

[51] *Ibid.*, p. 48.

[52] *The Estate of Poetry*, pp. 8-9.

[53] *An Autobiography*, p. 281.

[54] *One Foot in Eden*, p. 80.

[55] Butter (1), p. 94.

CHAPTER SIX

[1] To Norman MacCaig (April 1958), quoted in Butter (2), p. 290.

[2] *The Estate of Poetry*, pp. 9-10.

[3] Quoted in Butter (2), p. 272.

[4] Butter (2), p. 274.

[5] January, 1957. Quoted in Butter (2), p. 286.

[6] cf. Butter (2), p. 286.

[7] Quoted in Butter (2), p. 288.

[8] Archibald MacLeish, *Poetry and Experience* (New York, 1960), p. 64.

[9] *Ibid.*, p. 184.

[10] Butter (2), p. 284.

[11] Erich Heller, *The Hazard of Modern Poetry* (Cambridge, 1953), p. 47.

[12] The last lines here, "Spilling salt angry tears on the salt waves/My life waste water drawn down through a hole" are virtually identical to the lines in "The Last War": "Spilling salt angry tears in the salt waves/Their lives waste water sucked through a gaping hole." Had Muir lived to collect these poems into a volume, he would surely have ensured that such a striking image was not used twice.

[13] Quoted in Butter (2), p. 289.

[14] MacLeish, p. 165.

[15] Quoted in Butter (2), pp. 289-90.

SELECT BIBLIOGRAPHY

1. WORKS BY EDWIN MUIR

Full details of Edwin Muir's writings, including translation, criticism, reviews and American editions, may be found in Elgin W. Mellown's *Bibliography of the Writings of Edwin Muir*. Alabama (University of Alabama Press) 1964; revised ed. London (Nicholas Vane) 1966.

(a) *Verse*

First Poems. London (Hogarth) 1925.

Chorus of the Newly Dead. London (Hogarth) 1926.

Variations on a Time Theme. London (Dent) 1934.

Journeys and Places. London (Dent) 1937.

The Narrow Place. London (Faber) 1943.

The Voyage. London (Faber) 1946.

The Labyrinth. London (Faber) 1949.

Collected Poems 1921-1958. London (Faber) 1952.

One Foot in Eden. London (Faber) 1956.

Collected Poems 1921-1958. London (Faber) 1960; second edn. London (Faber) 1963.

Selected Poems. (ed. T. S. Eliot). London (Faber) 1965.

(b) *Prose*

We Moderns. Under pseudonym "Edward Moore." London (Allen & Unwin) 1918.

Latitudes. London (Melrose) 1924.

Transition. London (Hogarth) 1926.

The Marionette. London (Hogarth) 1927.

The Structure of the Novel. London (Hogarth) 1928.

John Knox: Portrait of a Calvinist. London (Cape) 1929.

The Three Brothers. London (Heinemann) 1931.

Poor Tom. London (Dent) 1932.

Scottish Journey. London (Heinemann) 1935.

Scott and Scotland. London (Routledge) 1936.

The Present Age, from 1914. London (Cresset) 1939.

The Story and the Fable. London (Harrap) 1940.

Essays on Literature and Society. London (Hogarth) 1949. Second edn. revised with six further essays, London (Hogarth) 1965.

An Autobiography. London (Hogarth) 1954.

The Estate of Poetry. London (Hogarth) 1962.

(c.) *Letters*

Selected Letters of Edwin Muir. (Ed. P. Butler). London (Hogarth) 1974.

2. WORKS ABOUT EDWIN MUIR

Full details of writings about Muir are listed in *A Checklist of Writings about Edwin Muir,* compiled by Peter C. Huy and Elgin Mellown, Troy (Whitston) 1971. I list here only those works which have been particularly useful to me or to which I refer most often in the text.

Blackmur, R. P. "Edwin Muir: Between the Tiger's Paws," *Kenyon Review,* Vol. XXXI, No. 2 (1959), 419-436.

Butler, Peter. *Edwin Muir.* Edinburgh, 1962.

———. *Edwin Muir: Man and Poet.* Edinburgh, 1966.

Cox, C. B. "Edwin Muir's 'The Horses'," *Critical Survey,* Vol. 1, No. 1 (1962), 19-21.

Gardner, Helen. *Edwin Muir.* The W. D. Thomas Memorial Lecture, (December 8, 1960). Cardiff, 1961.

Hall, J. C. *Edwin Muir.* London, 1956.

Hoffman, Daniel. *Barbarous Knowledge: Myth in the Poetry of Yeats, Graves and Muir.* New York, 1967.

Holloway, John. "The Poetry of Edwin Muir," *The Hudson Review,* Vol. XIII, No. 4 (Winter 1960-1961), 550-567.

Huberman, Elizabeth. *The Poetry of Edwin Muir: The Field of Good and Ill.* New York, 1971.

Jennings, Elizabeth. "Edwin Muir as Poet and Allegorist," *The London Magazine,* Vol. 7, No. 3 (March 1960), 43-56.

Mellown, Elgin W. "The Development of a Criticism: Edwin Muir and Franz Kafka," *Comparative Literature*, Vol. XVI, No. 4 (Fall 1964), 310-321.

Morgan, Edwin. "Edwin Muir," *The Review*, No. 5 (1963), 3-10.

Muir, Willa. *Belonging: A Memoir*. London, 1968.

Raine, Kathleen. *Defending Ancient Springs*. London, 1967.

———. "Edwin Muir: An Appreciation," *Texas Quarterly*, Vol. IV, No. 3 (Autumn 1961), 233-245.

Rosenthal, M. L. *The Modern Poets*. New York, 1965.

Watson, J. R. "Edwin Muir and the Problem of Evil," *Critical Quarterly*, Vol. 6, No. 3 (Autumn 1964), 231-249.

3. OTHER WORKS

Beebe, Maurice. *Literary Symbolism*. San Francisco, 1960.

Bowra, C. M. *The Heritage of Symbolism*. London, 1943.

Chadwick, Charles. *Symbolism*. London, 1971.

Davie, Donald. *Articulate Energy: An Enquiry into the Syntax of English Poetry*. London, 1956.

Eliade, M. *The Myth of the Eternal Return*. New York, 1954.

Engelberg, E. (ed.), *The Symbolist Poem*. New York, 1967.

Gross, Harvey. *Sound and Form in Modern Poetry*. Ann Arbor, 1964.

MacLeish, A. *Poetry and Experience*. New York, 1960.

Marwick, Hugh. *Orkney*. London, 1951.

Murphy, F. (ed.) *Poetry: Form and Structure*. Boston, 1964.

Symons, A. *The Symbolist Movement in Literature*. London, 1919.

Wilson, Edmund. *Axel's Castle*. New York, 1931.

INDEX